Urban Communication Systems
Neighborhoods and the Search for Community

MEDIA SOCIOLOGY

Series Editor:
David Demers, Washington State University

Urban Communication Systems: Neighborhoods and the Search
   for Community
      Leo W. Jeffres

forthcoming

Mass Media and Cultural Identities: The Dialectics of Integration
   and Fragmentation
         *Hanna Adoni, Dan Caspi, Akiba A. Cohen, Barbara Pfetsch,
         and Han-Juergen Weiss*

Urban Communication Systems
Neighborhoods and the Search for Community

Leo W. Jeffres
Cleveland State University

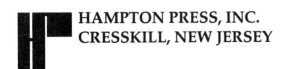

HAMPTON PRESS, INC.
CRESSKILL, NEW JERSEY

Printed in the United States of America

Library of Congress Cataloging-in-Publication Data

Jeffres, Leo W.
  Urban communication systems: neighborhoods and the search for community /
  Leo W. Jeffres
      p. cm. -- (Media sociology)
  Includes bibliographical references and indexes.
  ISBN 1-57273-411-6 (c. alk. paper) -- ISBN 1-57273-412-4 (p. alk paper)
      1. City and town life--United States. 2. Community organization--United States.
  3. Interpersonal communication. I. Title. II. Series.

HT123.J4 2002
307.76'0973--dc21

                                                        2002022201

Hampton Press, Inc.
23 Broadway
Cresskill, NJ 07626

Contents

Preface

My interest in communities and communication systems dates back many years and has its roots in several graduate programs and personal experience. In my undergraduate days at the University of Idaho, I developed a taste for research and participated in my first survey in a class taught by the late Professor Sydney Duncombe in the Department of Political Science. A classmate and I drew a rural area for our interviewing, forcing us to drive from farm house to farm house asking people for whom they were going to vote. As I recall, folks were initially skeptical but eventually cooperative when we approached them for our survey. Journalism Professor Bert Cross gave us assignments that took us off campus and into the community, a style that I inflict on my own students with a vengeance. In the process, I learned to be a "community observer" and developed an intellectual interest in understanding our environment. Later, as a reporter for the *Lewiston Morning Tribune,* I rotated through numerous beats and filled several editorial slots. One of those was regional editor, where I kept in touch with correspondents in a couple dozen small communities that ranged from small mining towns to prairie communities surrounded by wheat. In those days, the paper was still printing "cousins" items from the small towns—telling who was visiting whom and whose son was home from college. The sense of community was quite strong and the interpersonal communication patterns were reinforced by the newspaper itself.

Moving on to the University of Washington, where I received my master's degree, I want to cite two faculty in particular who had an impact that remains to this day. Professor Peter Clarke was my "boss" in the research center, and I was in charge of sampling students from rosters at various neighborhood schools. I did the full range of activities associated with surveys and can credit Professor Clarke with the fact that I still enjoy fieldwork and the research process itself. When that's no longer the case, I'll know it's time to retire. He taught me to become "intimate" with the data so there are no surprises and you know what the numbers mean. Another faculty member, Professor Richard Carter, taught me "how to think" as a creative scholar. Most of all, he taught me to not be afraid while developing "new" concepts that have descriptive power in helping us understand people's communication and other behaviors. I still employ some of the heuristics learned three decades ago when I encounter a situation that is largely "undiscovered" by communication scholars.

At the University of Minnesota, numerous faculty and fellow graduate students were influential, and some of them are cited in this book. Professor Dan Wackman helped to broaden my field experiences and Professor Phil Tichenor introduced me to some of the central influences cited here, including the community as a unit of analysis. My own dissertation was done in a small town in the western part of the state, and I still recall the close interpersonal ties of residents and the rapid diffusion of information that our interviewing created; it was reminiscent of my days as a youth in western Nebraska. A third professor, Roy Carter, told me something that has grown in importance now that I have jumped through all the requisite tenure and promotional hoops; do research because you want to learn something, to answer some question, not because you want to publish something. And that is the guiding motivation behind this book and the studies reported herein.

Cleveland and my home institution, Cleveland State University, have not only the most recent but the most direct impact on this volume. My own conception of communication grew out of interactions with colleagues not only in mass communication but also in interpersonal and organizational communication. As the book demonstrates, I think too many scholars infer communication and too few actually study symbolic activity. The first words leading to the current manuscript date back almost two decades. Always sensitive to the "unit of analysis" problem from my days in Seattle, I struggled to reconcile literatures in urban studies and sociology with those in communication. Only when I read a chapter by Chaffee and Berger (1987) did the "solution" dawn on me, that levels of analysis should be conceptualized "within" rather than "across" disciplines and theories should be developed to reconcile relationships. Thus, this book points out the need to look at both network and systems perspectives. If one begins with conceptualizations only within the urban context and then applies communication, the latter tends to be relegated to a variable status rather than fully developed across levels; thus, in this book, one begins defining neighborhoods and neighborhood systems in a fashion parallel with a similar process of conceptualizing communication units and networks. The Cleveland metropolitan area itself has been a marvelous laboratory for studying urban communication patterns and neighborhoods. Over the years, I have collected numerous data sets, many of them reported in this manuscript. Because I've collected and worked on some of those data sets with colleagues, their contributions are noted in the joint authorship of particular chapters. Although this book was almost two decades in the making, I view it as a temporary statement on a much longer road to study neighborhoods and the search for community.

—Leo W. Jeffres

1

The Continuing Significance of Neighborhoods

- The Importance of Neighborhoods
- Defining "Neighborhoods"
- A Brief History of the Neighborhood Concept
- Evolving Neighborhoods: Growth and Change
- The Relationship Between Neighborhoods and the City
- Summary

Three concepts dominate this book—*communication, community,* and *neighborhoods.* The three are intertwined in any discussion of society and social organization. Communication represents the symbolic activity that allows people to form associations, groups, and societies.[1] In the process, communication enables people to grow and change and pass along their cultures. Along Maslow's chain of needs from physical survival to self-actualization, humans have always searched for affiliation. For most people, this is a search for the second concept, community and a sense of belonging—represented by the formation of tribes, ethnic groups, interest groups and, more recently, lifestyles. In primitive "times," the "sense of place" was limited and localized but social organization eventually led to the development of communities and cities. In the longer history of time, the third concept—neighborhood—is a relative newcomer to the trio because it is seen as emerging only with the demise of the walking city in the 19th century. Neighborhoods themselves became a manifestation of the "search for community," although they were often combined with ethnicity and other ties. Neighborhoods, and the cities they comprised, combined a sense

1

of place with a sense of belonging and identity. Some of people's identity was associated with being from or belonging to a community and a neighborhood. Modern transportation and the mobility accompanying it changed the social organization of the city and decreased the utility of neighborhoods as an answer in the search for community. Furthermore, new communication technologies that allow people to gather in virtual communities provide another vehicle for finding commonalities and meaning in life. Yet neighborhoods still provide an alternative in the search for community, one that may see a renaissance as people discard less satisfying and less flexible alternatives.

In recent years, neighborhoods have not been viewed as "necessary" for modern society, where jobs and other sources of identity have been seen as more important. In fact, many observers of the post-World War II era have seen neighborhoods as a quaint relic limited to center cities and more traditional times.[2] However, there is a nostalgia associated with urban neighborhoods and increasingly they are seen as desirable options for "creating community," if only people would return to them and act accordingly. More upscale or diverse neighborhoods with healthy portions of singles and couples with no kids are quite trendy. But it still takes a pioneering spirit and urban ideology for middle-class families to return and live in urban neighborhoods.

Neighborhoods are answers to the search for community only when they offer a "sense of place" and "sense of belonging," whether it's based on a shared ethnicity or shared diversity.[3] To understand how modern center-city neighborhoods can fulfill people's search for community, research is needed to show how communication fits into this scenario and how all three concepts relate to people's sources of identity and meaning in life. How do communication processes operate to create the "weak ties" on which neighborhoods depend for their survival? How are residents' perceptions of the "quality of life" (QOL) dependent on neighborhoods relative to other sources of identity? And how do communication concepts fit in theories of social action and urban development?

This book is an effort to integrate several literatures while examining the relationships between these three concepts: communication, community, and neighborhood. Although scholars in urban studies, communication, and sociology often cite variables from each other's domain, seldom are the boundaries crossed in any systematic attempt to integrate literatures. The first third of the book looks at the urban literature and traditional approaches to studying neighborhoods and communication. How does social structure affect communication (e.g., pluralism and the linear hypothesis from sociology)? The direction of influence is reversed when the question asks how communication patterns affect neighborhoods and social relations.

Next, the empirical literature focusing on neighborhood communication patterns is examined, including interaction and interpersonal communication as well as neighborhood newspapers and media links. This evolves into a discussion of networks and systems as approaches to studying neighborhoods and communication.

The last third of the book examines social action in urban areas, including neighborhoods as development units and neighborhood participation as social action. This section focuses on communication and neighborhood development, with attention to diffusion research and more recent studies that examine communication technologies.

THE IMPORTANCE OF NEIGHBORHOODS

Perkins (1988) noted that the significance of neighborhoods continues despite increased geographical mobility and an expansion in the number of alternative settings for behavior, including computer networks. He added that "spatial aspects of a community still matter, but no longer to the exclusion of such phenomena as social networks, individuals coping in response to environmental stress, and the empowerment of residents to change the physical environment" (p. 946); this "person-in-context" perspective focuses on residential participation in neighborhood and community change.

Lerner (1957) long ago noted that the nostalgia for the small town should not be construed as an interest in the town itself but rather as a quest for community, a nostalgia for a compassable and integral living unit. The issue is whether American life will evolve any other "place" to replace the small town. Oldenburg (1989) noted that no new form of integral community has been found and the small town has yet to "greet its replacement" (p. 3). The automobile suburb in effect fragmented the individual's world, so that a person works in one place, sleeps in another, shops elsewhere, finds pleasure or companionship where he or she can and cares little about any of these places. Noting the lack of community life in residential areas today, Oldenburg (1989, p. 4) said:

> The typical suburban home is easy to leave behind as its occupants move to another. What people cherish most in them can be taken along in the move. There are no sad farewells at the local taverns or the corner store because there are no local taverns or local stores. Indeed there is often more encouragement to leave a given subdivision than to stay in it, for neither the homes nor the neighborhoods are equipped to see families or individuals through the cycle of life. Each is designed for families of particular sizes, incomes and ages. There is little sense of place and even less opportunity to put down roots (p. 4)

Oldenburg pointed out that observers disagree about the reasons for growing estrangement between the family and the city in U.S. society. Goodwin (1974) said, "There is virtually no place where neighbors can anticipate unplanned meetings" today, producing what Oldenburg called an absence of an informal public life that "provides the basis of community and the celebration of it" (p. 14). Domestic and work relationships are forced to supply everything for the U.S. middle class. This also has led to a growth in the home entertainment industry, he suggested. At the same time, some suburbs are attempting to create a "downtown" along classic small-town lines, whereas metropolitan areas are supporting new center-city housing developments that emphasize the "new urbanism" style of small lots and houses with porches that promote interaction. Thus, the quest for community continues across neighborhood contexts.

DEFINING "NEIGHBORHOODS"

Keller (1968) point out that most definitions of neighborhood involve two components, the social and the physical (see Table 1.1). The basic elements are people, place, interaction system, shared identification and public symbols. Schwirian (1983) defined a *neighborhood* as "a population residing in an identifiable section of a city whose members are organized into a general interaction network of formal and informal ties and express their common identification with the area in public symbols" (p. 84). He distinguished a *neighborhood* from *residential areas* by the degree of social organization among residents. Residential areas have few or no patterned relations among residents. Areas may become neighborhoods and vice versa, depending on the "viability and extent of the network of social relationships among residents" (p. 84).[4] Keizer (1997) asked whether community can exist apart from place, with no promise of continuance, without interdependence or without a core of shared values.

In addition to neighborhood, several related concepts have emerged to describe similar units, almost all reflecting some aspect of social ties or interdependence. Crenshaw and St. John (1989) introduced the concept of *organizationally dependent community* to describe those in which sentiment and attachment among residents is a result of participation in formal organizations—generally created to protect the community from outside threats—than of informal social networks. In their study of Oklahoma City, Crenshaw and St. John found that renovating urban neighborhoods were an example of such organizationally dependent communities, lacking an informal social foundation on which to build community commitment. This contrasts with R. E. Park, Burgess, and McKenzie's (1925) concept of *natural communities*, based on ascribed statuses and social interaction. R. A. Park (1952) and his Chicago School associates argued that a natural area involves the following:

1. A geographic area physically distinguishable from adjacent areas.
2. A population with unique demographic, social, or ethnic composition.
3. A social system with norms, rules, and regularly recurring patterns of social interaction that function as mechanisms of social control.
4. Aggregate emergent behaviors or ways of life that distinguish the area from others around it.

The Chicago School believed that any change in the population of a natural area—through mortality, fertility, migration—necessarily was followed by changes in other elements of the social system as the area adjusted to a declining population or accommodated newcomers (Schwirian, 1983). Crenshaw and St. John (1989, p. 413) say that the "natural community has been replaced by the **community of limited liability**."

> Janowitz and Suttles (1978) proposed that the urban community has evolved from natural communities based on in-group solidarities into a multitiered hierarchy of community organization. The "social bloc" is the smallest unit of community organization. At this level a sense of community is built on person-to-person contact, shared demographic and social characteristics, and a similar view of the residential area. The social bloc is the heir of Park and Burgess's natural community. (Crenshaw & St. John, 1989, p. 413)

The concept of *neighborhood* is often used interchangeably with notions of *community*.[5] Allen (1990) pointed out further that the relationship between community and neighborhood must be more clearly delineated because the terms often are used interchangeably in much of the literature, some suggesting that neighborhood is a subunit of community, which is geographically defined (Deseran, 1978; Marans & Rodgers, 1975), whereas others suggest that neighborhoods can be viewed as "creating community" (Ahlbrandt, 1986). However, community also can be viewed as both a geographic unit or the consequence of interdependence and interaction, or communication (also see Hillery, 1955).[6] Haeberle (1988) said "the concept of neighborhood is deceptively simple. It encompasses space, people, shared experiences, and human interaction" (p. 619). In a study of Birmingham, Alabama, he looked at how neighborhood activists described their neighborhoods, finding that 45% of the descriptors used to define neighborhoods were physical, 22.4% human interactive descriptors, 11.8% human demographic descriptors, and 18.4% mixed and unclassifiable.

L. Allen (1990) noted that community can be viewed from a social-psychological perspective that focuses on a psychological sense of community or from an ecological-functional perspective that focuses on a set of services, opportunities, and characteristics. Or these perspectives can be integrated into one conceptualization (Wilkinson, 1986). Looking at residential environments, Sanoff (1971) offered a matrix of environmental variables,[7] attitudinal variables,[8] and individual and social differences (demographic variables, social status, length of residence, and household composition). Bridger (1996) looked at the role that collective images play in maintaining or altering community environments by shaping the political debate and providing residents stories and language for discussing their neighborhoods. "Communities are defined, in large part, by the stories people tell about them" (Bridger, 1996, p. 355). "Through

TABLE 1.1
A Taxonomy of Neighborhood Characteristics

Concept/Source	Defining Characteristics
Neighborhood (Keller, 1968)	Social and physical components, including identifiable section of city; residents organized into general interaction network of formal, informal ties; residents express common identification in public symbols.
(Marans & Rodgers, 1975)	A subunit of community, that is geographically defined.
(Ahlbrandt, 1986)	Neighborhoods can be viewed as creating community.
(Haeberle, 1988)	Encompasses space, people, shared experiences, and human interaction.
(Downs, 1981)	Geographic units within which certain social relationships exist, although the intensity of these relationships and their importance in the lives of the individuals vary greatly, a view that merges the territorial view with the notion of limited liability.
(Winters, 1979)	Neighborhoods today evolve in part because of their "reputations."
(Bennett, 1993)	Identifies three approaches for examining neighborhoods: physical sites, neighborhood systems (which examine the social threads—personal ties, shared habits, and institutions—that hold neighborhoods together) and neighborhood stage (a complex overlapping of diverse social practices set in a bounded physical space).
(Schwirian, 1983)	Looks at neighborhoods as interaction systems.
(Mandelbaum, 1985)	Viewing neighborhoods as systems focuses attention away from total size and physical form and toward the ways in which communication networks influence social integration and governance.
Natural community (Park, Burgess, & McKenzie, 1925)	Based on ascribed statuses and social interaction, involving 1. a geographic area physically distinguishable from adjacent areas; 2. a population with unique demographic, social or ethnic composition; 3. a social system with norms, rules, and regularly recurring patterns of social interaction that function as mechanisms of social control; and 4. aggregate emergent behaviors or ways of life that distinguish the area from others around it.
Community of limited liability (Janowitz, 1952/1967)	Seen as replacing natural community, based not on in-group solidarities but hierarchy of community organization where residents maintained ties with religious, ethnic, occupational, or other types of communities while interact-

TABLE 1.1 (cont.)

Concept/Source	Defining Characteristics
	ing with the neighborhood to the extent it fits their interests and lifestyles.
Organizationally dependent community (Crenshaw & St. John, 1989)	Communities in which sentiment and attachment among residents is a result of participation in formal organizations, generally created to combat outside threats, rather than informal social networks.
Social bloc (Crenshaw & St. John, 1989)	The smallest unit of community organization, where a sense of community is built on person-to-person contact, shared demographic and social characteristics, and a similar view of the residential area. Seen as heir to Park and Burgess' natural community.
Residential area (Keller, 1968)	Few or no patterned relations among residents.
Community concept	Many applications with neighborhood concept:
(Hillery, 1955)	Definitions emphasize geographic distinction and/or interaction.
(Allen, 1990)	Sociopsychological perspective focuses on sense of community.
(Allen, 1990)	Ecological-functional perspective focuses on a set of services, opportunities, and characteristics.
(Sanoff, 1971)	A matrix of environmental and attitudinal variables, individual and social differences.
(Bridger, 1996)	Communities are defined by the stories people tell about them.
(Hunter, 1974b)	Communities based on use of symbols.
(Gardner, 1996)	Community has 10 attributes: wholeness incorporating diversity, shared values, mutual obligations, effective internal communication, links beyond itself, concern for youth, forward-looking viewpoint, and well-developed community maintenance.
Longo (1995)	Four dimensions as continua along which communities can be described: choice–chance, time–space, abstract–concrete, affinity–proximity.
Neighborhood economy (Wiewel, Brown, & Morris, 1989)	Notion of neighborhood economic system fuzzy but useful.
Neighborhood social fabric (Ahlbrandt, 1986)	Includes personal ties to the neighborhood (dependency links to friends, relatives, and neighbors), neighboring (helping activities), participation in neighborhood organizations, and use of neighborhood institutions.
(D. Warren, 1986)	Distinguishes between neighboring and close friendships; concept of a good neighbor depends on perceptions, social norms rather than feelings of closeness.

the telling, hearing, and reading of stories like this, we gain a sense of familiari-
ty with, and a common basis for talking about, particular places and their inhabitants ([B.] Johnstone 1990)" (p. 355). Implicit in Bridger's comments is the
view that community emerges through communication, a position articulated by
Y. Kim (1977, 1978, 1979, 1982, 1988, 1994, 1995a, 1995b) in her research on
how ethnics acculturate (i.e., people "become Americans" by learning how to
communicate in the culture). Bridger called such stories "heritage narratives"
that tell a community's origins, history, character, trials, and triumphs; these
stories "are central to the temporal persistence of the community as a unit of
social organization" (p. 355).

Melvin (1987) provided a history of the scholarly interest in neighborhoods. He noted that "neighborhoods emerged as identifiable units of concern
in the American cityscape at that point when urban centers underwent the transformation from the pedestrian city of the eighteenth and early nineteenth cen-
turies to the expanded and differentiated urban structure of the early twentieth
century" (p. 257). Thus, neighborhoods emerged when changes in transportation allowed people to segregate themselves and abandon the crowded conditions of the "walking city." At the turn of the century, scholars began looking at
neighborhoods as unifying units that were the building blocks making up cities.
Each historical era has viewed neighborhoods somewhat differently. By the
1920s, the focus was on forces pulling cities apart and neighborhoods were seen
as more parochial units—united by ethnicity, and the like—that fought for local
interests and against outside threats. After 1930, academic interest in neighborhoods declined, but the emerging planning profession soon was to see neighborhoods as territorial units representing the staging ground for urban projects.
This was accompanied by a shift away from viewing the neighborhood as a central element in U.S. cities toward an increasing concern about the metropolitan
or regional unit. In the 1940s and 1950s, Janowitz suggested viewing neighborhoods as communities of "limited liability"—where residents maintained ties
with religious, ethnic, occupational, or other types of communities while interacting with the neighborhood to the extent it fit their interests and lifestyles. The
1960s and 1970s saw a renewed interest in neighborhoods with the urban crisis
and positioning of neighborhoods as staging grounds for solving urban problems. A merger of the territorial perspective with Janowitz's notion of communities of limited liability seems to capture the prevailing notion of neighborhood
today.

A BRIEF HISTORY OF THE NEIGHBORHOOD CONCEPT

C. Abbott (1974) suggested that neighborhoods existed as early as the colonial
era in New York City. However, most students of the American city date the
"emergence of neighborhood consciousness with the demise of the walking
city" (Melvin, 1987, p. 258), when cities no longer were small, compact, and

relatively integrated, as was the case before 1860.[9] A series of innovations in transportation broke the "casement of the walking city" between 1840 and 1860—steam railroads, horse cars, cable cars, electrification, allowing first the wealthy and later the middle class a chance to abandon the crowded conditions of the walking city (Melvin, 1987, p. 258). "With the emergence of residential neighborhoods as identifiable units, interest grew in their definition and role in the life of the metropolis" (p. 258).

At the turn of the century, urban observers began scrutinizing neighborhoods and their relationship to the city, some viewing the city as a "'cluster of interlacing communities' (or neighborhoods), 'each having its own vital ways of expression and action, but altogether creating the municipality which shall render the fullest service through the most spirited participation of all its residents'" (Woods, 1923, cited in Melvin, 1987, pp. 258-259). Like Woods, Phillips (1940) visualized the nation as a "grand union of neighborhoods that, when linked, comprised cities, counties, states, and ultimately the nation as a whole" (Melvin, 1987, p. 259).

In subsequent analyses and views of neighborhoods, their relationships with cities shifted with the historical period (Melvin, 1987). By the mid-1920s, emphasis was on forces that seemed to pull cities apart and produced urban forms characterized by particularlism rather than unifying interaction described by Woods, Phillips, and others. Thus, studies by the Chicago sociologists Robert Park, Ernest Burgess, Louis Wirth, Roderick D. McKenzie, and Harvey W. Zorbaugh revealed a view that neighborhoods "operated within the larger city structure as 'natural areas,':: communities defined in terms of the 'common experiences of the group,' which evoked a sense of 'territorial parochialism'" (Park, 1925, cited in Melvin, 1987, p. 259). Thus, neighborhoods were seen as fragmented by economic, racial, and cultural factors, which provided the points of identification for neighborhood residents, who, when they mobilized as groups, sought to protect the community from outside influences or groups.

At this point, neighborhoods were seen as parochial in nature, and cities were viewed as "conglomerations of groups intent on protecting their own interests rather than working for the interests of the community at large" (Melvin, 1987, p. 260). "The general crisis over the apparent loss of community during the 1930s and 1940s was accompanied by a shift away from viewing the neighborhood as a central element in American cities toward an increasing concern about the metropolitan or regional unit. Such a shift dampened research efforts that focused on the neighborhood and its role in the American urban structure" (indirect quote, cite of Smith, 1982, in Melvin, 1987, p. 261). One wrote that technological innovations had rendered the neighborhood obsolete (Steiner, 1929) as people sought satisfaction within a less narrow circle.

Between the wars, little attention was directed toward analyzing the historical experience of the neighborhood. However, "neighborhood activity persisted during the period when social scientists studying urban areas [1930-1960] often discounted its importance in understanding the city" (Melvin, 1987,

p. 262). However, although academics were less interested in neighborhoods, members of the nascent U.S. planning profession displayed a lively interest, emphasizing the neighborhood unit as a territorial unit (Melvin, 1987). In the 1940s and 1950s, Janowitz suggested the view that individuals were the only real units of society, arguing for the notion of the community of "limited liability"—where residents maintained ties with other types of communities, religious, fraternal, occupational, but interacted with the neighborhood as their interests and lifestyles dictated.

During the urban crisis of the 1960s, interest was renewed in the territorial view of neighborhood, which was to be a staging ground for solutions to contemporary problems through such programs as Community Action Programs and the Office of Economic Opportunity—which sought to "revitalize neighborhoods." Jacobs' popular book served as a critique of the planning profession and directed attention to the destruction of neighborhoods, sparking renewed interest in them. The 1970s witnessed neighborhood activists and a spirit of strident localism, including such slogans as "power to the neighborhoods." Bulmer (1985) said that a decline in community studies in Britain followed skepticism in the 1960s about the relationship between built form and social relationships and whether rural and urban concepts were useful for distinguishing forms of social relations.

In the 1980s, Hunter (1974b) and others focused on "symbolic communities." Downs (1981) defined *neighborhood* as "geographic units within which certain social relationships exist, although the intensity of these relationships and their importance in the lives of the individual may vary tremendously," a view that suggests a merger of the territorial view of neighborhoods and Janowitz's notion of communities of limited liability, "capturing the prevailing spirit of neighborhood today" (Melvin, 1987, p. 265). Bulmer (1985) said that rejuvenation of community studies is linked to a renewed interest in the primary group, of ties between kin, friends, neighbors and of informal relationships in formal settings. Bulmer (1985) said that "a major virtue of shifting the emphasis from the study of 'community' to the study of the primary group—whether made up of neighbours, friends or kin— is that it gets away from the metaphysical problem of community" (p. 434). He continued, "Ways of life indeed do not coincide with settlement patterns, but in studying neighbours one is not studying settlement patterns but social networks and the ways in which people construct their primary group relationships" (p. 434). Thus, again there is a need to examine not just geographically proximate relationships but communication networks.

EVOLVING NEIGHBORHOODS: GROWTH AND CHANGE

Regardless of the historical account of how neighborhoods have evolved, Winters (1979) noted that individual neighborhoods today evolve in part because of their "reputations." In cities today, each neighborhood tends to acquire a different reputation, and these reputations become self-fulfilling as new people are attracted to those that appear likely to be most congenial. Thus, a sorting process occurs and "divergent forms of self-identification have been projected into urban space," producing many types of specialized neighborhoods based on cultural commonalties of one type or another. Jacob (1971) also underscored the importance of "neighborhood culture" as a variable. Hoover and Vernon (1959/1962) suggested that neighborhoods follow a series of stages generally marked by progressive decreases in social status after the early development from low density, rural uses to more dense urban uses; however, Guest's (1974) study of census tracts representing Cleveland neighborhoods did not particularly support a life cycle concept.[10] Bennett (1993) contended that the notion of neighborhood stage helps us to understand public policies aimed at contemporary big city neighborhoods.[11] He looked at three approaches for examining neighborhoods: physical sites, neighborhood systems (which examine the social threads—personal ties, shared habits, and institutions—that hold neighborhoods together), and neighborhood stage (a complex overlapping of diverse social practices set in a bounded physical space).

> The social area perspective is closely tied to a general theory of social organization and social change (Greer 1962). Accordingly, the degree of social differentiation in life-styles among individual urbanites and among characteristics of city neighborhoods is a function of the "societal scale." Societal scale refers to the extent of the division of labor within a society and the degree of elaboration of integrative mechanisms and institutions centering on transportation and communication. High-scale societies such as those of North America, are characterized by complex occupational and industrial differentiation, an intricate transportation network, and an elaborate system of electronic communication. Low-scale societies, such as those of emerging Africa and Asia, have much more rudimentary occupational and industrial systems, embryonic transportation systems, and incomplete communication networks. As societies increase in scale they increase in social differentiation; this is reflected in the increasing specialization of urban land use and in the social characteristics of the population. (Schwirian, 1983, p. 85)

Furthermore, people's lives are organized around three basic dimensions: social status, ethnicity, and familism (urbanism, measured by items concerning home and family). Schwirian (1983) noted that few studies have analyzed patterns of change in social areas. An example is Hunter's (1971, 1974a) study of Chicago from 1930 to 1960; he identified four stages of neighborhood change that involved the interplay of family characteristics and social status.

Looking at neighborhoods as interaction systems, Schwirian (1983) noted that most ethnographics of particular areas do not deal with changes in the "relationship network." Suttles (1972) proposed that the social organization of neighborhoods may exist at several levels, ranging from an organization that is almost a primary group to a formalized set of relations structured to deal with outside institutions and groups. The most basic form of city neighborhood, Suttles said, is the single block consisting of residents whose homes share common egress and who use the same local facilities regularly. The next level of organization is the defended neighborhood, a residential social system shut off from other areas through social or physical mechanisms. It has a corporate identity to local residents and outsiders. Residents of the defended neighborhood "share a common fate at the hands of the city and other key decision-making organizations" (Schwirian, 1983, p. 87). Two other types of neighborhoods cited by Suttles are the community of limited liability and the expanded community of limited liability, which develop in response to administrative districts found in cities for such things as education or urban renewal.[12]

THE RELATIONSHIP BETWEEN NEIGHBORHOODS AND THE CITY

As Melvin (1987) noted, the growth of the literature describing scholarly interest in neighborhoods fails to provide much insight into the relationship between the neighborhood and the rest of the city.[13] There is an interesting parallel that can be drawn between the city-neighborhood relationship and the city-region or nation relationship. Goheen (1974) noted that any theory of the modern city must analyze how urban influence and control have diffused throughout the nation, as well as provide a theoretical rational for an urban form or structure and construct a chronology of major turning points and events in the history of the city. The literature on the rational for the neighborhood as a structure and the historical development of neighborhoods has been reviewed, but the neighborhood-city relationship (in terms of power and influence) remains.

This book views the metropolitan area as a functional system composed of subsystems. A review of the historical literature suggests that it probably would not be profitable viewing neighborhoods as subsystems until the latter part of the 19th century. However, as von Bertalanfry's (1968) notion of systemness suggests, the extent to which neighborhood units are subsystems is an empirical question. Mandelbaum (1985, p. 141) noted that, although the systems approach has not "swept the [urban studies] field," it has penetrated the language of both planners and urban historians. He noted that the cities viewed as systems in the work of well-known urban observers are limited sets of well-specified interacting variables. Furthermore, "cities are not physical entities but mental constructs that must be justified pragmatically" (p. 143). Mandelbaum added that systems thinking "focuses attention away from total size and physical form and towards the analysis of the ways in which communication networks influence social integration and governance. As a planning tool, systems thinking generates network design principles that are simultaneously more general and more far-reaching than those that inform architectural theories of public spaces and legible environments" (p. 146).[14]

Although urban studies and sociology clearly can claim neighborhoods and urbanism as primary turf, other disciplines also should contribute to our understanding of the area.[15] Thus, economists can analyze the extent to which neighborhoods are functionally intact economic systems or, at the other end of a dimension of dependence-interdependence, completely dependent on the rest of the urban system. Wiewel et al. (1989) noted that the concept of neighborhood economy is even fuzzier than that of regional economy, but they offer definitions that allow us to see to what extent a neighborhood is linked to the larger urban area, and how. They show how such familiar concepts as dependency, self-sufficiency, local development, and empowerment can be used to describe neighborhood economies and their relationships with the larger economic system.[16] Neighborhoods generally are economically dependent on city and regional labor, capital and real estate markets, and efforts to resist or shape change are more likely to be successful if they are directed at political mobilization and access to the larger labor markets rather than direct job creation within the neighborhood itself (Teitz, 1989).[17]

Similarly, sociologists and other urban scholars can show the extent to which neighborhoods are unified socially by bonds of family, race, ethnicity, or religion; here several dimensions may be represented—diversity-heterogeneity by life cycle, social units, and individual differences.[18] Teitz (1989) noted that neighborhoods are strongly influenced by economic conditions but are "best seen as social communities" (p. 111). Such a definition of neighborhood is based largely on culture and social relations that may be influenced by economics, politics, and physical structure. "Nonetheless, the common interests that people within an area express are mediated primarily through the local sphere. It is this quality that makes neighborhoods different from larger areas within which people live and with which they also identify themselves" (Teitz, 1989, p. 114). Ahlbrandt (1986) described a neighborhood social fabric as including personal ties to the neighborhood, neighboring, participation in neighborhood organizations, and use of neighborhood institutions. The first represents dependency links to friends, relatives, and neighbors.[19] Neighboring includes helping activities.[20] Participation in neighborhood organizations include those concerned with issues or problems in the neighborhood as well as belonging to other groups such as church, civic, fraternal, and similar groups. As would be expected, Ahlbrandt (1986) found in one city that numerous measures of these four aspects of the "social fabric" were correlated with neighborhood attachment and satisfaction. Ahlbrandt (1986) noted that "neighborhood life has a variety of dimensions, and where those features of the neighborhood—personal, physical and institutional—offer strong inducements for involvement, communal feelings will be high. When neighborhoods provide disincentives for involvement by their residents, the sense of community will be low" (p. 303).[21] He added that neighborhoods can be viewed as "creating community" in conjunction with their residents. D. Warren (986) distinguished between neighboring and close friendships; what constitutes a good neighbor depends on perceptions and social norms rather than feelings of closeness. However, as Fried (1986) noted, there are few "monolithic neighborhood values" at the individual level, and observers can go too far in concluding what residents seek and prefer in their neighborhood and what produces neighborhood satisfaction.22 Tomeh (1967) looked at four types of informal associations in urban communities—neighbors, relatives, co-workers, and other friends—during three periods in the 1950s, finding that interaction with relatives was most frequent, then friends, neighbors, and lastly co-workers (contact outside the work situation).

Interaction often is cited as a central factor in defining neighborhood units or characterizing activity within them. The Ahlbrandt (1986) study incorporated aspects of interpersonal communication within his view of a neighborhood's "social fabric." And neighboring activities are dependent on communication most of the time; in fact, the exchange of greetings over the back fence is often an expression of the sociability attached to notions of neighboring (D. Warren, 1986). Sanoff (1971) mixed social factors with communication variables and family relationships in a grab bag called attitudinal variables. E. Hill and Bier (1989) noted that neighborhoods earlier could be characterized in terms of long-term social relationships, which is less so today. Mackensen (1986) noted that the quality of urban life heavily depends on the quality of social relationships in neighborhoods, which is more important than the physical environment (also see Bandura, 1986). Treinen (1965, cited in Mackensen, 1986) demonstrated that perception of the urban environment considerably depends on the density of social relations in an urban area. Mackensen (1986) said that a detailed understanding of the social meaning of a neighborhood requires knowing the density and content of social networks in housing areas.

However, communication scholars have largely ignored this area, and communication concepts are central to understanding the extent to which neighborhood units are integrated-disconnected, and independent-dependent in their links to the larger urban system. Even when scholars have focused on networks defined in terms of interpersonal relationships, little research has actually focused on the messages or symbolic activity that represent communication networks (e.g., Sodeur, 1986). This is examined further in the next section.

Clearly, the relationship between neighborhood and the larger urban unit has strong policy consequences. Mier (1989) noted that any evaluation of local public investment forces one to confront the linkage between neighborhood and regional economies. Recently, the movement to describe land-use policies not just in terms of economic growth but in terms of the consequences to those in the inner city points out that neighborhoods, cities, and suburbs are part of a regional system, where changes in modes of transportation, and so on are not neutral in their impact on center city neighborhoods. This view stresses that the urban center is an integrated system in economic terms. Policies that make it easy to relocate jobs and homes influence the existing tax base and quality of life for those left behind and the metropolitan quality of life requiring support from the entire metro system (e.g., the more distant residents are less likely to join different aspects of public and organizational life when they are far removed).[23] Similarly, improvements in communication affect the relationship between the individual resident and the city. Many of those who work through the Internet no longer need to commute to a job and, thus, they can select neighborhoods or communities independent of employment considerations, often choosing to leave the city and live elsewhere.

By extrapolation, communication networks can be viewed as linking people within neighborhoods and externally linking them to the rest of the city and the society. Clearly, the notion of neighborhoods as subsystems—with varying degrees of "independence"—can be applied in both communication and socioeconomic terms.

In a recent essay, Greer (1989) viewed cities in urban-dominated societies as "differentiated parts of large-scale organizational networks" (p. 342). He noted that with increasing societal scale, cities have become more interdependent on other cities and continents while the city's culture has diffused widely. He concludes that the city today no longer controls much of its own destiny because so many decisions occur beyond its boundaries and because the culture of urban residents that once separated them from rural folk is now shared by most of society, leaving few differences. Greer said there are two major systems in the United States today—market and government. Greer (1989) said the "intrinsic city" is a

> social structure operating in a physical container, a continuous and stable population in a pattern of physical structures and spaces. The social structure is that complex of habits that organizes behavior, allowing the city to produce and reproduce over time with considerable predictability. The two levels of structure interplay, and each is in some degree imposed by extrinsic conditions. The city's terms of trade with its markets and its role in the network of government influence its wealth and its interests; these, in turn, influence the kinds of private and public physical structures and the nature of open spaces the city can afford. (p. 344)

The city's physical structure "constrains and channels the nature of settlement, density, and scatteration" (p. 344). Thus, the relationship between neighborhood and city has a parallel in the relationship between city and the larger regional system and society.

SUMMARY

The significance of neighborhoods continues despite changes in technology, family patterns, and the mobility associated with employment. Public nostalgia for small towns and neighborhoods is largely the quest for community and personal ties. The neighborhood concept itself needs to be distinguished from several others, including the community concept, natural community, the community of limited viability, the organizationally dependent community, social bloc, and residential area. A "neighborhood" has both social and physical components as well as a pattern of interaction and ties and a common identification and experience. Definitions of the other concepts share many of these features but make further distinctions that qualify and reduce the "turf" to which they refer.

A brief history of the neighborhood concept in the United States begins as early as the colonial era in New York City but most scholars date the emergence of neighborhood consciousness with the demise of the walking city as cities grew in size and diversity. By 1900, cities came to be viewed as clusters of neighborhoods that created the city. Observers shifted their view throughout the 20th century, from emphasizing forces that pulled cities apart in the 1920s, to focusing on the larger municipal unit or metro area, to a renewed interest in the territorial view of neighborhoods in the 1960s and an emphasis on symbolic communities in more recent years.

Neighborhoods evolve over time and develop images that contribute to those changes and operate along with demographic, economic, and other forces. Some see neighborhoods following a series of stages marked by decreases in social status and changes in density. The social area perspective views neighborhoods through social organization and social change, whereas an interaction view emphasizes changes in the relationship network.

The relationship between neighborhoods and the larger city often is ignored. Here a systems view is employed, which also allows for the integration of work by urban studies scholars and sociologists with contributions by other social scientists, including those in economics, political science, and communication. Thus, questions can be raised as to what extent neighborhoods are economically dependent on the city and region, how common interests and cultures lead to political activities used to advance neighborhood interests, and the extent to which neighborhood interaction still defines neighborhoods.

2

Urbanism, Pluralism, and Communication

- Size and Social Structure
- Pluralism and Communication
- Urbanism, Neighborhood Characteristics, and Social Relations
- Empirical Evidence of Link Between Social Relations and Urbanism, Neighborhood Characteristics
- Summary

This section begins by examining the relationship among size, social structure, and communication, then looks at consequences of communication for neighborhoods. Within sociology, the traditional line of impact goes from population size to social structure. Following a similar logic, pluralism theory argues that changes in social structure affect patterns of communication, producing a line of impact from size to social structure to communication. The direction of influence generally depends on the home discipline from which a scholar comes, but arguing which is the chick and which is the egg is not a particularly fruitful approach to understanding the complex relationships among the three concepts.

      Neighborhoods may be fairly "recent" phenomena but a "sense of place" is arguably one of the most important ideas in a world beset by constant change. Societies and "nation states" as phenomena are themselves being affected by globalization and increased interdependence across boundaries of place and identity—nation, society, and culture. Communication is not a single variable but a set of processes that link people and help form associations and violate boundaries of place and identity. A more profitable approach is to ask what aspects of communication are affected by social structure, which aspects are not affected, and, reversing the order, how do communication processes affect neighborhood development and the search for community. Thus, influences in both directions can be examined.

SIZE AND SOCIAL STRUCTURE

The classic model in the tradition of Toennies (1957/1887) and Wirth (1938) says that size and density are the primary factors influencing social behavior; thus, urbanism is seen as weakening community kinship and friendship bonds, affectional ties for the community, and social participation in local affairs. What has sometimes been called the *linear hypothesis* begins with the notion of community size and argues that it affects social diversity. Wirth argued that social heterogeneity increases with community size, but, Wilson (1986) noted, he offered no rationale outside the occupational sphere. Fischer (1975a, 1975b, 1984) offered a rationale for a general link between population size and social heterogeneity in his subcultural theory of urbanism, which says that size increases such heterogeneity by increasing the variety of subcultures, defined as "sets of modal beliefs, values, norms and customs associated with a relatively distinct social subsystem" existing in the larger social system (Fischer, 1975b, p. 1323). Wilson (1986) tested the notion that size also leads to heterogeneity in values and attitudes, using a national data set that compared residents in the 12 largest standard metropolitan statistical areas (SMSAs) with those in the next 88 largest SMSAs and those living in smaller communities. Dependent measures of social heterogeneity included several sexual and political attitude measures in the 1980 General Social Survey (e.g., a political liberalism scale, a scale measuring tolerance of communism, and scales measuring tolerance for extramarital sex and homosexuality). In the analysis, all the dependent variables varied with community size, except for equalization of wealth (highest in largest areas but lowest in medium-sized areas) and satisfaction (inversely related to community size). In general, the pattern persists even after controlling for population characteristics such as income, education, age, marital status, and race. Abrahamson and Carter (1986) analyzed national data sets from 1947 to 1982 to study the effects of city size and region on indicators of tolerance, finding the effect of city size declined while the effect of region remained.

PLURALISM AND COMMUNICATION

The "pluralistic perspective" is probably the most popular view expressing the relationship between the community and communication.[24] In this view, communication networks—including mass and interpersonal communication—are constrained by the community and environment in which people live. Huckfeldt and Sprague (1987) noted that people may choose their friends and have some control over their conversations,[25] but these are bounded by the environment. In their study of South Bend, Indiana, both individual preference (whether or not neighbor discussants shared their voting preference) and context (preference of the neighborhood in which one lives) affected the accuracy of predicting voting preference of one's neighbors. Straits (1991) found that people discuss politics more often with closer associates, with people from the same social status, and with politically compatible discussion partners. The classic literature on the "two-step flow" in political communication similarly focuses on how influence occurs through interpersonal communication and personal relationships (see J. Robinson, 1976).

In addition, media themselves in the pluralistic tradition reflect the community they serve. The media are viewed as operating in support of the larger system, as agents of social control (Tichenor, Donohue, & Olien, 1980; Viswanath & Demers, 1999). The macro variable to which influence is generally attributed in the pluralistic perspective is power, sometimes operationalized as status at the individual level. The key notion of structural pluralism is the distribution of power,[26] which is seen as being more widely distributed and decentralized in larger, more heterogeneous communities. The media are viewed as operating in support of the larger system, as agents of social control (Viswanath & Demers, 1999). In smaller, more homogeneous communities, that has been interpreted to mean that papers avoid conflict and engage in consensus reporting, not upsetting the apple cart when people share common values and interests—called "distribution control processes" by Tichenor et al. (1980, p. 85). In larger, more heterogeneous communities, papers are expected to focus on conflict, getting it out in the open so it can be dealt with and problems solved—called "feedback control processes" by Tichenor and his colleagues (1980). Each strategy is seen as functional for the community as a social system. In political science and sociology, the same perspective has been used to examine how people participate in policy making in communities and societies (e.g., Gunnell, 1996; Sartori, 1997; Schumaker, 1991; Waste, 1987).[27] Scholars in mass communication using the pluralism model to study mass media and communities have examined the knowledge gap (C. Gaziano, 1989; E. Gaziano & Gaziano, 1999; Griffin, 1990; Viswanath & Finnegan, 1991), the critical nature of corporate newspapers located in larger, more pluralistic communities (Demers, 1996b, 1998), an increased emphasis on conflict in newspapers located in more pluralistic communities (D. Hindman, 1996), greater use of ethnic minorities as news sources by editors in more ethnically pluralistic communities (E. Hindman, Littlefield, Preston, & Neumann, 1999), the relative constancy hypothesis and use of structural pluralism to predict changes in advertising expenditures (Demers, 1994), the relationship between journalists and news sources as members of interpretive communities (Berkowitz & TerKeurst, 1999), how community heterogeneity or pluralism affect journalists' prioritizing of values (Viall, 1992), greater interactivity of online newspapers in more pluralistic communities (D. Hindman & Homstad, 2000), and a greater likelihood for newspapers to lay blame rather than downplay environmental risks in larger communities (Dunwoody & Griffin, 1999).

URBANISM, NEIGHBORHOOD CHARACTERISTICS, AND SOCIAL RELATIONS

In the urban literature, traditional theory has linked social relations in neighborhoods to traditional urban indicators and neighborhood characteristics. This also has been studied as the "linear hypothesis," as noted earlier. Lindstrom (1997) argued that social bonds and solidarity have been transformed from affective ties into more diffuse relationships. "One of the classic questions in urban sociology is how social relations and solidarity are maintained in an urbanized, industrialized, bureaucratic society. The central theoretical and research focuses have been the issues of (1) the persistence of territorially based affective ties and primary relations in an urban world and (2) the micro/macro links connecting community residents and the larger society" (p. 19). The assumption of the early Chicago School and theorists concerned with preindustrial solidarities in urban neighborhoods was that common locality, territorial boundaries, organizational activity, and population characteristics were necessary for intimate social bonds and social order (Wirth, 1938). Once successful individuals move from immigrant neighborhoods, the link between affective ties and territory was expected to dissolve. In the 1970s, researchers using network analysis found evidence that people who moved beyond their immigrant neighborhoods maintained strong ties with family and friends (Fischer, 1982; Granovetter, 1973; Kadushin, 1966; Laumann, 1973; Wellman, 1979). This concept of community was defined as a personal community rather than a territorially bounded set of relations. Both theoretical approaches conclude that territorially based solidarities are only viable in immigrant enclaves and mobility destroys territorially based social order (Lindstrom, 1997).

Since the 1980s, two theoretical approaches centered on the importance of place have emerged that move away from the debate on territory and affective ties (Lindstrom, 1997). First, the interdisciplinary perspective on *place identity* explores the ways that individuals integrate culturally constructed meaning systems encoded in U.S. houses and communities in constructing their identities (e.g., Csikzentmihalyi & Rochberg-Halton, 1987; Cuba & Hummon, 1993; Duncan, 1976). Second, the neo-Marxian perspective on *place stratification* emphasizes that "place inequality provides the foundation for social inequality" (Lindstrom, 1997, p. 20). In these views, a metropolitan area offers residents a mosaic of communities from which to choose the one that best fits their preferences and values. Households intentionally seek housing and communities that mirror their values and preferences, creating solidarity not necessarily as warm intimate ties or even social relationships. A sense of community is seen as occurring because people occupy the same social position and share common symbolic understandings of home and community (Lindstrom, 1997). However, although these perspectives emphasize "commonalities" in terms of social class and shared values, they do not rule out the importance of relationships and communication.[28] The next section examines the empirical research linking neighborhoods and social relations, followed by a similar review of the research linking communication to neighborhoods and social relations.

EMPIRICAL EVIDENCE OF LINK BETWEEN SOCIAL RELATIONS AND URBANISM, NEIGHBORHOOD CHARACTERISTICS

Like communication, social relations represent more than a single variable. Thus, there is evidence examining choice in social relations, the impact of urban variables on *neighboring behaviors*, and the impact of urbanism on a host of measures tapping *community attachment, community attitudes*, and similar factors. That evidence shows that urban structure does have an impact on socializing, with less socializing in urban areas than in small towns; however, neighboring appears to be greater in central-city neighborhoods than in suburbs. Social structure also constrains one's choices for association (e.g., ethnic diversity encourages interaction among people from different groups). There also is some evidence that socializing has declined in the United States over the past few decades. Community attachment and ties are lowest in those neighborhoods with high residential mobility, and analysis at the individual level shows that the length of one's residence in a community is the strongest predictor of neighboring activities and community attachment. Objective neighborhood characteristics—crime and housing—are more important for an individual's integration into a community than is size of population. Clearly, the links between urbanism, neighborhood characteristics, and social relations are more complex than traditional theory suggests. The following studies lay out the complexity of those relationships.

Blum (1985) tested Blau's (1977) macrostructural theory about the rate of *social contacts* between different social characteristics using a California data set. Differentiation and integration are opposites in Blau's schema, the former providing barriers to associations and the latter resting on bonds established by ingroup association.[29] Blum's research shows that social structure does constrain choice (e.g., religious and ethnic heterogeneity encourages social interactions among people from different ethnic or religious groups). Measures of *intergroup relations* were based on the number of people with whom respondents reported socializing during the 3 months prior to the survey. Palisi and

Ransford (1987) looked at patterns of socializing with friends in and out of the neighborhood using the General Social Surveys in the United States for 1974, 1975, 1977, 1978, 1982, and 1983; population size was used as a measure of urbanism, and a modest but positive relationship was found with socializing with friends outside the neighborhood—thus, urban residents socialized more than less urban people. Income and education were positively correlated with socializing with friends outside the neighborhood. Urbanism was negatively associated with socializing with neighbors, as was income but not education. Thus, those in larger cities socialized less with neighbors than did those in smaller cities or rural areas; those with more income—who generally live in larger homes on larger lots—socialize less with their neighbors than do those with less income. Being married, age, and having children were negatively associated with socializing in and out of the neighborhood. All correlations are very small but statistically significant, so the impact of urbanism is minor.

Concerned with the "decline of community" question, Guest and Wierzbicki (1999) used the General Social Survey to see whether there was a decline in socializing with neighbors and with friends outside the neighborhood from 1974 to 1996. Some 15 of the surveys during that period asked respondents to tell how frequently they "spend a social evening" with someone from their neighborhood. A second question asked how often they "spend a social evening with friends who live outside the neighborhood." Results showed a positive relationship between the two variables—social people are social across contexts. Across the two decades, socializing with neighbors declines somewhat, whereas socializing with friends outside the neighborhood shows an increase, and the decline within neighborhoods is not offset by the external increase, providing some support for the "community-lost perspective" and an overall decline in socializing in the United States (Guest & Wierzbicki, 1999, p. 103). The youngest and those without children had the highest absolute neighborhood activity patterns. The absolute levels of socializing with neighbors showed little change over the decades for seniors. There was little evidence of different trends by education, gender, or other social categories. Bleiker (1972) noted that in a Massachusetts study of a complex, heterogeneous urban area, the nature of *personal relations* was not adequately explained by proximity, age, or social class; even hippies and old-timers established friendly ties. Greider and Krannich (1985) found data refuting the popular notion that *primary neighboring interaction* declines with the onset of rapid population growth and heterogeneity. Schwirian (1983) noted that a major interest in human ecology is the extent to which neighborhoods maintain their social organization in the face of continued population turnover. Research by Moore (1972, cited in Schwirian, 1983) and by Schwirian and Berry (1982, cited in Schwirian, 1983) suggests that population turnover and neighborhood change are independent processes. Neighborhoods may change under conditions of low turnover and they may remain socially stable under conditions of high turnover.[30]

Kasarda and Janowitz (1974) focused on the length of residence as the key exogenous factor affecting *attitudes and behavior toward the community*. Kasarda and Janowitz (1974) found that length of residence was positively related to *local friendships, community sentiment,* and *participation in local affairs,* independent of urbanization, density, socioeconomic status (SES), and life cycle. The longer people live in a neighborhood or community, the stronger their affective attachments with the area, regardless of other factors.

Sampson (1988) used a national sample of 10,905 residents in 238 localities in Great Britain to examine *friendship ties* and *community attachment.* He sought to examine macro-social determinants of community social organization and effects of community structure on individual behavior. Hypotheses were that community residential stability positively affects macro-social variations in the extent of community-based friendship ties, the level of collective attachment, and social activity patterns (participation in local organizations and leisure activities). The major prediction was that length of residence and community residential stability would be positively related to one's local friendships, community attachment, and participation in local activities. Residential stability was defined as the percentage of residents brought up in the area within a 15-minute walk of home. Local friendship ties was defined as the percentage of community residents with half or more of their friends within a 15-minute walk of home. Collective attachment was the level of sentiment and attachment to community, measured as the percentage of residents reporting they would be "very sorry" to leave the local area. Five items measured social participation (average number of nights went out of the home in the week for leisure, social, or other spare-time activities; visiting friends and relatives; leisure entertainment; going to sporting events; and organizational participation). Individual-level measures were length of residence, local friendships living in the area, community attachment (how sorry to move from area), and social activity (nights outside home for leisure activities).

Results showed that collective levels of attachment are lowest in communities with residential mobility, higher urbanization, density of youth, and high levels of fear about crime. Rates of total leisure and social activity were explained by three community characteristics: residential stability, urbanization, and levels of fear.

Looking at the effect of community structure on individuals, Sampson (1988) found the length of community residence was the largest predictor of individual local friendships, as hypothesized. However, residential stability also had an impact, positively affecting local friendship ties (so both the context and individual-level variables had an impact).

Individual-level length of residence increased every type of community participation. The largest contextual effect was on local entertainment and leisure activities. As the systemic model of community (Kasarda & Janowitz, 1974) would suggest, length of residence had direct effects on the individual's local friendships, attachment to community, and participation in local social activities. Community residential stability also had significant contextual effects on the individual resident's local friendships and participation in local social activities. Furthermore, social-network theory (see, e.g., Fischer et al., 1977; Freudenburg, 1986; Wellman, 1983) "suggests that the density of friendship ties in a community comprises a structural constraint that does not characterize any one individual. For example, a sparse or nonexistent pattern of local friendship networks probably indicates fewer opportunities for individuals from new local ties, regardless of length of residence" (Sampson, 1988, pp. 776-777).

In further analysis looking at both the contextual and individual level, Sampson found that residents of areas where the level of attachment is high also report greater sentiment for the community; all other things being equal, the impact of urbanization was not statistically significant once collective attachment was controlled. At the macro level, analysis showed that local friendship ties vary widely across communities and that the variations are positively related to community stability. Specifically, macro-level stability strongly increased local friendship ties at both ends of the urban-rural continuum. Residential stability also had less powerful but independent effects on collective attachment to community and participation in local leisure and social activities, such as visitation, entertainment, and sporting events. Data also showed that the community's level of friendship ties had a significant and important contextual effect on an individual's local friendships. The structural constraints imposed by aggregate friendship patterns and the normative climate reflected in levels of collective attachment apparently exert independent influences on residents' behavior and attitudes toward the community.

Sampson (1988) concluded:

> Overall, the data suggest that the important social forces that undermine an individual's integration into the local community are not urbanization or the compositional factors (e.g., low social class) as suggested in traditional theory. Rather, they are multilevel systemic factors such as residential mobility and sparse friendship ties, and other factors anticipated but just beginning to be understood [fear of crime, attenuated collective attachment]. (p. 778)

Ginsberg (1975) compared two Tel Aviv neighborhoods, finding significant differences in the degree of social activities between a homogeneous, close-knit community and a neighborhood that was heterogeneous. In the close-knit community, married men shared their activities much less with their wives than did married men in the heterogeneous community.

Silverman (1986) found that the correlation between urbanism and *neighboring* was an artifact of how neighboring is defined. Analyzing a 1,050-person survey from 1977 to 1978 in northern California, she measured neighboring as the number of neighbors who were not kin but who could be called on to take care of the home. The association between urbanism (population) and neighboring dropped out when local variables (housing, ethnicity) were included in the model.

Jeffres, Perloff, Atkin, and Neuendorf (2000) looked at different neighborhoods and suburban communities from a major midwestern metropolitan area in a project examining relationships between the nature of the community and behavioral patterns within them. Six center-city neighborhoods, three first-ring suburbs, and three outer-ring suburbs were selected and U.S. Census data matched with the communities to allow for classification in subsequent analysis. A sample of residents from each of the 12 neighborhoods was drawn for a survey that measured neighboring,[31] neighborhood activity,[32] community attachment,[33] and other variables.[34] Results showed that neighboring was greatest in the central city neighborhoods and lowest status neighborhoods, but the relationship was not perfectly linear by location. However, neighborhood activity was lowest in the city and lower status neighborhoods and highest in the first ring and middle status communities. Community attachment did not differ by neighborhood location or status, but relationships with perceived community solidarity approach significance, with perceived solidarity highest in the outer ring and highest status suburbs and lowest in the central city communities. Both neighborhood location and status have an impact on perceived neighborhood quality of life, with a more positive QOL perception as one moves outward from the city or upward in status. When the three measures of affect were combined into a single scale, there was a strong additive effect

Blau (1977) noted that the importance of neighborhood for social interaction decreases as residential mobility increases. Thus, proportionally less communication with neighbors and more communication with those outside neighborhoods among higher SES people would be expected. In contemporary society, modern transportation, mobility, and mass media help overcome obstacles of physical distance to social associations (Blau, 1977). Homel, Burns, and Goodnow (1987) found that the SES of a neighborhood affected a child's social involvement with peers and friendship patterns.

Palisi and Palisi (1984) noted that urbanism has affected the way in which people relate to each other. He studied social participation in three contexts: Los Angeles; Sydney, Australia; and London, England. He noted the literature arguing that *formal associations* arise and thrive because of the attenuation of primary relationships (with immediate family and kin) in urban areas (Fischer, 1975c); the logic is that family and kin relationships are no longer supported by the city's structure so friends are more important in one's social life. He found that membership in formal associations was substantial in all three cities (only 19% of Los Angeles residents were not members, and only 23% to 25% of those in Sydney and London were not members). Also, 40% reported they had attended at least monthly meetings, so memberships were not passive. However, respondents tended to share relatively little "intimacy with kin." In Sydney and Los Angeles, only 33% reported intimate discussions with extended kin once a month or more often; in Sydney, 37% were never intimate with extended kin. A similar picture was found for friendships; respondents visited frequently but did not often have intimate discussions.

Respondents were more likely to visit frequently with friends (at least 50% visited weekly or more) than with kin. Thus, urban respondents interacted more often with friends than with kin and had more intimate discussions with friends than with kin (38% had such discussions with friends weekly or more often, compared with some 15% who shared such intimate discussions with kin). Thus, the image of social isolation and detachment in the city portrayed by Wirth (1938) and others was not supported in urban areas on three different continents. The data also supported the interaction view that interacting with friends was positively correlated with involvement with kin in each city. Being involved in a variety of social activities did not lead to decreased well-being, and those who shared intimacy with friends, extended kin, spouse, and others in the household were happier (also see Palisi, 1985).

SUMMARY

This chapter focused on the relationship among size, social structure, and communication. The impact of social structure on communication processes is expressed in both the linear hypothesis and pluralism theory. The former says that size and density are primary factors influencing social behavior, with urbanism weakening community bonds and ties; studies show some impact of city size on attitudes but not on satisfaction. The latter says that communication networks—mass and interpersonal—are constrained by the community and environment in which people live, particularly by its social structure (conceptualized as the distribution of power but often measured in terms of community characteristics such as status and diversity); politics has been the prime target of scholars examining interpersonal communication using this logic. A much larger literature exists in mass communication, where the pluralistic tradition initiated by Tichenor et al. (1980) has generated evidence that media content and operations often reflect community size and social characteristics.

The key factors in the linear hypothesis, size and social structure, exert their influence through social relationships, the notion being that the common characteristics of neighborhoods and community are necessary for social bonds and warm relationships. Evidence linking social relations with urbanism has examined neighboring behaviors, community attachment, and community attitudes. Thus, ethnic diversity encourages social interaction among people from different backgrounds, urban residents socialize more than less urban people, community attachment is lowest in more urban areas but mobility and friendship ties are more important than urbanism for one's integration into a community. Furthermore, diversity does not affect neighboring activity, which is greater in the central city. A study on three continents does not support the image of social isolation and detachment in the city portrayed by Wirth (1938) and others. Although there clearly is support for the impact of size and social structure on some variables operationalizing social relation-ships, it does not extend across the range of variables tapping neighboring, community attachment, and community attitudes. The next chapter examines empirical evidence for the relationship between communication variables and community linkages.

3

Communication and Community Linkages: Empirical Evidence

- Community Ties and Communication
- Community Location, Status and Communication
- Neighborhood Pluralism, Diversity and Communication
- Significance of Influences at Different Levels
- Summary

Community linkages have been related to media use since R. E. Park's (1925) work in Chicago more than half a century ago. The multidimensional concept is employed in several disciplines and is associated with such notions as community integration. Rothenbuhler (1991) noted that community ties have operationally been defined to include the following:

1. Structural ties such as owning a home, having a job.
2. Social network ties such as the number of relatives and friends in an area and frequency of interaction with them.
3. Participation in local organizations and "localness of the activity" (e.g., extent to which one shops, works, engages in leisure activities locally).
4. Cognitive ties such as knowledge about local issues.
5. Personal identification with the local area.
6. Affective ties (e.g., having affection for the area and being happy living there).[35]

Clearly, the emphasis shifts with the disciplinary focus of the researcher. Looking at community integration, media use, and democratic processes, McLeod et al. (1996) used 15 indicators drawn from integration studies to test the hypothesis that community integration is a multidimensional concept. Their research identifies five dimensions: psychological attachment (like living in area, view it as home, likelihood will move away), interpersonal discussion networks (indexed by discussion with neighbors, discussing area problems, getting together with neighbors, and the proportion of friends who live in the area), city versus group (identify with city or with social group), localism versus cosmopolitanism (local news more interesting than national, best organizations are local), and city versus neighborhood (concern with larger community rather than concern with local town or neighborhood and identification with neighbors).[36]

COMMUNITY TIES AND COMMUNICATION

Four different ties to a community were related to media use by Viswanath, Finnegan, Rooney, and Potter (1990); they found civic and political involvement related to newspaper subscription. Emig (1995) found a significant relationship between community ties—including voting in local elections—and keeping up with local news and certain media use.[37] Collins-Jarvis (1992) found community identification predicted community newspaper use. In a long program studying community involvement, Stamm (1985, 2000) found people's use of newspapers linked to their integration into a community (Stamm & Guest, 1991), but some media contribute more to individual involvement in a community than do others (Stamm, Emig, & Hesse, 1997). Most recently, Stamm (2000) found evidence that community newspaper readership was related to a variety of community involvement measures, including working for change, attending a community forum, and participating in local organizations. Janowitz (1952/1967) found that people in smaller communities thought local newspapers should promote social consensus; he also thought that participation in and identification with local facilities and institutions would be linked to greater use of local newspapers. Blau (1977) noted the importance of neighborhood for social interaction. In contemporary society, modern transportation, mobility, and mass media help overcome obstacles of physical distance to social associations (Blau, 1977, p. 4; also see Blum, 1985[38]). In their research on community integration, McLeod et al. (1996) found strong relationships between local media use and the dimensions of community integration. In addition, media use was significantly related to community knowledge, local political interest, and measures of community involvement, attending forums, and institutional activities. Interpersonal communication variables—included in the community integration concept—also were correlated with community attachment and an emphasis on localism versus cosmopolitanism.

COMMUNITY LOCATION, STATUS,
AND COMMUNICATION

The survey by Jeffres and associates (2000) reported in chapter 2 also included measures of communication, including a scale of items tapping the strength of one's involvement in the neighborhood communication network,[39] interest in neighborhood news and reliance on various communication channels,[40] and two global measures of interpersonal communication links[41] and mass media use.[42] Results showed that both neighborhood location and status affect the strength of communication patterns linking people to their neighborhoods, with the strongest patterns found in the central neighborhoods and those with the lowest status, followed by outer ring and middle status communities. This is the reverse of what was hypothesized. Another research question asked whether there would be any impact of neighborhood location and status on interest in neighborhood news and preferred channels. Interest in neighborhood activities was greatest in the lowest and highest status neighborhoods and differences by location approach significance. The importance of sources of neighborhood news also vary by neighborhood location and status, with people—interpersonal communication—more important for the center-city and lower status communities, the chain weekly more important in the more distant suburbs—where they are more available, and television more important in center-city neighborhoods. Neither of the two general communication measures—tapping overall interpersonal contact and overall mass communication—is affected by neighborhood location and status.

NEIGHBORHOOD PLURALISM, DIVERSITY,
AND COMMUNICATION

Jeffres, Cutietta, Sekerka, and Lee (2000) applied the pluralism model in a national study examining the impact of community characteristics on neighborhood newspapers and reporting styles in the 25 largest metropolitan areas of the country.[43] The study draws on several measures designed to tap conflict versus consensus reporting styles as advanced by Tichenor and his colleagues, but it imbeds these measures in a larger set of newspaper goals and functions as described by newspaper editors (also see Jeffres, Cutietta, Lee, & Sekerka, 1999),[44] allowing them to ask if other goals and functions are affected by community pluralism. The study separates out size of population from measures of pluralism and diversity and relies on Blau's (1977) distinction between heterogeneity and inequality (group diversity and status) in constructing measures of pluralism and diversity.[45] The former was conceptualized as the distribution of status via occupational differentiation, income differentiation, and educational differentiation. The latter was conceptualized as heterogeneity in terms of race, ethnicity, and language use. In addition, the study adds differentiation by life-cycle factors—age, marital status, and household size—which represent sources of distinction and life style that affect diversity and are not synonymous with pluralism. Most of the studies of structural pluralism in mass communication and sociology "infer" the distribution of power through measuring the number of groups, schools, or by using similar indicators. The notion is that larger numbers of groups and institutions represent the potential for power to be distributed more diffusely rather than concentrated. The potential political power held by groups is illustrated by the turmoil in China in 1999 over the Falun Gong, a mediation group banned by the government as a threat to the Communist Party because of its ability to mobilize millions of people. However, most of the operationalizations utilize measures of central tendency (e.g., levels of income, percentages of workforce not in agriculture) rather than measures of dispersion. This study used measures of dispersion of social status within a community because access to resources—whether through income, education, or occupational status—is one basis for power.[46] Population of a community was related to numerous measures of community diversity and pluralism, and was highly correlated with the summary measure of diversity–pluralism.[47] Editors' perceptions of who wields power in the community are related to several measures of community diversity and pluralism in the census data.[48]

The actual test of Tichenor et al.'s conflict-reporting styles is found in relationships between measures of consensus and conflict reporting and census measures of status differentiation and diversity. Life-cycle diversity was positively correlated with both conflict and consensus reporting. Thus, in communities with greater differentiation by household size and marital status, editors emphasize consensus reporting. The correlation between racial diversity in the community and emphasizing consensus reporting approaches significance, as does the negative relationship between consensus reporting and household income differentiation (i.e., the greater income differentiation, the less the emphasis on consensus reporting).

Measures of pluralism and diversity also were related to other newspaper goals and functions.[49] The index measuring overall diversity–pluralism in the census data is correlated with only one dimension—the relative importance of advertising and theater as goals or functions. The three census measures of status differentiation (income, occupational status, and education) are relatively unimportant, although household income differentiation is positively correlated with an emphasis on people—features and photos. The measures of ascriptive diversity in the census—race, language, and gender—also appear in a couple of significant relationships, and the index of ascriptive diversity is positively correlated with the relative importance of civic journalism and activism as newspaper goals and functions. One could argue that status has been replaced by social ethnic differences as the basis of conflict, and, thus, there is a need to view such group differences as the basis of power conflicts that are reflected in newspaper reporting styles. Life-cycle diversity is much more important and all measures are related to one or more newspaper goals and functions. The index tapping life-cycle diversity is positively correlated with an emphasis on civic journalism/activity and with the importance of ethnic news and social services. The less life-cycle diversity in the community, the more important are advertising and theater in editors' ratings. Thus, in communities with a greater mixture of singles, retirees, married couples, and other combinations, the social differences lead to an emphasis on activism and coverage of social services that cater to the different groups. There also is strong evidence that in communities composed largely of families (and less diversity on marital status), editors emphasize church news, organizational news, and personal items, as would be expected.

Although pluralism is a valuable perspective for examining the relationship between the community and mass media, this study suggests that a straightforward reflection hypothesis is clearly too simple an application, and there is a need to treat the relationship more as a complex process than a static position. Communication phenomena are more complicated than that and, in a given situation, media not only reflect but affect aspects of the communities they serve.

SIGNIFICANCE OF INFLUENCES AT DIFFERENT LEVELS

In an additional analysis, Jeffres and Lee (1999) examined influences at different levels—the community level, the organizational level, and the individual level—to see whether community, organizational, or individual characteristics were more important factors influencing journalists' perceptions of their community. In their portrait of U.S. journalists, Weaver and Wilhoit (1996) described the background of U.S. news people, their characteristics, education, job conditions, professional values and ethics. Their national sample paints a picture of American journalists as individuals and as members of both organizations and professions, but not as residents of their communities. The pluralistic model used by Tichenor and his associates (1980) views the media themselves as reflecting the community and operating within the structural constraints imposed by size. Thus, they found that editors in more complex, pluralistic communities see planning as a part of maintaining community social order and control more than editors from smaller communities (Olien, Tichenor, Donohue, Sandstrom, & McLeod, 1990). To some extent, these traditions miss an important link—that between journalists and the communities they reflect and affect.

Studies focusing on journalists detached from communities suggest that family, education, and role pressures (from other journalists) are key influences on journalists, and no doubt they are; management policies, whether one is college educated, and experiences gained from being a member of a minority

group all can influence reporting processes. Demers and Merskin (1998) found
that structurally complex newspapers were seen by sources as being more critical. At the same time, the pluralistic model could be viewed as placing control
in sources and audiences or in several potential relationships, those between
journalist and source, between journalist and audience, or between ownership
and local influentials. These factors also are important (e.g., journalists cannot
report conflict that's not present and a multitude of equally powerful sources
surely influences the nature of local news). D. Hindman and Richardson (1998)
explored the ways a community's social and economic conditions shape a local
newspaper editors' perception of the problems facing the community.
Following the pluralistic tradition, they argue that individualistic interpretations
of journalists' performance fail to consider the social organization underlying
the media system. They surveyed 85 Minnesota and 51 North Dakota newspaper editors in two studies that used three indicators of pluralism: county population; the number of residents with college degrees; and the percentage of adults
not employed in agricultural, fisheries, or forestry occupations. They found that
editors in less pluralistic communities were more likely to see a lack of growth
as a major community problem in contrast to editors in more pluralistic communities. The logic was that papers in smaller communities would tend to feel the
impact of declining economic conditions and the paper's profitability would be
more closely tied to the local economy. Demers and Merskin (1998) also pointed out that more structurally complex papers are likely to be in more pluralistic
communities.

The task is to lay out the links and influence processes that include
individual journalists, their professions and organizations, and the community.
Clearly, the results produced using each of these traditions show that no single
model has the final word in determining outcomes of the reporting and news-
writing processes. It is an empirical question that must be answered periodically
as communities, the industry, the journalistic profession, and audiences change
in a media system that continually reinvents itself when confronted with changing technologies.

Journalists are trained to be expert observers of their communities
because their professional performance depends on such assessments. By examining these assessments, further information can be obtained to help sort out the
power of the different research traditions. In their roles, editors assign stories
and act as final arbitrators of news values and the importance attributed to specific stories. In smaller papers, they also write editorials commenting on community issues and local civic disputes. Thus, the accuracy and nature of their
perceptions is important to audiences. To what extent are journalists' perceptions and assessments of their community dependent on the structure of the
community, the media organization, the personal background of journalists, or
the journalist's place in the community being served by his or her newspaper?
These issues were examined in a national survey of community newspaper editors in major metropolitan areas of the United States by Jeffres and Lee (1999).

Their analysis asked three questions: (a) What is the *impact of community characteristics* (including census data and characteristics reported by editors) on editors' perceptions of their community? This research question reflects issues raised by the pluralism model in mass communication research as well as those emphasizing sociological traditions; (b) What is the *impact of newspaper characteristics* (from circulation, frequency and ownership to economic factors, all as reported by editors) on editors' perceptions of their community? This research question reflects the tradition followed by those emphasizing consequences of organizational and industrial structure on "news-making";[50] (c) What is the *impact of social categories* on editors' perceptions of their community? This research question reflects the long line of research on demographics and individual differences (e.g., portraits of journalists by Weaver and Wilhoit, 1996, and others).

The Jeffres and Lee (1999) survey of community newspaper editors in the 25 largest U.S. metropolitan areas used a series of items that tapped perceptions of both audiences and the community. The study is part of the Urban Grassroots Journalism Project, which focuses on urban community newspapers in urban areas, whose size and location insure diversity. The project matched the editors' communities with census data. The questionnaire contained sections to operationalize the three sources of influence:

1. *Community Diversity–Pluralism Measures*—As described earlier, these are based on U.S. Census Bureau data of gender, race, age, household size, marital status, language use, education, occupation, and household income in the communities, using Blau's (1977) formula for variance across categories; in addition, *Reports on Community Size and Population* were included as independent variables along with the census data. Editors provided the size of the population served, whether it included city and/or suburban neighborhoods, the number of square miles of the community and the number of zip codes represented by the target population.

2. *Newspaper Background and Characteristics*—Several items in the survey questionnaire obtained information about the newspaper, its organization and distribution, including: the paper's circulation, frequency of publication, whether it is a member of a chain, and the percentage of revenue from advertising, sales and other sources. An open-ended question solicited major problems facing the community paper and these were coded as financial, news-gathering, distribution, audience or other; the range was 0-2.

3. *Editors' Background and Place in the Community*—Editors were asked for their age, gender, level of education and whether they lived in the neighborhood or elsewhere. The dependent variables included three broad areas of the community perceptions—editors were asked about the following three areas: *Quality of Life*—the quality of life,

community image, community assets and liablities;[51] *Residents Behaviors*—residents' attachment to the area, residents interaction, activities, and level of information;[52] *Community Characteristics*—distribution of social categories (including measures of pluralism), an inventory of major community/neighborhood institutions, sources of local power, and types of local conflicts.[53]

In their analysis, Jeffres and Lee (1999) found that the *editor's backgrounds and characteristics* did affect their perceptions, but these social categories played a minor role in comparison to community characteristics and newspaper characteristics (see Table 1 in the appendix).[54] Of the individual characteristics, age—perhaps a proxy for experience—and education appear as the most significant influences.

Newspaper characteristics as a group appear as key predictors in 14 instances (see Tables 2 and 3 in the appendix). *Newspaper characteristics* were significant predictors of variables in each of the three categories of dependent variables—perceptions of community QOL,[55] perceptions of residents' behaviors,[56] and perceptions of community diversity and pluralism.[57] The key newspaper characteristic influencing editors' perceptions was the source of revenue—whether newspapers depend on advertising or other sources for their income. The percentage of advertising was a predictor in three instances, the most of any single variable. An allied variable, whether the paper was distributed free or sold, garnered another slot as a predictor. The origins of the community newspaper—whether founded by activists, an individual entrepreneur, or others—emerged as a major source of influence in five instances; thus, it would appear that the "nature" or "purpose" of the paper—whether it was founded as a business, as the voice of activists or for other goals—was particularly important. Because this affects both the content and targeted audiences, it should come as no surprise. Two other newspaper characteristics—circulation and frequency of publication—were predictors in three instances.[58]

Community characteristics were second to newspaper characteristics as a set of predictors, and the importance of specific measures appeared to be linked to specific dependent variables rather than running across all five (see Table 3.1, which gives the relationships between general community characteristics obtained in the survey—size and the type of community served—and editors' perceptions,[59] and Table 3.2, which gives the relationships between variables based on census data—measures of diversity and pluralism—and editors' perceptions[60]). Each of three census measures of diversity—one reflecting status, one reflecting an ascriptive factor, and one a life-cycle marker—were key predictors twice: household income diversity, language diversity, and marital status diversity. Other census measures generating predictive strength once were occupational diversity, racial diversity and educational diversity. Also, three community characteristics reported by the editors, population, serving the central city, and the number of zip codes served by the paper, were key predictors once.

TABLE 3.1
Relationships Between Community Characteristics Reported by Editor and Editor's Community Perceptions

	Community Characteristics Reported by Editors					
	Square Miles	Pop.	No. Zips	Serve suburbs	Serve city	Serve both
Quality of Life Variables						
Quality of Life Ratings						
Editor's community QOL rating	-.05	-.20*	-.15	-.20*	.24**	.00
How think residents rate QOL	.03	-.17#	-.11	-.09	.17#	-.03
Residents' Image of Area						
People focus	.10	-.14	-.03	-.10	.17*	-.01
Nature-Physical emphasis	-.03	.02	-.06	.01	.02	.05
Housing-Culture	-.07	-.09	-.03	-.03	.03	.05
Negative	-.09	-.13	-.12	.06	-.06	.04
Positive	-.07	-.02	-.02	.07	.04	-.07
Attitude	-.09	.08	-.04	.03	.10	-.12
Major Assets of Area						
Physical	-.14	-.01	-.05	-.05	.04	.09
People	.03	-.08	-.09	-.05	-.10	.15#
Leisure opp.	.19*	-.00	.10	-.03	.02	-.10
Economic factors	.12	-.00	.07	-.05	.12	.03
Services avlb.	.06	.02	.09	.03	.13	-.08
Feelings, attitudes	-.10	.24*	-.01	.07	.08	-.08
Area's Major Liabilities						
Economic	.09	.06	.01	.10	.03	-.10
People	-.09	.06	-.16#	-.01	.00	-.02
Poverty	-.06	.02	.14	.07	.07	-.08
Housing	.09	-.24*	-.06	-.13	-.04	.20*
Crime	.16#	.06	.13	.07	-.11	.03
Roads	.06	-.02	.13	.10	-.05	-.01
Government	.07	-.07	-.09	-.16#	.29***	.01
Schools	-.07	-.02	.04	-.01	-.04	.05
Public services	-.04	-.06	-.04	.16#	-.12	-.02
Urban ills	.02	.08	-.02	.19*	-.07	-.10
Racial factors	.04	.08	-.03	-.03	.00	.10
Environment	.02	.01	-.01	.07	.04	.14
Perceptions of Residents' Behaviors						
Level of commitment to area	-.01	.02	-.03	.02	.05	-.02
Talkfreq (frequency talk)	.10	.02	-.05	-.08	-.11	.15
Inout (internal–external links)	-.08	.05	-.01	-.10	.10	.06
Wheretlk (street/public activity)	.04	.13	.06	.08	.04	-.09
GR1 (amount of formal group activity)	.14	.22*	.14	-.04	.04	.03
GR2 (how much group activity exists)	.02	.08	.03	-.11	.16#	.03

(continues)

TABLE 3.1 (cont.)

| | *Community Characteristics Reported by Editors* | | | | | |
	Square Miles	Pop.	No. Zips	Serve suburbs	Serve city	Serve both
Informd (informed about current events)	.10	-.02	.14	.20*	-.24**	.01
Demrep (who won last pres. race in community vote)	.02	-.08	-.07	.03	-.27**	.31***
Community Perceptions						
Diversity Perceptions						
Total Perceived Diversity	.15	-.00	.21*	.05	-.09	.09
Racial Diversity	.11	.04	.24*	-.09	-.02	.10
Religious Diversity	.07	.07	.22*	.02	-.10	.06
Educational Diversity	.07	-.04	.05	.09	-.15	.04
Life-cycle Diversity	.03	-.11	.07	.07	-.08	.10
SES Diversity	.14	-.03	.13	.04	.01	-.02
Institutions Reported in Community by Editors						
No. institutions cited (Instcom)	.11	.29**	.25*	.21*	.08	-.17*
Major factory (Factry)	-.01	.19*	.11	.09	.05	-.07
Library (Libry)	.09	.07	.12	.05	.05	.02
Park (Park)	.09	-.06	.06	.14#	.08	-.06
Manufacturing areas (Mfg)	.01	.23*	.10	.20*	.02	-.18*
Local hospital (Hosptl)	.16#	.24*	.20*	.01	.08	-.01
Recreation center (Recon)	.05	.19#	.19*	.20*	-.01	-.10
Several churches (Church2)	.06	-.08	.05	.08	.11	-.04
Shopping mall (Mall)	.12	.38***	.20*	.21**	.02	-.25**
Private ethnic club (Club)	.11	.21*	.22*	.19*	.02	-.14#
Retail stores (Retail)	.08	.10	.02	.11	.13	-.16#
Small convenience stores (Constor)	.04	-.02	-.03	.05	.05	-.04
Local schools attended by area youth (Locsch)	.01	.13	.14	.18*	.05	-.15#
Editor's Perceptions of Who Has Power in Community						
Neighborhood groups (Powngrps)	-.07	-.01	.06	-.03	-.01	.13
Money (Powmoney)	-.01	.07	-.03	-.03	.17*	-.12
Institutions (Powinst)	-.07	-.19*	-.16#	-.08	.19*	-.00
Media (Powmedia)	-.05	.03	-.13	.05	-.01	-.13
Government (Powgov)	-.08	.00	-.00	.01	-.02	-.02
Editor's Reports of Neighborhood Conflicts						
Social, group conflicts (Consocl)	.02	-.07	.07	.04	-.06	.03
Political conflicts (Conpol)	-.06	-.10	-.03	-.00	.05	-.03
Economic conflicts (Conecon)	-.00	-.02	-.04	-.03	.00	.09

Note. Sample sizes for variables in the survey are 141, with occasional missing data. The sample size for correlations involving one of the variables based on census area are 81, with occasional missing data.

TABLE 3.2

Relationship Between Community Characteristics (Census Variables) and Editor's Perceptions

	Total Census Div.	Gender Div.	Racial Div.	Age Div.	House-hold Div.	Marital Status Div.	Lang-uage Div.	Ed. Div.	Occup. Div.	Income Div.
								Community Diversity Variables Based on Census Data		
Quality of Life Variables										
Quality of Life Ratings										
Editor's QOL rating	-.27*	-.02	-.31**	-.06	-.28*	-.27*	-.14	-.02	-.33**	.37***
How think residents rate QOL	-.31**	-.03	-.26*	-.01	-.30**	-.30**	-.21#	-.00	-.31**	.34**
Residents' Image of Area										
People focus	-.03	-.14	-.01	.10	.14	-.09	-.11	-.17	-.05	-.05
Nature-physical emphasis	-.04	.07	-.14	.06	-.12	.07	-.01	-.06	-.16	.03
Housing-culture	.00	.04	.09	.07	-.01	.18#	.22*	.14	.07	-.01
Negative	-.07	.06	.03	-.13	.03	.03	-.02	-.05	.10	-.24*
Positive	.00	.05	-.04	.07	-.02	-.00	.09	.07	.00	.15
Attitude	.13	.07	-.04	-.02	-.10	-.05	.03	-.01	.01	.06
Major Assets of Area										
Physical	-.21#	-.01	-.15	-.16	-.28**	.08	-.12	.10	-.03	.08
People	.06	-.13	.08	-.04	-.04	.09	-.07	-.02	-.05	-.01
Leisure opp.	.09	.08	.13	-.30**	-.20#	-.04	.11	.06	-.07	.18
Economic factors	-.06	.10	-.11	.00	-.07	.01	-.21#	-.15	.06	.14
Services avlb.	.12	-.01	.09	.22*	.32**	-.14	.16	.15	.16	-.07
Feelings, attitudes	.10	.07	-.12	-.01	-.18	-.01	-.10	-.08	-.33**	.16
Area's Major Liabilities										
Economic	-.05	-.02	-.16	-.13	-.01	-.15	-.08	-.04	.01	.01
People	-.19#	.09	-.16	-.23*	-.02	-.12	-.04	.06	-.26*	-.12

(continues)

TABLE 3.2 (cont.)

	Total Census Div.	Gender Div.	Racial Div.	Age Div.	House-hold Div.	Marital Status Div.	Lang-uage Div.	Ed. Div.	Occup. Div.	Income Div.
Community Diversity Variables Based on Census Data										
Poverty	.37***	.08	.19#	.02	.01	.16	.23*	.07	.07	.07
Housing	-.04	-.08	.12	-.04	.02	.19#	.01	-.02	.15	-.23*
Crime	.15	-.02	.40***	-.06	.09	.28*	.06	-.03	.17	-.16
Roads	.01	-.15	.03	.08	-.03	-.06	.06	.15	-.08	.22*
Government	-.15	-.05	-.35***	.03	-.14	-.21#	-.27*	-.16	-.19#	.20#
Schools	.23*	-.02	.03	.06	.09	.07	.03	-.04	.20#	-.05
Public services	-.02	.03	.07	.01	.09	.01	.11	.11	.07	.02
Urban ills	-.11	.06	-.08	.03	-.40***	.07	-.07	.16	-.16	.23*
Racial factors	.06	.05	-.04	.20#	.10	.02	-.08	.12	.05	.02
Environment	-.13	.06	-.06	.11	.13	-.08	-.03	.04	.03	.12
Perceptions of Residents' Behaviors										
Commitment to area	-.02	.08	-.11	-.06	.09	.08	-.01	-.02	.24*	-.23*
Talkfreq (frequency talk)	-.05	-.09	.22#	.00	-.05	.12	.01	.01	-.15	.09
Inout (internal–external links)	-.01	.03	-.03	-.12	-.16	-.10	-.02	.24*	-.17	.31**
Wheretlk (street/public activity)	-.08	.05	-.21#	.19#	.14	-.29**	-.08	-.01	.10	.04
GR1 (amount of formal group activity)	.16	-.01	-.01	.25*	.23*	.09	-.04	-.20#	.18	-.19#
GR2 (how much group activity exists)	-.10	.08	-.25*	-.00	.05	-.14	-.20#	-.12	.16	.02
Informd (informed about current events)	.11	-.09	-.13	.05	.14	.07	-.06	-.12	.32**	-.13
Demrep (who won last										

pres. race in community vote)	.03	-.03	.20#	-.04	-.06	.38***	-.02	.15	-.04	-.07
Community Perceptions										
Diversity Perceptions										
Total Perceived Diversity	.03	-.06	.07	.03	-.14	.14	-.16	.16	.06	.16
Racial Diversity	.27*	-.03	.60***	-.03	.06	.23#	.33**	.25*	.19	-.22#
Religious Diversity	.13	.13	.05	-.06	-.25*	.08	-.14	.06	.13	.26*
Educational Diversity	-.03	-.06	-.01	.07	.10	.15	-.13	.10	.21#	-.10
Life-cycle Diversity	-.08	-.11	-.03	.02	-.22#	.09	-.17	.02	-.23*	.07
SES Diversity	.00	-.03	-.02	-.10	-.21#	.23#	-.16	.12	-.01	.11
Institutions Reported in Community by Editors										
No. institutions cited										
(Instcom)	.31**	.01	.15	-.04	.12	.09	.05	-.06	.29**	-.02
Major factory (Factry)	.12	.07	.10	.11	.28*	.26*	.12	-.21#	.38****	-.27*
Library (Libry)	.10	.25*	.01	-.03	-.10	-.04	-.07	-.04	-.00	.26*
Park (Park)	-.04	-.04	.00	-.04	-.14	-.05	-.11	.08	-.01	-.01
Manufacturing areas (mfg)	.17	.10	-.06	-.04	.16	-.06	-.02	-.04	.14	-.02
Local hospital (hosptl)	.25*	-.12	.19#	-.05	.07	.12	.11	-.06	.20#	-.14
Recreation center (recon)	.25*	-.10	.13	.03	.08	.13	.17	.05	.10	.10
Several churches (church2)	.04	-.05	.04	-.09	-.15	.01	-.08	-.02	.00	-.11
Shopping mall (mall)	.20#	.11	.10	-.09	.07	-.05	-.01	.06	.21#	.12
Private ethnic club (club)	.28*	-.04	.26*	-.03	.08	.18#	.17	-.05	-.06	-.11
Retail stores (retail)	.11	-.06	.04	-.10	-.07	.02	-.04	.03	.29**	-.11
Small convenience stores (constor)	-.06	-.06	-.15	.09	.01	-.09	-.18#	-.01	.07	.02
Local schools attended by area youth(locsch)	.15	-.06	.07	.02	.03	-.3	-.04	-.01	.25*	.17
Editor's Perceptions of Who Has Power in Community										
Neighborhood groups (Powngrps)	.11	.06	.21#	.10	.04	.32**	.19#	.18	.10	-.02

(continues)

41

TABLE 3.2 (cont.)

	Community Diversity Variables Based on Census Data									
	Total Census Div.	Gender Div.	Racial Div.	Age Div.	House-hold Div.	Marital Status Div.	Lang-uage Div.	Ed. Div.	Occup. Div.	Income Div.
Money (Powmoney)	-.05	.08	-.25*	.08	-.03	-.12	-.15	.04	.03	.18
Institutions (Powinst)	-.17	-.06	-.04	-.03	.00	-.28**	-.15	.06	.05	-.21#
Media (Powmedia)	-.09	.07	.05	.13	.11	-.01	-.07	-.20#	-.06	-.03
Government (Powgov)	.09	-.08	-.07	-.10	-.13	-.00	-.07	.05	-.05	.19#
Editor's Reports of Neighborhood Conflicts										
Social, group conflicts (Consocl)	-.04	.06	-.02	-.05	.02	-.11	-.17	.04	-.07	-.14
Political conflicts (Conpol)	-.06	.07	.08	.11	.07	.13	.06	.10	.00	-.06
Economic conflicts (Conecon)	-.03	.06	-.05	-.06	-.06	.04	.11	.11	.02	.12

Note. Sample sizes for variables in the survey are 141, with occasional missing data. The sample size for correlations involving one of the variables based on census area are 81, with occasional missing data.

An examination of *the relative importance* of the three sets of characteristics on editors' community perceptions was limited only to those found related in the bivariate relationships. This was done because of the small sample size. Five types of variables were selected as representative of editors' community perceptions—the dependent variables: (a) perceptions of the QOL, (b) perceptions of residents' commitment to the area, (c) overall perceived diversity on social categories, (d) perceptions of who has power in the community, (e) perceptions of the number of key institutions, and (f) perceptions of conflict in the community. As Table 3.3 shows, only two variables emerged as predictors of editors' perception of the quality of community life—the percentage of revenue derived from other sources, and the census measure of household income diversity. Other income is likely to include sponsorships and grants, as opposed to sales and advertising. Thus, the more income from these sources the lower the QOL assessments. And the greater the income diversity, the higher the QOL ratings. As Table 3.4 shows, three variables are significant predictors of how editors assess community commitment, and two predictors come from the same set—newspaper characteristics. First, one personal characteristic was important—the older the editor, the less commitment he or she sees. The other two predictors were newspaper circulation and whether the paper was founded by "others" (than merchants, development corporations, entrepreneurs, activists). The higher the circulation, the greater the perceived community commitment, and editors of papers founded by "others" were more likely to give higher ratings of residents' commitment to their neighborhoods. As Table 3.4 shows, only one factor, an individual characteristic, the editor's educational background, was a significant predictor of overall community diversity, and that relationship is positive. Editors with more education see more differentiation within their communities. In predictors of editors' accounting of community institutions, again only one variable was a significant predictor—the greater the occupational diversity in the census data, the greater the number of institutions. This is a straightforward reflection of the urban studies literature, which says that growth leads to occupational differentiation, which leads to differences in power reflected through institutional diversity (see Table 3.4). Questions soliciting how residents got along and the types of conflict generated three major categories of community conflict: social, political, and economic (see Table 3.5). Perceptions of social conflict were predicted by two newspaper characteristics; thus, editors of papers founded by activists and individual entrepreneurs were less likely to see such conflicts. The sole predictor of editors' perceptions of political conflict was the percentage of revenue from advertising, where political conflict was less likely to be cited the higher the reliance on advertising. And none of the variables were significant predictors of economic conflict.

In analyses of editors' perceptions of community power, two equations failed to produce any significant predictors, one indicating perceptions that power lies in money and the other that power rests in government. However, several variables emerged as significant predictors of perceptions that commu-

TABLE 3.3

Predicting Editors' Quality of Life Perceptions Based on Three Sets of Variables: Editors' Characteristics, Newspaper Characteristics, and Community Characteristics

Dependent Variable = Editor's QOL Rating		
	Betas	*Sig. T*
Editors' Characteristic		
Age	.04	
Newspaper Characteristics		
% Revenue from Advertising	.05	
% Revenue from Other Sources	-.31	*p* < .03
Member of a chain	-.10	
Community Characteristics (reported by editor)		
Population	-.30	
Serves City	.09	
Community Diversity/Pluralism Variables (Census Data)		
Racial diversity	-.15	
Household diversity	-.11	
Marital status diversity	-.19	
Occupational diversity	-.11	
Household income diversity	.37	*p* <. 05

Multiple R = .61, R Squared = .37, F = 3.10, p < .01, N = 80

Dependent Variable = Editor's Perception of How Residents Rate Community QOL		
	Betas	*Sig. T*
Editors' Characteristic		
Age	.06	
Newspaper Characteristics		
% Revenue from Advertising	.19	
% Revenue from Other Sources	-.33	*p* < .02
Member of a chain	-.08	
Community Characteristics (reported by editor)		
Population	-.28	
Serves City	.05	
Community Diversity/Pluralism Variables (Census Data)		
Racial diversity	-.11	
Household diversity	-.17	
Marital status diversity	-.21	
Occupational diversity	-.10	
Household income diversity	.34	*p* < .08

Multiple R = .62, R Squared = .38, F = 3.22, p < .01, N = 80

TABLE 3.4
Predicting Editors' Perceptions of Community Commitment, Diversity, and Institutions Based on Three Sets of Variables: Editors' Characteristics, Newspaper Characteristics, and Community Characteristics

Dependent Variable = Editors' Perception of Residents' Community Commitment		
	Betas	Sig. T
Editors' Characteristics		
Age	-.26	p < .02
Newspaper Characteristics		
Free/Paid (Hi=paid)	.08	
Circulation	.26	p < .06
% Revenue from Advertising	-.06	
Founded by Ind. Entrepreneur	-.19	
Founded by Other	.35	p < .02
Published by Dev. Corp./Org.	.01	
Community Characteristics (reported by editor) (none)		
Community Diversity/Pluralism Variables (Census Data)		
Occupational diversity	.05	
Household income diversity	-.22	

Multiple $R = .59$, R Squared $= .34$, $F = 3.65$, $p < .01$, $N = 80$

Dependent Variable = Editors' Perception of Community Diversity		
	Betas	Sig. T (none sig.
Editors' Characteristics		
Age	-.11	
Education	.25	p < .08
Newspaper Characteristics		
Circulation	-.07	
Founded by Ind. Entrepreneur	-.14	
Published by Individual	.00	
Age of newspaper	-.11	
Community Characteristics (reported by editor):		
No. zip codes covered	.12	
Community Diversity/Pluralism Variables (Census Data)		
Language diversity	-.19	

Multiple $R = .42$, R Squared $= .18$, $F = 1.48$, $p < .18$, $N = 80$

(continues)

TABLE 3.4 (cont.)

Dependent Variable = Editors' Perception of Number of Community Institutions

	Betas	Sig. T (none sig.)
Editors' Characteristics		
Education	.16	
Newspaper Characteristics		
Circulation	.30	
Frequency of publication	-.26	
No. full-time editorial staff	.12	
Member of chain	.27	
% Revenue from advertising	-.02	
Year founded	-.06	
Published by ind. entrepreneur	-.13	
Community Characteristics (reported by editor)		
Population	.28	
No. of zips served	.10	
Serves suburbs	.02	
Serves city & suburbs	-.07	
Community Diversity/Pluralism Variables (Census Data)		
Occupational diversity	.29	$p < .03$

Multiple $R = .59$, R Squared $= .34$, $F = 2.12$, $p < .03$, $N = 80$

TABLE 3.5
**Predicting Editors' Perception of Types of Community Conflict Based on Three
Sets of Variables: Editors' Characteristics, Newspaper Characteristics,
and Community Characteristics**

Dependent Variable = Editors' Perception of Social Conflict

	Betas	Sig. T
Editors' Characteristics		
Lives in community	-.14	
Newspaper Characteristics		
% Revenue from advertising	.13	
Published by ind. entrepreneur		
Founded by ind. entrepreneur	-.28	$p < .01$
Founded by merchants	.02	
Founded by activists	-.22	$p < .01$
Community Characteristics (reported by editor)		
Population	-.17	
Community Diversity/Pluralism Variables (Census Data)		
Marital status diversity	-.04	
Language diversity	-.17	

Multiple $R = .44$, R Squared $= .19$, $F = 1.86$, $p < .08$, $N = 80$

(continues)

TABLE 3.5 (cont.)

Dependent Variable = Editors' Perception of Political Conflict		
	Betas	*Sig. T (none sig.)*
Editors' Characteristics		
Lives in community	.13	
Newspaper Characteristics		
% Revenue from advertising	-.35	*p<*.01
Published by ind. entrepreneur		
Founded by ind. entrepreneur	-.04	
Founded by merchants	.01	
Founded by activists	.00	
Community Characteristics (reported by editor)		
Population	-.15	
Community Diversity/Pluralism Variables (Census Data)		
Marital status diversity	.07	
Language diversity	.06	

Multiple R = .40, R Squared = .16, F = 1.51, p < .17, N = 80

Dependent Variable = Editors' Perception of Economic Conflict		
	Betas	*Sig. T (none sig.)*
Editors' Characteristics		
Lives in community	-.13	
Newspaper Characteristics		
% Revenue from advertising	-.04	
Published by ind. entrepreneur		
Founded by ind. entrepreneur	-.01	
Founded by merchants	.17	
Founded by activists	-.09	
Community Characteristics (reported by editor)		
Population	-.07	
Community Diversity/Pluralism Variables (Census Data)		
Marital status diversity	.01	
Language diversity	.11	

Multiple R = .27, R Squared = .07, F = .60, p < .77, N = 80

nity groups, institutions or the media have power in the community. As Table 3.6 shows, editors were more likely to see community groups having power when their papers were founded by activists and their communities were smaller but served multiple zip codes, and when the census data showed language diversity and marital status diversity but not racial diversity. Perceptions of institutional power were associated with serving the city, with not having language or

TABLE 3.6
Predicting Editors' Perception of Who Has Power in Community Based on Three Sets of Variables: Editors' Characteristics, Newspaper Characteristics, and Community Characteristics

Dependent Variable = Editors' Perception that Community Groups Have Power

	Betas	Sig. T (none sig.)
Editors' Characteristics		
Age	-.08	
Lives in community	.18	
Newspaper Characteristics		
Free/Paid (Hi=paid)	.06	
Frequency of publication	-.11	
% Revenue from advertising	.07	
Published by chain	.09	
Founded by individual	.24	
Founded by dev. corp.	.21	
Founded by merchants	.08	
Founded by activists	.51	$p < .01$
Founded by others	-.07	
Community Characteristics (reported by editor)		
Population	-.39	$p < .02$
No. of zip codes served	.39	$p < .02$
Serves city	-.05	
Community Diversity/Pluralism Variables (Census Data)		
Racial diversity	-.38	$p < .02$
Marital status diversity	.33	$p < .02$
Language diversity	.25	$p < .07$
Education diversity	.16	
Household income diversity	.04	

Multiple $R = .70$, R Squared $= .48$, $F = 2.27$, $p < .01$, $N = 80$

Dependent Variable = Editors' Perception That Power Lies in Money

	Betas	Sig. T (none sig.)
Editors' Characteristics		
Age	-.22	
Lives in community	.15	
Newspaper Characteristics		
Free/Paid (Hi=paid)	.23	
Frequency of publication	.18	
% Revenue from advertising	.02	
Published by chain	.01	
Founded by individual	.13	
Founded by dev. corp.	.17	
Founded by merchants	.35	

TABLE 3.6 (cont.)

Dependent Variable = Editors' Perception That Power Lies in Money

	Betas	Sig. T (none sig.)
Founded by activists	.26	
Founded by others	-.01	
Community Characteristics (reported by editor)		
Population	-.12	
No. of zip codes served	.04	
Serves city	-.06	
Community Diversity/Pluralism Variables (Census Data)		
Racial diversity	.07	
Marital status diversity	-.14	
Language diversity	-.11	
Education diversity	.02	
Household income diversity	.24	

Multiple R = .48, R Squared = .23, F = .73, $p < .15$, N = 80

Dependent Variable = Editors' Perception That Power Lies in Institutions

	Betas	Sig. T (none sig.)
Editors' Characteristics		
Age	-.05	
Lives in community	-.06	
Newspaper Characteristics		
Free/Paid (Hi=paid)	-.03	
Frequency of publication	.23	$p < .10$
% Revenue from advertising	.21	$p < .09$
Published by chain	.18	
Founded by individual	-.06	
Founded by dev. corp.	.01	
Founded by merchants	-.17	
Founded by activists	-.20	
Founded by others	.02	
Community Characteristics (reported by editor)		
Population	.02	
No. of zip codes served	-.10	
Serves city	.32	$p < .02$
Community Diversity/Pluralism Variables (Census Data)		
Racial diversity	.22	
Marital status diversity	-.27	$p < .06$
Language diversity	-.27	$p < .06$
Education diversity	.15	
Household income diversity	-.20	

Multiple R = .69, R Squared = .47, F = 2.14, $p < .02$, N = 80

(continues)

49

TABLE 3.6 (cont.)

Dependent Variable = Editors' Perception That Media Have Power

	Betas	Sig. T (none sig.)
Editors' Characteristics		
Age	.46	$p < .01$
Lives in community	-.10	
Newspaper Characteristics		
Free/Paid (Hi=paid)	-.27	$p < .05$
Frequency of publication	-.28	$p < .05$
% Revenue from advertising	-.28	$p < .03$
Published by chain	-.07	
Founded by individual	-.02	
Founded by dev. corp.	-.07	
Founded by merchants	.06	
Founded by activists	.28	
Founded by others	.28	$p < .08$
Community Characteristics (reported by editor)		
Population	-.05	
No. of zip codes served	-.24	
Serves city	-.04	
Community Diversity/Pluralism Variables (Census Data)		
Racial diversity	.07	
Marital status diversity	.02	
Language diversity	.13	
Education diversity	-.31	$p < .02$
Household income diversity	-.05	

Multiple $R = .68$, R Squared $= .47$, $F = 2.11$, $p < .02$, $N = 80$

Dependent Variable = Editors' Perception That Government Has Power

	Betas	Sig. T (none sig.)
Editors' Characteristics		
Age	.03	
Lives in community	-.16	
Newspaper Characteristics		
Free/Paid (Hi=paid)	-.02	
Frequency of publication	-.27	
% Revenue from advertising	-.19	
Published by chain	.23	
Founded by individual	.06	
Founded by dev. corp.	.11	
Founded by merchants	.07	
Founded by activists	.02	
Founded by others	-.01	
Community Characteristics (reported by editor)		
Population	.11	

TABLE 3.6 (cont.)

Dependent Variable = Editors' Perception That Government Has Power		
	Betas	*Sig. T (none sig.)*
No. of zip codes served	-.10	
Serves city	.01	
Community Diversity/Pluralism Variables (Census Data)		
Racial diversity	-.19	
Marital status diversity	.16	
Language diversity	-.05	
Education diversity	.12	
Household income diversity	.12	

Multiple $R = .45$, R Squared $= .220$, $F = .62$, $p < .87$, $N = 80$

marital status diversity (census data), and with more frequent publication and higher revenue from advertising. Editors were more likely to see the media as having power in the community if they were older, the paper was distributed freely and not for sale, publication was less frequent, the percentage of revenue from advertising was lower and the paper was not founded by "others."

The choice of dependent measures no doubt influences the relative importance of the three sets of predictors, but it seems reasonable to argue that the two overall QOL ratings are reliable measures of environmental assessments. Furthermore, because news often focuses on issues of conflict and power, the two sets of measures based on open-ended measures of editors' perceptions in these areas would seem to capture important aspects of journalists' jobs. This study focused only on community newspapers in the 25 largest metropolitan areas of the country; however, the results do caution us to limit attributions of influences on newspapers to single sources, whether that's the distribution of power and diversity in a community—the "pluralism model"—or the impact made by individuals from their backgrounds. In fact, the most important influence may be the journalistic enterprise itself—the goals, functions, and origins of the newspaper itself (also see Jeffres et al., 1999).

SUMMARY

Communication scholars have long viewed the relationship between communication variables and community linkages as having major significance. This multidimensional concept is associated with such notions as community integration and community ties; the latter has been defined to include structural ties such as owning a home, social network ties such as the number of friends and relatives and interaction with them, participation in local groups, cognitive ties, personal identification with the neighborhood, and affective ties with an area.

Media use in general and newspaper reading in particular have been closely related to measures of community ties and integration, including voting, keeping up with local news, civic involvement, local political interest, community knowledge, attending forums, and institutional activities. Some evidence also supports a positive correlation between interpersonal communication variables and community integration.

Measures of urbanism—community location (city vs. suburb) and status—also have been linked directly with communication variables; thus, interpersonal sources are more important in the center city than in suburban neighborhoods but overall interpersonal contact and the overall volume of media use are unaffected by neighborhood location and status.

A national study of community newspapers in urban areas found that some measures of neighborhood pluralism and diversity were related to editors' perceptions of who wields power in the community. Similarly, consensus and conflict reporting styles of editors were related to particular measures of community diversity and pluralism. The index tapping overall diversity–pluralism was correlated with only one newspaper goal, or function, but specific diversity–pluralism measures were associated with several newspaper functions. In particular, the measure of ascriptive diversity (race, language, gender) was correlated with the importance of civic journalism and activism, suggesting that status has been replaced by social ethnic differences as the basis of conflict, and such group differences should be viewed as the basis of power conflicts reflected in newspaper reporting styles.

In additional analyses, influences at the community, organizational, and individual levels were pitted against each other to see which was more important as an influence on journalists' perceptions of their community. Results showed that editors' backgrounds and characteristics did affect their perceptions but these social categories played a minor role in comparison to community characteristics and newspaper characteristics. Of the individual characteristics, age—perhaps a proxy for experience—and education appear as the most significant influences. Newspaper characteristics as a group appeared as key predictors in 14 instances, as significant predictors of variables in each of the three categories of dependent variables—perceptions of community QOL, perceptions of residents behaviors, and perceptions of community diversity and pluralism. The key newspaper characteristic influencing editors' perceptions was the source of revenue—whether newspapers depend on advertising or other sources for their income. Community characteristics were second to newspaper characteristics as a set of predictors, and the importance of specific measures appeared to be linked to specific dependent variables rather than running across all five. The study suggests that a straightforward reflection hypothesis is too simple and there is a need to treat the relationship between community characteristics and communication phenomena as more complicated.

4

Communication's Consequences for Neighborhoods

- Some Evidence of the Impact of Communication on Neighborhoods
- Impact of New Technologies on Neighborhood Communication and Neighborhoods
- Summary

Although many scholars have examined communication variables in neighborhood settings, there has been relatively little attention to neighborhood communication patterns and few efforts to employ or develop communication theories in this context. Here, the flow of influence is reversed to look at potential consequences of communication for neighborhoods. Clearly, communication—generally viewed as interpersonal interaction—has been viewed as central to the life and existence of neighborhoods. It is one of the defining features of neighborhoods cited earlier. However, often scholars have assumed communication in language that focused on social relationships. Thus, there is less actual theorizing or data that speak to the impact communication patterns have for neighborhoods.

Because the evidence for the strength of the "linear hypothesis" is quite meager, size and social structure should not be expected to account for all the variability in communication variables. Clearly, patterns of symbolic activity are more complicated than mere reflections of occupational structure and neighborhood or community size. Over time, the arrows of influence would go in both directions,[61] as dense communication networks help neighborhood residents to fight off threats and solve problems, thus helping the neighborhood to persist even as its social structure changes. Neighborhoods are formed through communication, and interdependence persists through the same patterns of symbolic activity that are the "fodder" of the discipline. Thus, at a point in time communication variables can affect different aspects of neighborhoods and neighborhood behavior (e.g., making it easy or difficult to engage in social mobilization or action that maintains or rejuvenates the community, or weakening/strengthening the social ties that link people within the neighborhood and affect its future).

This chapter summarizes the research showing that both mass and interpersonal communication patterns can affect community behaviors (e.g., reading the newspaper is associated with a stronger sense of community). The research is rather meager, but one study found residents using both communication and community ties to form beliefs and attitudes about their community, which in turn led to their intention to stay or leave the neighborhood. The Internet is seen as one more communication vehicle pulling people out of their physical neighborhoods and into "virtual communities." However, a study focusing on urban neighborhood Web sites found evidence that the Web can operate to strengthen weak ties in communities, and a national study found Internet use strengthening civic participation.

SOME EVIDENCE OF THE IMPACT OF COMMUNICATION ON NEIGHBORHOODS

Sense of community has been linked to both mass and interpersonal communication. Edelstein and Larsen (1960) found that readership of the urban weekly served as a facilitating agent for community, and Bogart and Orenstein (1965) found similar support looking at the supplemental role of urban weeklies to daily papers. As Doheny-Farina (1996) suggested, one's sense of community arises out of interest group interactions that occur during communication at public celebrations and events such as school board meetings dealing with a controversy. Greer (1962) noted the importance of communication—interpersonal and mass media—for interdependent social groups to coordinate their behavior in cities. He added, "communication in the neighborhood may take place at many levels, but viewing it as an organizational unit, the most important level is in casual interaction among those whose paths must cross, in adjoining backyards, at bus stop, school and corner grocery, on sidewalks . . . interaction is unavoidable with the 'neighbors'" (p. 112). Keller (1977) observed that "communication is not only necessary for the formation of human communities, it is also indispensable for sustaining them" (p. 282).

Jeffres, Dobos, and Sweeney (1987) used the Fishbein and Ajzen (1975) theory of reasoned action to examine decisions by residents that commit them to neighborhoods, operationalized as the individual resident's intention to continue living in a community or neighborhood. In their application of the theory, residents use communication and community ties to form beliefs and attitudes about their community, which in turn led to their intention to leave or remain. The path model of neighborhood commitment is supported by the data, with interpersonal communication and structural ties each predicting beliefs about neighborhood problems and readership of neighborhood newspapers predicting beliefs about attitudes; these two predict attitudes toward the neighborhood, which is a strong predictor of neighborhood commitment. Another path model of commitment to the metropolitan area also received support, but attitudes were a better predictor of intention to stay in a neighborhood than they were to remain in the metro area (also see Jeffres et al., 1988). Recently, Scheufele, Shanahan, and Kim (2000) found that the heterogeneity of a person's discussion network and measures of local media use affected one's interest in local politics and neighborhood affairs.

IMPACT OF NEW TECHNOLOGIES ON NEIGHBORHOOD COMMUNICATION AND NEIGHBORHOODS

Doheny-Farina (1996) believes that electronic communication pushes people toward "virtual community"[62] while they ignore "real, dying communities" that are tied to a geographic place. It is the latter that give "meaning to virtual experiences" (p. 8).[63] Another view of the significance is provided by Furlong (1989), who argued that computers and online opportunities for communication and social interaction give older adults a way to be part of contemporary culture along with a new network of social support. In addition, Rubinyi (1989) found that more successful nonprofit organizations used computer technology for community networking.[64]

"In physical communities we are forced to live with people who may differ from us in many ways. But virtual communities offer us the opportunity to construct utopian collectivities—communities of interest, education, tastes, beliefs, and skills. In cyberspace we can remake the world out of an unsettled landscape" (Doheny-Farina, 1996, p. 16). Ironically, some urban sociology literature says that homogeneous neighborhoods have allowed people to do much the same, and cable TV and media in general also allow people to "tailor" their tastes. Still, it's a useful point that diverse environments force people to react in different ways and cope with differences. Doheny-Farina (1996) argued:

> The mass media as we know it [*sic*] is dead. Newspapers don't give us news, because in the time frame of the net what newspapers print is old news before ink meets paper. Book publishing is dead when anyone's words can reach millions of potential readers moments after the final draft is finished. The music industry withers away when any musician can make high-quality digital recordings at home and distribute them to the world via

the net. Television networks are inconsequential when everyone has the power to produce programming for everyone else. Governments as we know them are increasingly powerless because nations become irrelevant when communication technologies make borders as porous as air. Power goes to those who can control the flow of information. But when all information, all music, all art, all words, all images, all ideas are digitalized, then everyone can access, alter, create, and transmit anything, anywhere, anytime. (pp. 20-21)

The point may be overstated, but it's still important. Kemmis (1990) also argued that considerations to reinvigorating political structures and processes that are not tied to place weaken the effort. Doheny-Farina (1996) added, "I fear that the continual virtualization of community reveals that geophysical community is dying. As we invest ourselves in simulation, the simulated phenomena disappear" (p. 27).[65] The Internet does allow people to look for other sources of identity outside their communities by joining chat groups—political, social, lifestyle, or other interests—and "seeking community online." The Internet also reduces the need for institutional gatekeepers by allowing anyone to be a "mass communicator" but it does not eliminate the significance of institutions and professionals; the bulk of the message construction on the Internet is not a solitary activity, and most participants rely on professional Internet support to help them sort through the rubble. Research is needed to see to what extent people have "needs" to be "mass communicators" via the Internet and who is content to treat the new communication channel as another mass medium, albeit one with interactive features for audiences (see Jeffres & Atkin, 1996).

Doheny-Farina (1996) said that what are called virtual communities resemble what Bellah, Madsen, Sullivan, Swidler, and Tipson (1985) called "lifestyle enclaves." He added that

> a true community is a collective (evolving and dynamic) in which the public and private lives of its members are moving toward interdependency regardless of the significant differences among those members. In contrast, lifestyle enclaves [skiing community, criminal justice community, etc.] are segmental because they describe only parts of their members private lives—usually their behaviors of leisure and consumption—and celebrate the "narcissism of similarity" through the common lifestyles of their members.

However, the urban and other sociological literature suggests a decline in the importance of immediate place.

"Lifestyle enclaves flourish where individuals need not depend on others for much beyond companionship in their leisure lives. As individuals rely more on national and global ties than on local ties, the need for complex, integrated communities—collectivities of interdependent public and private lives—

is replaced by the need for isolated individuals to bond through lifestyle enclaves, which provide only the 'sense' of community" (Doheny-Farina, 1996, p. 50). However, virtual communities are likely to be sought out by people who find their geophysical communities lacking, thus supplementing rather than supplanting them. And it's an empirical question whether the Internet will only be used to pull people out of their geographic communities rather than help strengthen their ties to them.

> One kind of local public space has largely disappeared: the places for public discourse about the issues, problems, and celebrations that affect a locality as a whole. Life in American cities and suburbs is notorious for having eliminated public space for public discourse. When we combine the belief that our economies have relieved us of the need to rely on our neighbors for our economic well-being, the hostile environments that plague our cities and isolate our suburbs, and decades of urban and suburban planning that have inhibited the creation and maintenance of space in which individuals can easily interact, we come to believe that public life beyond work is either nonexistent or so remote it is irrelevant to daily life. (Doheny-Farina, 1996, pp. 51-52)

Doheny-Farina noted surveys of communities that are wired or facing such changes. Some surveys suggest that the net may do what civic activists and community net proponents hope it will do—reinvigorate the geophysical community. For example, in Blacksburg, electronic mail (e-mail) is becoming as ubiquitous as making a phone call or receiving mail. A survey for the Blacksburg Electronic Village found that members use the community system for three general purposes: to communicate via e-mail with family and friends (97%), to obtain information related to recreation and entertainment, and to connect to discussion forums related to information and entertainment. Doheny-Farina (1996) cited data showing that "community nets are indeed making it possible for some individuals and some organizations to connect to other people in their geophysical communities. But for some nets this phenomenon represents only a part—probably the lesser part—of their actual functions" (p. 159). He also noted that observers in the early 1970s were saying that cable and public access TV would do what they are saying the Internet may do today.

Although most of the Internet studies just cited focus on small towns or college communities, a project in Cleveland, Ohio recently focused on using the Internet to strengthen urban neighborhoods. As noted earlier, neighborhood communication systems today are composed largely of "weak ties," links between people who are not relatives or enduring friends but acquaintances and friendships built on proximity and other ties (Granovetter, 1973). Although many people do live amidst relatives and close friends, mobility has reduced the number of such neighborhoods. And, although many people seeking community find it in geographic communities represented by neighborhoods, many more find it at work, in peer groups, in professional ties, in extended families or patterns surrounding their children. As Bulmer (1985) noted, weak ties are indispensable to individuals' opportunities and to their integration into communities. This project focused on the issue of whether neighborhood Web sites could be designed to "strengthen weak ties" and improve communication within the urban communities by involving residents in a grassroots process.[66] Five center-city neighborhoods were selected, and teams of graduate students combed their communities for potential neighborhood stakeholders to be represented on the Web site—divided into the following domains: shopping-retail, industry and major employers, social services, local organizations, entertainment, recreation, churches, schools, media, public offices, and neighborhood development. Participation in Web site construction was solicited and those interested were invited to attend a Neighborhood WebFair held at a local university or to contribute information and materials that could be used to construct pages. Once each neighborhood website was up and running, it was diffused through communication interventions that included a demonstration at a community event or location, articles in community newspapers covering the neighborhoods, providing information at branch libraries, and sending postcards announcing the Web site and public access points to samples of residents in each neighborhood. Participants in neighborhood Web site construction completed questionnaires that provided information about the stakeholder they represented (organization, business, social service, etc.[67]) and its relation to the community. The participants rated 14 items assessing their expectations for their organization's web pages. Rated most highly was informing residents of their services and activities, followed by informing nonresidents of their services. Sharing information with another organization and building community support came next in importance. Advertising the neighborhood as a nice place to live came fifth, followed by linking residents within the community. More than 60% of participants said half of their organization's volunteers live in the neighborhood being served by the Web site, and a similar figure said half of their clients or customers live in the neighborhood. Some 48% said half of their part-time employees live in the community and 25% said half of their full-time employees live in the Web site community.

In addition, a survey of a random sample of residents from each neighborhood was conducted using a computer-aided telephone-interviewing (CATI) system. The project also called for a tabulation of Web site "hits" used as a measure of interest and diffusion. Within 15 months of the project's initiation, the home page introducing the five neighborhoods had received more than 5,000 hits.

Further evidence that the Internet may stimulate civic involvement is found in a recent secondary analysis of the 1999 DDB Needham Life Style Survey, which was based on panels of respondents drawn from commercial lists that were weighted to match the demographic composition of the target population (Shah et al., 2000). That analysis found that time spent on the Internet was a positive and significant predictor of civic participation (volunteering, working on community projects, and attending club meetings), public attendance (visiting art galleries and museums, going out to see movies, attending classical concerts, going to the zoo, and going to rock concerts), and informal socializing (entertaining people at home, giving or attending dinner parties, playing cards, and cooking outdoors). They conclude that time spent on the Internet does not dampen people's social ties and may help people discover ways to be active in their communities and strengthen ties of social organizations.

SUMMARY

Given the fairly meager evidence for the linear hypothesis, size and social structure should not be expected to account for all the variability of communication patterns found in communities. Over time, influence should flow in both directions as dense communication networks help community residents to fight off threats and solve problems. Neighborhoods are formed through communication and their viability through time is likely to depend on maintenance of particular forms of symbolic activity, but there is relatively limited empirical evidence of these processes.

Sense of community has been linked to both mass and interpersonal communication variables. Studies also link communication to residents' commitment to their area. Residents use communication and community ties to form beliefs and attitudes about their community, which in turn lead to their intention to leave or remain.

The new communication technologies are seen as potential threats to neighborhoods. Some observers see the Internet as one more vehicle pulling people from their geographic neighborhoods as residents substitute virtual communities for their neighbors. Others see the Internet doing what civic activists hope it will do—reinvigorating the geophysical community; research on the Blacksburg Electronic Village provides some support for this hope.

5

Social Relationships and Communication

- Types of Community Relationships
- The Significance of Social Relationships for Neighborhoods
- Linking Relationships and Communication
- Summary

Social relationships are often treated as synonyms for communication, and although the two are closely linked, they are not the same thing. An example illustrates this. In a community setting, one individual may have no relatives but a strong pattern of communication with friends and neighbors, "weak ties." Another individual may live in the same neighborhood as do numerous relatives and maintain a strong pattern of communication with the extended family but interact infrequently with others. Clearly, the pattern of one's social relationships in the community is not automatically "reflected" in a specific pattern of communication.

TYPES OF COMMUNITY RELATIONSHIPS

Scholars have conceptualized community relationships in various ways, identifying them in terms of people-to-people relationships—as friendships, family/relatives, causal acquaintances or distinguishing between primary and secondary, formal and informal or causal, and so on—or in terms of community-to-people relationships or attachments. Park (1916) thought communality of interests gave rise to association. Groups such as trade and labor unions, based on common interest, differ from neighborhood and similar forms of association because the latter are based on contiguity, personal association, and the common ties of humanity. Citing four levels of organization in residential areas (household, neighborhood, residential community, and municipality), Greer (1962) described three social types to describe how people participate in different organization systems: isolates, neighbors, and community actors. Isolates are disengaged from the organizational structure of their geographic space in the city and "they operate as neighbors little if at all, and they belong to none of the voluntary organizations in the area." They are poor voters and not as attentive to newspapers for news. Neighbors are involved in their household and its immediate social environment. They are involved in casual interaction and family friendships. They participate less in local politics but are more likely to read the local paper than are isolates. Community actors are involved in the local area, belong to local organizations, read the local paper for local news, engage in neighboring for news, are better educated, and are "a part of the communication flow of the area" (p. 120).[68]

THE SIGNIFICANCE OF SOCIAL RELATIONSHIPS FOR NEIGHBORHOOD

Max Weber established in his town analyses that the preindustrial town was based on the neighborhood principle of association, which basically meant "proximity in space" (Lenz-Romeiss, 1973, p. 48). "The neighbourhood-contacts of an earlier age have been replaced in the modern city by a person's circle of intercourse" (p. 84) as people have become more mobile. In pre-industrial towns, belonging to a neighborhood was important to everyone, based on the need for social help and assistance in part.

> Today no social community is based on the neighbourhood concept. The neighbourhood now depends far less on the kind of mutual dependence, social control and emotional give-and-take among neighbours which we described in connection with the pre-industrial town. Instead, the whole life of the neighbourhood tends to be permeated by behavior patterns of aloofness which correspond to the description of public behaviour. (Lenz-Romeiss, 1973, p. 94)

Rosel (1983) looked at a neighborhood where elderly residents who have known each other for years developed a closely knit network of mutual assistance and support. She noted that "neighborhood networks such as this one show that social integration may be modest in scale, yet grand in results."

Neighborhood networks not only alleviate isolation and loneliness but help people to maintain independent lifestyles—through interdependent neighboring.

Neighborhood relationships and communication patterns also are linked to neighborhood attachment. Hunter's (1974a) findings suggested that one's social connections to nearby friends, neighbors, and facilities determined one's emotional attachment to the neighborhood. Slovak (1986) tested residents' attachment to neighborhood and the larger community. Slovak looked at the city of Newark, New Jersey as the community of limited liability, separate from the neighborhood; Janowitz's (1952/1967) community of limited liability is distinct from the block and the neighborhood in terms of attachments and interactions. Slovak found that use of city facilities, normlessness, and neighborhood attachment determined city attachment. Perceived safety and length of residence predicted neighborhood attachment; length of residence was correlated with both informal neighboring and sociability satisfaction. Bell and Force (1956) looked at four census tracts in San Francisco in the early 1950s, finding that men of higher social status were more likely to belong to formal associations; however, holding individual SES constant, those living in higher SES neighborhoods still had more participation in formal associations than those living in lower status neighborhoods, suggesting that the neighborhood reference group may set expectations for such activity. Wandersman and Giamartino (1980) found that several factors influence residents' participation in block organizations, including perceptions of problems on the block, a sense of community, neighboring behaviors, importance of the block, perception of one's personal ability to change the block, and the locus of control.

LINKING RELATIONSHIPS AND COMMUNICATION

Young (1986) noted that "the ideal of community arises" as a

> response to the individualism perceived as the prevailing theoretical position, and the alienation and fragmentation perceived as the prevailing condition of society. Community appears, that is, as part of an opposition, individualism/community, separated self/shared self. In this opposition each term comes to be defined by its negative relation to the other, thus existing in a logical dependency. I suggest that this opposition, however, is integral to modern political theory, and is not an alternative to it. (p. 6)[69]

Young noted that those who advocate an ideal community argue that small group, face-to-face relations are essential to the realization of that ideal, but, he added, media today expand the richness, creativity, diversity, and potential of a society to expand and he suggested that there are no conceptual grounds for considering face-to-face relations "more pure, authentic social relations than relations mediated across time and distance" (p. 16). He suggested that community theorists prefer face-to-face relations "because they wrongly identify mediation and alienation" (p. 16).[70]

The community context for interpersonal communication or neighborhood media is infrequently examined in studies focusing on interpersonal and mass media influences. An exception to that is the extensive work on media use and community attachments (e.g., Rothenbuhler, Mullen, DeLaurell, & Ryu, 1996; Stamm, 1985), where the political variables emphasize involvement in community problem solving. Those studies provide evidence for the interrelationships among media use, measures of community involvement, and measures of community attachments (affective and cognitive). In general, there is considerable evidence that both interpersonal and mass communication variables are linked to people's community ties. Jeffres and Dobos (1983) found that readership of neighborhood newspapers was correlated with social interaction with neighbors and use of local neighborhood facilities. Interest in news about people in the paper also was correlated with participation in social activities with neighbors and use of local facilities. Demers (1996a) found that personal community experience and attachments were linked to reading the local community weekly but not the metropolitan newspaper.

In the Jeffres et al. (2000) survey of central city and suburban community residents reported earlier, both perceived community attachment and community solidarity are positively related to the strength of neighborhood communication. They also found that the strength of neighborhood communication patterns was positively related to measures of neighborhood activity, with a particularly strong relationship involving neighboring. The study also found that the strength of interpersonal communication links was positively associated with both neighborhood activity and neighboring but not to measures of neighborhood feelings or perceptions.

The pattern for media use was more mixed. The higher one's media use overall, the stronger the pattern of neighborhood activity and the more positive the perceived neighborhood QOL. However, those two relationships and a correlation with perceived community attachment that approaches significance fail to achieve statistical significance once the two macro variables—community status and location—are controlled. The study also examined the importance of different channels for neighborhood news and interest in neighborhood activities. Results showed that interest is positively related to all of the other neighborhood measures and the pattern is retained when the macro variables were controlled. The importance of interpersonal channels—neighbors in general—and neighborhood organizations was positively related to all of the neighborhood activity and feelings variables, again a pattern retained once the macro variables are controlled. The importance of both community media channels was related to the two activity measures and perceived community attachment but not to perceived community solidarity or the neighborhood QOL. Using the metro daily was positively related to neighborhood activity but not neighboring and to perceived community attachment but not solidarity of QOL. The importance of broadcast channels is unrelated to any of the community activity or feelings measures. Thus, "local" communication channels were relatively more important, although daily newspaper readers appear to be stimulated toward higher neighborhood activity as well.

Jeffres, Perloff et al. (2000) also arrayed the variables in a path model (see Fig. 5 1). Because efforts to mobilize residents focus on getting people involved in their communities, they selected neighborhood activity—a much broader measure of how residents "use" their neighborhoods than just belonging to organizations—as the criterion for the model. The key macro variable— neighborhood status—was located as the key exogenous measure, with the rest of the variables arrayed from left to right as follows: achievement-oriented (income and education), life-cycle (age) and ascriptive (gender) measures; interest in neighborhood news; communication variables (neighborhood communication and local media linking people to the community, and mass media use); neighboring and neighborhood affect; and neighborhood activity.

Results showed that neighborhood status was positively associated with corresponding measures of achievement at the individual level (income and education), and also had direct paths to four other variables in the model: a negative relationship with neighborhood communication, a positive relation with the importance of local papers, a positive relation with neighborhood affect, and a positive impact on the criterion variable, neighborhood activity.

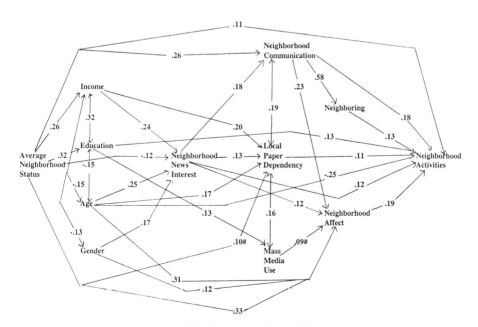

FIG. 5.1. A path model.

Interestingly, the two achievement measures, income and education, operate differently on interest in neighborhood news. Thus, those with higher incomes have a greater interest, whereas those with higher educations show less interest. Age and gender (being a woman) have relationships with interest. Those who are more interested in what's going on in their communities also have stronger neighborhood communication patterns, higher mass media use and attribute greater importance to local papers as neighborhood news sources. Education was positively related to media use.

Neighborhood communication is the only variable with a direct path to neighboring. Neighborhood affect has direct paths from both neighborhood communication and media use, as well as age and gender and the macro neighborhood status measure. Eight variables have direct paths to neighborhood activity, which is promoted by neighboring, neighborhood communication, and the importance of local papers as channels, as well as the level of interest in neighborhood news, the level of neighborhood affect and two status measures—individual education and neighborhood status. Age has a direct negative link.[71]

SUMMARY

Social relationships often are treated as synonyms for communication, and although the two are closely linked, they are not the same thing. The pattern of one's social relationships in the community is not automatically "reflected" in a specific pattern of communication. Scholars have conceptualized community relationships in terms of people-to-people relationships (friendships, kinship, casual acquaintances, primary vs. secondary, formal vs. informal, etc.) or in terms of community-to-people relationships, or attachments. With mobility, people's relationships became tied less to proximity than to communication. Neighborhood relationships and communication also are linked to neighborhood attachment expressed in terms of use of facilities, belonging to local groups and organizations, and feelings of attachment.

Studies examined provide considerable evidence for the interrelationships among media use, measures of community involvement and measures of both affective and cognitive community attachments. The strength of interpersonal communication links in the neighborhood was positively associated with both neighborhood activity and neighboring. In one study, a path model that featured involvement in neighborhood activities as the criterion variable showed direct paths from strength of neighborhood communication and dependency on the community newspaper.

6

Neighborhood Communication Patterns

Leo W. Jeffres
Kimberly Neuendorf
David Atkin
Larry Erbert

- Urban Neighborhood Communication Channels
- Personal Communication Networks
- Mapping Personal Communication Networks
  First Study
  Second Study
- Neighborhood Communication Informants
- Summary

Every neighborhood has a unique communication system that reflects the pattern of communication needs distributed among residents as well as the constraints of geography and social environment. Thus, a tightly knit ethnic neighborhood bound by family relationships may have a dense communication network in which almost everyone is connected by reliable communication channels. Another ethnic community with different traditions and needs may have a much looser network, with pockets of "isolates" and loosely tied groups. The literature search located no studies that have tried to document a neighborhood's communication network through a formal network analysis.[72] However, case studies identify some patterns and more quantitative empirical work provides descriptive data on aspects of neighborhood communication systems and also examines people's individual networks and the extent to which they are contained within the neighborhood.

URBAN NEIGHBORHOOD COMMUNICATION CHANNELS

Davison (1988) said urban neighborhood channels can be divided into three categories: those based on person-to-person ties, those that come into existence
with the establishment of organizations (themselves communication networks),
and mass media. "The amount of information about community affairs that
flows through person-to-person channels is enormous, even though a relatively
few individuals play a disproportionately large role in this network. Some people are much more active communicators and are more widely known than others" (p. 13). Four types of organizational channels were identified in the
Kingsbridge neighborhood study: organizational gatherings that act as conduits
for information flow; facilities in which the gatherings take place—auditoriums,
meeting halls, classrooms; mechanisms like bulletin boards, handbills, direct
mail, posters, and phone campaigns used to reach large numbers of people; and
organizational media, newsletters, newspapers, or radio stations (p. 14).
Davison (1988) reported that all community leaders interviewed read the local
community weekly in that Bronx neighborhood. Also cited as part of people's
interpersonal networks were the public library, seniors' meetings, bingo parties,
and so on. "Community leaders who have an active interest in national and
international affairs, as well as local affairs, often use an impressive number of
channels" (p. 21).

> On the basis of our observations in Kingsbridge, we would characterize the
> role of the local media in helping to establish community identity some-
> what differently. The Riverdale Press is one of the major community insti-
> tutions in which many local residents take pride. Its very existence makes
> it an important cohesive influence. In addition, by reinforcing the content of
> the less formal channels of communication, it gives wider currency to the
> topics and concerns that people are talking about or would like to talk
> about. But we found no indications that the Press, in spite of its popularity,
> puts an imprint on the community. Instead it gives expression to existing
> interests and values, accentuates these, and helps link those who share
> them. (Davison, 1988, pp. 23-24)

All communication channels were important for building a "shared
resolve to resist urban decay" (p. 25), for building community morale (by providing people with instructive examples), or for lowering morale and helping
public opinion to form on issues affecting the community.

PERSONAL COMMUNICATION NETWORKS

Focusing on how widespread use of the telephone plays a key role in keeping
personal community networks connected, Wellman and Tindall (1993) viewed
each individual as the center of a unique social network composed of the 10 to

20 relationships outside of their households with whom people are actively and significantly in contact; some of these communication relationships are within the neighborhood, some aren't—they include informal ties with friends, neighbors, relatives and workmates.[73] They surveyed East York near Toronto, finding 344 active relationships with 137 socially close intimates and 207 somewhat less intimate significant persons with whom they also were actively in contact. The median active network had four intimate ties and seven significant ties. Most networks contained a mixture of friends and relatives, nearly half being kinfolk, principally immediate kin such as parents, adult children, and siblings. "Immediate kin tend to have close, intimate relations. 'By contrast, those few extended kin' who are active network members tend to have weaker non-intimate relations. Similarly, 'friends' tend to be intimate while active neighbors and 'organizational ties' (including 'co-workers' seen socially outside of work) tend to have non-intimate relations" (Wellman & Tindall, 1993, p. 71).[74] In their Canadian study, only a small portion of network members were within walking distance of the respondents' homes or jobs and most active network members live more than 9 miles from the respondents. Only 22% live within 1 mile, whereas 32% live more than 30 miles away.

   East Yorkers are involved in "private home societies" rather than the "street corner societies" described by Whyte (1943). They interact privately rather than in groups (Wellman, 1992). The private nature of many interactions also is reflected in the low density of most networks. Only 33% of the members of the median network have direct ties with each other, although all are indirectly linked through others. Some 88% of network members meet inside others' homes—the most prevalent meeting place except for co-workers and other organizationally focused ties. Telephones provide the second most widely used context for network interaction: 85% of all network members talk on the telephone. Only a minority of network members interact on street corners, organizational venues, or such informal centers of activity as pubs. Intimates keep in touch by phone somewhat more frequently than significant, nonintimate, network members. Intimates use telephone contact as much as face-to-face contact. Nevertheless, frequency of contact varies greatly among both intimates and significants: from thrice-daily visits with invalid mothers, socially and geographically close neighbors, and co-workers to less-than-yearly contact with friends who have moved overseas, or extended kin who have moved elsewhere. Wellman and Tindall (1993) found no difference between types of respondents in either their frequency of telephone contact with network members or their proportional use of the telephone to communicate with network members. There were no differences by age, gender, working outside the home or not, occupational status, or marital status. Thus, the extent to which people use telephones was relatively constant for broad sections of the North American population.

   Wellman and Tindall (1993) also asked respondents for 18 types of social support, later grouped into six dimensions: emotional aid, small services, large services, financial aid, companionship, job/housing information. Network members specialized in the kinds of help given and most provided one to three dimensions of support. Support was more likely to come from intimates than from significant but nonintimate, active ties. Intimate friends and siblings provide the bulk of companionship. Neighbors and others seen frequently provided most small services. All dimensions of support were provided through the telephone as well as through face-to-face contact. Network members who frequently talk on the phone tend to provide more support.

In neighborhood research, kinship is emphasized because family relationships often are the core of many people's social networks, and considerable family social interaction is highly localized. In a survey of Albany-Schenectady-Troy, New York, Logan and Spitze (1994) found that 15% of respondents had an adult child and 7% a parent living within the neighborhood. Yet, despite their small numbers, a substantial share of all social interaction with nonhousehold members (15%–25%) was with family neighbors. The best predictor of three forms of neighborhood interaction (neighborhood telephone talks, visiting and receiving help from neighbors) was the number of family neighbors. Few other variables consistently predicted neighborhood interaction, such as visiting (e.g., predicted by number of years in neighborhood, income, being a homeowner, and a contextual variable, the number of neighborhood families with children).

Bolan (1997) considered variables associated with an individual's most recent move into current residence as predictors of neighborhood attachment, using the 1978-1979 Seattle Community Attachment Survey. He noted one way to study micro-level determinants of community attachment is the "community of limited liability" approach, which suggests that attachment is a function of residents' economic and social investments in a community. Past research has demonstrated that such factors as home ownership and raising children influence residents' feelings about their community and their social involvement (Stinner, Van Loon, Chung, & Byun, 1990; Woolever, 1992). In addition, the Chicago School perspective highlights how residential stability affects attachment. Studies show that longer term residents have greater community sentiment and involvement, and the process of becoming emotionally and cognitively attached to a place evolves over time (Kasarda & Janowitz, 1974; Sampson, 1988; Tomeh, 1967). Bolan (1997) said that social investment and residential stability act with social categories such as age and education in predicting attachment (also see Gerson, Stueve, & Fischer, 1977). However, such predictors explain only some of the variation in attachment, and additional variation may be explained by considering more macro-level predictors such as population density, population heterogeneity, and physical features of the landscape[75] (Bolan, 1997; see Gerson et al., 1977; Guest & Lee, 1983; Sampson, 1988; Woolever, 1992).

> Contemporary research has ignored a valuable class of microlevel predictors . . . motivations and attitudes shaping an individual's entry into a new neighborhood affect subsequent feelings about and behavior within this

environment. The "mobility experience" reflects an individual's past and recent experience with the selection of a new residence measured by four elements: history of migration, the motivation for the move, the time involved in the move, and the spatial distance traveled during the move. (Bolan, 1997, p. 225)

Bolan found that levels of communication with local neighbors was especially low for "family migrants" (those moving for marriage, divorce, to be near family or friends), evidence of the constraining impact of kinship-related transitions on the formation of neighborhood sentiments and involvements. Interaction was significantly higher for those who moved for housing reasons that included landlord problems, decisions to buy, build or sell or unreasonable housing costs, compared to those who moved for family reasons.

MAPPING PERSONAL COMMUNICATION NETWORKS

Models and communication projects that begin with the core definition of symbolic activity need to be constructed rather than beginning with perspectives whose referent begins in the mass, organizational, or interpersonal context and collects the others as an afterthought. This is particularly true as new technologies erase differences between forms of communication. As Jeffres and Atkin (1996) noted, the Internet is pulling together group communication, organizational communication, point-to-point communication, and mass communication.[76] When real-time visual images and audio transmissions of people talking are added, the conditions for interpersonal (face-to-face) communication also will have been more closely proximated with the communication matrix.

Cronkhite's (1986) definition of communication as symbolic activity is a sound basis for viewing people as participating in communication through their roles as encoders and decoders, as well as the patterned interaction that ensues over time. Encoding includes talking with neighbors; sending letters and memos; asking a stranger for directions; issuing orders at work; calling loved ones on the phone; regaling a group of friends with one's latest exploits; and professional writing, filming, or other message construction for large audiences. Decoding includes listening to neighbors; reading the memos; listening to a stranger ask for directions; hearing one's marching orders for the day; processing messages of affection from family, and processing media messages as members of audiences.[77]

Efforts to construct systems of political communication or systems similarly restricted by context inevitably abstract slices of relevant symbolic activity (e.g., defined by the nature of the topic) from what here is conceived as the overall communication system. However, a recent study took a broader approach by looking at frequency of communication about a host of different topics across several contexts. Wyatt, Kim, and Katz (2000; Wyatt, Katz, & Kim, 2000) asked people how often they discussed not just happenings in national and statement government, but also the economy, personal and family matters, religion, entertainment, and so on; furthermore, they asked respondents to estimate how much they talked about these topics in different contexts—in general, at home and in the homes of friends, with friends and strangers at bars, restaurants and malls, at work, at places of worship, at clubs and organizations, and via e-mail/Internet. In factor analyses of talk variables by context/locus, they identified two factors, political talk and personal talk. Their findings across the six loci and general talk suggest that politics are talked about relatively frequently and are not discussed in "sharp isolation" from other topics of conversation. Wyatt and his colleagues link the communication patterns to demographic predictors and political activity.[78]

The importance of communication to individuals' ties to their communities is demonstrated in a recent study by Rothenbuhler et al. (1996). Although focusing only on mass communication behaviors, they found that newspaper reading made important contributions to both community attachment and involvement, independently of other variables in the model; television news viewing did not. Their measure of community attachment tapped respondents' assessments of several items, including the extent to which they felt a part of the community, were proud to be from it, were happy living in it, and would be unhappy to leave. Community involvement included getting together with people, keeping up with the local news and having ideas for improving the community. Using similar involvement measures but adding interpersonal communication, Stamm et al. (1997) found level of involvement correlated not only with newspaper use but also radio listening, TV viewing and frequency of interpersonal communication in the community; however, they identified respondents in terms of their community attachment (settled, relocating, drifting, or settling) and found media contributions varied by stage, with newspaper use and TV viewing, each correlated with community involvement among settlers (those just settling in), radio use linked to involvement among the settled, and interpersonal communication correlated with involvement among settled, settlers, and those relocating. Clearly, the nature of community ties is a complex notion.

Efforts to construct a communication system are more fruitful if the goals are clear. Descriptive mapping of symbolic activity is worthwhile but rudderless without guiding hypotheses. Communication links people to each other and their environment. Thus, the strength of communication links should predict stronger "ties" and greater awareness.

Neuendorf, Jeffres, and Atkin (1998) conducted two exploratory studies designed to "map" people's involvement in communication in a project that treats contextual communication variables as operationalizations of the larger concepts of communication. There are many studies of political systems, organizational systems, and various social and cultural systems. However, although communication variables occupy prominent places in such systems, seldom do scholars attempt to study communication systems that cover more than a "single" communication context. As a result, the target of generalizeability is often the context rather than symbolic activity in the context. Efforts to build such communication systems would seem to be a priority for those concerned with building the core of a discipline of communication.

First Study

The first study by was conducted in early 1993, when items mapping people's communication links were included in a regional survey of a metropolitan area in the midwest. Using a CATI (computer aided telephone interviewing) system, 331 adults age 18 or older were interviewed. In operationalizing communication links, items used give an indication of the strength of each link, whether measured by number of individuals talked to or the volume of mass communication activity measured by frequency or hours. Person-to-person communication links were obtained with a series of requests for how many people respondents talked with "yesterday," starting with "people in your household, including spouse, children or others." Subsequent items asked for the number of people talked with in the following categories: neighbors; people in your neighborhood at stores; on public transportation or in public places; people outside of your neighborhood in stores, on public transportation or in public places; people elsewhere in the city; people at a job outside the home; people in the metro area talked with on the telephone; people outside the metro area talked with on the telephone; and number of times one sent or received a fax in the past month.

Mass communication links were measured using the traditional items. Because some mass communication activity is so infrequent, they asked respondents to gage their behavior over longer time spans (i.e., the amount of television watched yesterday and the number of books read over the past 6 months). Measures included the following: number of hours of television watched yesterday; number of hours listened to the radio yesterday; number of days last week read a newspaper; number of magazines read regularly; number of books read in the past 6 months; number of videos watched in the past month; number of movies seen at a theater in the past month. Some of the mass communication links are measured over longer time spans because they are such infrequent behaviors. Certainly, an accurate diary system spanning a longer period of time would be more accurate.

Two sets of analyses are appropriate. First, the communication system as tapped by the survey is described, showing how members of this urban area distribute their communication links across the different channels and contexts. Second, individual patterns are examined, showing how people emphasize person-to-person and mass communication links. Given the different scales used in measuring communication links, responses were standardized for individual comparisons.

A summary of the number of raw links via interpersonal or phone/fax communication is found in Table 6.1. Except for communication within the household, the modal frequency is 0 for all other categories. The largest number of links

TABLE 6.1
Number of People Talked to Yesterday by Context—1993 Study

	A	B	C	D	E	F	G	H	I
0	41	183	144	151	206	168	155	219	222
	12.7%	56.3%	44.9%	46.9%	64.6%	51.4%	47.8%	67.4%	67.1%
1	61	54	28	23	17	4	13	37	15
	18.8%	16.6%	8.7%	7.1%	5.3%	1.2%	4.0%	11.4%	4.5%
2	64	43	35	27	16	2	31	25	16
	19.8%	13.2%	10.9%	8.4%	5.0%	.6%	9.6%	7.7%	4.8%
3	49	19	20	28	16	6	31	14	3
	15.1%	5.8%	6.2%	8.7%	5.0%	1.8%	9.6%	4.3%	.9%
4	29	7	22	13	10	3	22	5	8
	9.0%	2.2%	6.9%	4.0%	3.1%	.9%	6.8%	1.5%	2.4%
5	28	3	19	15	12	3	14	5	8
	8.6%	.9%	5.9%	4.7%	3.8%	.9%	4.3%	1.5%	2.4%
6-10	37	14	21	26	24	34	30	7	10
	11.4%	4.3%	6.5%	8.1%	7.5%	10.4%	9.3%	2.2%	3.0%
11-15	7	1	8	14	5	23	5	3	11
	2.2%	.3%	2.5%	4.3%	1.6%	7.0%	1.5%	.9%	3.3%
16-25	2	0	5	9	5	25	7	3	11
	.6%		1.6%	2.8%	1.6%	7.6%	2.2%	.9%	3.3%
26+	6	1	19	16	8	59	16	7	27
	1.9%	.3%	5.9%	5.0%	2.5%	18.0%	4.9%	2.2%	8.2%
Total:	324	325	321	322	319	327	324	325	331
Average:	4.0	1.2	4.7	4.7	2.9	11.1	4.4	2.0	4.6
Median:	2.0	0.0	1.0	1.0	0.0	0.0	1.0	0.0	0.0
Std. Dev.:	6.8	2.8	10.3	9.7	7.8	15.9	9.0	6.9	9.8

A: People in your household, including spouse, children, others.
B: Any of your neighbors.
C: Any people in your neighborhood in stores, on public transportation, or in public places.
D: Any people outside of your neighborhood in stores, on public transportation or in public places.
E: Any people elsewhere in the city.
F: People at a job outside the home.
G: People in the metro area by phone.
H: People outside the metro area by phone.
I: Number of faxes sent, received in past month.

is found in the job place, as might be expected; here there was an average of a little more than 11 links, despite the fact that 39% of respondents did not work outside the home. Communication with people in the neighborhood and in other public places were next in frequency. A summary of the volume of mass communication linkages is found in Table 4 in the appendix; respondents watched an average of 2.8 hours of television yesterday, listened to the radio for an average of 2.1 hours, read a newspaper an average of 5.1 days last week, read 2.9 magazines regularly, read an average of 4.9 books in the past 6 months, watched an average of 4.5 videos (borrowed or rented), and went out to see an average of 1.3 films in a theater.

Next, a summary score was computed across items for a total "interpersonal" (face-to-face plus phone and fax) linkage score and a total "mass communication" score. Because the mass communication items were measured on different scales, those scores were standardized first. Measures of variability within the two types of communication linkages, mass and interpersonal communication, also were computed.

The relationships among summary and variability measures are in Table 6.2, which shows that the greater one's average interpersonal communication links across contexts, the higher the average volume of one's media use across media, but the correlation drops out when age, education, household income, and gender are controlled. Also, the maximum for interpersonal links is correlated with the maximum for mass communication links. As research has shown in the past, "the more, the more" operates here once again. The average of one's interpersonal links is related to variability across mass communication channels, but the reverse is not true. Thus, people with lots of interpersonal communication links (average and maximum) show more selectivity, perhaps specialization, in their use of media channels.

Table 6.2 also shows the correlations between interpersonal summary and variability measures and the individual media activity measures. In general, greater interpersonal linkage is negatively related to the amount of television viewing but positively related to listening to the radio, reading magazines, and going out to see films. It is not correlated with the other two print media variables—books and newspapers—suggesting they are less "social." As the frequency distributions indicate, newspaper reading as measured is ubiquitous and may show little variation in its relationship with interpersonal links.

Next, the correlations between mass communication summary and variability measures and individual measures of interpersonal communication links were examined. Results show that mass communication activity is positively related to the number of people talked to in one's household and the number of neighbors one talked to. Talking to other people in the neighborhood and at work are unrelated to mass media activity. However, there are hints suggested by correlations approaching significance that talking with people in public places and by phone is related to minimal levels of media use. Also, those who use faxes may specialize in their media use and are likely to be heavy users of at least one medium.

TABLE 6.2
Relationships Among Communication Variables

Correlations Between Interpersonal and Mass Communication Summary and Variability Measures

	Interpersonal Communication Measures			
	Mean	*Variance*	*Minimum*	*Maximum*
Mass Communication Measures				
Mean	**.123***	.077	.036	.103#
	(.04)	(.02)	(.01)	(.06)
Variance	.120*	**.089**	.082	.123*
	(.11*)	(.08#)	(.09#)	(.11*)
Minimum	.081	.054	**.031**	.051
	(.04)	(.02)	(-.00)	(.04)
Maximum	.103	.081	.030	**.113***
	(.08)	(.08)	(.02)	(.10*)

Correlations Between Interpersonal Summary and Variability Measures and Individual Measures of Mass Communication Activity

	Interpersonal Measures			
	Mean	*Variance*	*Minimum*	*Maximum*
Media Activity Measures				
Hours watched TV Yesterday	-.120*	-.109*	-.092#	-.102#
	(-.11*)	(-.11*)	(-.08)	(-.11*)
Hours listened to radio yesterday	.146**	.088	.000	.114*
	(.07)	(.03)	(-.02)	(.05)
No. days read paper last week	-.030	-.026	.031	-.079
	(-.01)	(-.02)	(.03)	(-.05)

	Mean	Variance	Minimum	Maximum
No. magazines read regularly	.168** (.10#)	.143* (.10#)	.046 (-.01)	.138* (.11*)
No. books read in past 6 months	.042 (.05)	.044 (.06)	-.002 (-.03)	.060 (.08)
No. videos watched in past month	.059 (-.06)	.032 (-.06)	.034 (.03)	.059 (-.05)
No. films seen in theater	.118* (.08#)	.059 (.03)	.101# (.09#)	.118* (.07)

Correlations Between Mass Communication Summary and Variability Measures and Individual Measures of Interpersonal Communication Activity

	Mass Communication Measures			
	Mean	Variance	Minimum	Maximum
Interpersonal Communication Measures				
No. people talked to....				
in household	.145** (.16**)	.285*** (.31***)	-.007 (.01)	.170** (.19***)
neighbors	.166** (.16***)	.148** (.15**)	.080 (.07)	.122* (.11*)
others in neighborhood	.071 (.06)	.054 (.03)	.018 (.02)	.078 (.04)
others outside neighborhood	.027 (.04)	.001 (.02)	.104# (.07)	.013 (.04)
in public places elsewhere in city	.105# (.05)	.077 (.09#)	.102# (.07)	.069 (.08)
at job	.025 (-.02)	-.013 (-.05)	.054 (.06)	.004 (-.02)

(continues)

TABLE 6.2 (cont.)

	Mass Communication Measures			
	Mean	*Variance*	*Minimum*	*Maximum*
locally by phone	.041	-.028	.112*	-.023
	(-.03)	(-.06)	(.09#)	(-.08#)
outside metro area by phone	.025	-.025	.069	-.001
	(-.04)	(-.04)	(.02)	(-.04)
by fax/sent, received	.089	.229***	-.088	.166**
	(-.00)	(.22***)	(-.18**)	(.15**)

Correlations Between Individual Mass Communication Measures and Individual Measures of Interpersonal Communication

	Mass Communication Measures (Frequency/Volume)						
	TV	*Radio*	*News-paper*	*Maga-zines*	*Books*	*Videos*	*Films*
Interpersonal Communication Measures							
No. people talked to							
in household	-.046	.053	-.004	.086#	.111*	.090	.205***
	(-.04)	(.04)	(.03)	(.09#)	(.16**)	(.07)	(.25***)
neighbors	.035	.111*	.056	.155*	.107#	-.011	.100#
	(.03)	(.13*)	(.05)	(.19**)	(.12*)	(-.03)	(.11*)
others in neighborhood	-.016	.119*	-.006	.020	.027	.010	.065
	(-.07)	(.07)	(-.05)	(.06)	(.04)	(-.04)	(.05)
others outside neighborhood	-.090	.021	.022	.126*	.049	-.061	.028
	(-.07)	(.06)	(-.02)	(.15**)	(.01)	(-.06)	(.03)
in public places							

elsewhere in city	-.119*	.039	.074	.122*	.060	.092#	.080
	(-.10#)	(-.04)	(.10#)	(.00)	(.09#)	(.07)	(.12*)
at job	-.075	.080	-.074	.076	-.001	.019	.028
	(-.09#)	(.03)	(-.01)	(.03)	(.02)	(-.09#)	(-.02)
locally by phone	-.032	.089	.005	.087	.003	-.007	.004
	(-.03)	(.01)	(.03)	(.06)	(.02)	(-.07)	(-.03)
outside metro	-.057	.066	.010	.070	.017	.003	-.032
area by phone	(-.08)	(.04)	(.05)	(.01)	(-.03)	(-.09#)	(-.06)
by fax/sent, received	-.096#	.093#	-.102#	.115*	-.020	.115*	.166*
	(-.10#)	(.01)	(-.14*)	(-.04)	(-.02)	(.08)	(.18**)

***$p < .001$; **$p < .01$; *$p < .05$; #$p < .10$

In parentheses are partial correlations controlling for age, education, household income, and gender.

The final section of Table 6.2 relates the two sets of individual media activity and interpersonal communication links by context to each other. Talking to people at work and by phone are unrelated to mass communication measures. Listening to the radio is associated with neighborhood links. Magazine reading was associated with neighborhood links as well as talking to more people in public places in the neighborhood and elsewhere in the city.

Table 6.3 shows relationships between social categories and communication summary and variability measures. Household size is negatively related to minimal levels of mass media use, but the other life-cycle measure—age—is relatively more important. Age is negatively related to the level and variability of interpersonal communication linkages; thus, older people talk to fewer people and have less variability across contexts. Education is positively related to most of the interpersonal summary measures and negatively related to variability across mass communication measures. Household income also is positively correlated with all interpersonal measures and one mass communication variable. Gender and race appear to be relatively unimportant (see Table 5 in the appendix for correlations between social categories and individual measures of interpersonal and mass communication).

Second Study

A second study incorporating measures of people's mass and interpersonal communication was conducted in 1996 by Neuendorf, Jeffres, and Atkin. This study also was an omnibus survey of the same metropolitan area, utilizing the same CATI system and introductions. The range of communication behaviors was expanded to include the following:

1. **Interpersonal/Point-to-Point Communication Activity**: including reports on the number of people talked to today: in one's household, in one's neighborhood (combining two measures used in the first study), at one's job, elsewhere in the city, locally by phone, and outside the area by phone.
2. **Mass Communication Activity**: including reports on TV viewing (number of hours watched yesterday and the number usually watched), radio listening (number of hours listened yesterday), newspaper reading (number of days last week read a newspaper), magazine reading (number of different magazines read regularly), book reading (number read in past six months), video viewing (number watched in past month, whether borrowed or rented), and film viewing (number times went out to see a film in a theater in past month).
3. **Communication Needs**: including items tapping the need to send and receive messages across both mass and interpersonal roles.[79]

TABLE 6.3
Correlations Between Communication Summary and Variability Measures and Social Category Measures

	No. in house-hold	No. child-ren in hsehold	Age	Educa-tion	House-hold Income	Gender	Race
Interpersonal							
Mean	.073	.031	-.239***	.235***	.301***	-.086	-.055
Variance	.041	.031	-.171**	.176**	.230**	-.066	.004
Minimum	.076	.095#	-.057	.097#	.116*	-.072	-.071
Maximum	.034	.028	-.254***	.190***	.231***	-.071	-.020
Mass Communication							
Mean	.001	-.007	-.048	-.014	.074	-.042	.037
Variance	.035	.040	-.102#	-.118*	-.004	.023	.011
Minimum	-.124*	-.097#	.148*	.078	.145*	-.018	.037
Maximum	.000	-.017	-.070	-.086	-.000	-.013	.029

***$p < .001$; **$p < .01$; *$p < .05$; #$p < .10$

4. **Communication Routines**: including reports of communication patterns rather than measures of communication links (volume or frequency).[80]

In addition to measures of communication activity, the interviews tapped respondents perceived QOL, personal identification, and community knowledge.[81]

Table 6.4 gives the number of people talked to by context in the 1996 study. The average number of people talked to in one's household was 3.15, compared to 4 in the first study. In this study, the three neighborhood measures from the first study were combined into a single measure to increase what was seen as a potential reliability problem in the first study; the average was 5.44, compared to almost double that figure in the first study. However, the figure for the number of people talked to elsewhere in the city went from an average of 2.9 in 1993 to 5.63 in 1996, suggesting that boundaries may be problematic. In the 1993 study, the average number of people talked to at a job outside the home was 11.1, a figure that was 9.14 in the 1996 study. The number of people talked to by phone locally and outside the metro area was 4.63 and 2.44, respectively, figures similar to those in the first study.

Table 6 in the appendix gives the strength of mass communication linkages in 1996. The number of hours of TV viewing was 3.04 yesterday, compared to 2.8 hours in 1993, whereas radio listening went from 2.1 hours to 2.32 hours. Newspaper reading averaged 5.1 days in 1993 and 4.77 days in 1996. The average number of magazines read was 2.9 in 1993 and 3.10 in 1996. The number of books read was 4.9 in 1993 and 5.33 in 1996, whereas an average of 4.5 videos was watched in the past month in 1993 and 3.36 in 1996. The average number of films seen at a theater was 1.3 in 1993 and 1.2 in 1996.

The second study also added a set of items measuring communication needs across a variety of contexts and roles (see Table 7 in the appendix) and communication routines (see Table 8 in the appendix). Respondents show great variability across the measures

NEIGHBORHOOD COMMUNICATION INFORMANTS

The use of "informants" is a technique popularized by linguists, anthropologists, and sociologists trying to get insights into a language or culture. The informant "role" also relies on the interview technique but the individual is selected because he or she is believed to have insight into the culture and, by being one step removed, provides a selective screen for the investigator (Webb, Campbell, Schwartz, Sechrest, & Grove, 1981). Jeffres, Dobos, and Lee (1991) extended the concept to examine neighborhood communication patterns. They selected "communication informants" to ascertain perceptions of neighborhoods and interactions within them from individuals who shared a history with the

TABLE 6.4
Number of People Talked to Yesterday by Context—1996 Study

	A	B	C	D	E	F
0	43 11.4%	92 24.4%	204 54.1%	142 37.7%	80 21.2%	189 50.1%
1	93 24.7%	41 10.9%	6 1.6%	22 5.8%	72 19.1%	63 16.7%
2	57 15.1%	48 12.7%	5 1.3%	37 9.8%	73 19.4%	52 13.8%
3	60 15.9%	39 10.3%	4 1.1%	31 8.2%	42 11.1%	20 5.3%
4	45 11.9%	27 7.2%	10 2.7%	18 4.8%	13 3.4%	7 1.9%
5	40 10.6%	22 5.8%	7 1.9%	22 5.8%	24 6.4%	12 3.2%
6-10	32 8.5%	67 17.8%	46 12.2%	61 16.2%	40 10.6%	20 5.3%
11-15	2 .5%	13 3.4%	18 5.3%	8 2.1%	11 2.9%	6 1.6%
16-25	3 .8%	16 4.2%	36 9.5%	17 4.5%	12 3.2%	3 .8%
26+	2 .5%	12 3.2%	41 10.9%	19 5.0%	10 2.7%	5 1.3%
Average:	3.15	5.44	9.14	5.63	4.63	2.44
Median:	2.00	3.00	0.00	2.00	2.00	0.00
Std. Dev.:	3.96	9.00	15.98	10.71	9.74	7.35
Total:	377 for all variables					

A: People in your household, including spouse, children, others.
B: People in your neighborhood, including neighbors, people at local stores, in public places, or on public transit.
C: People at a job outside the home.
D: Any people elsewhere in the city.
E: People in the metro area by phone.
F: People outside the metro area by phone.

area and were knowledgeable about it. Because informants are interested in the neighborhoods and integrated into local networks, they share the same context with editors but have different jobs, thus providing a point of comparison with editors. Informants were selected from each of 16 neighborhoods in the Cleveland, Ohio area over a 3-year period—in 1988, 1989, and 1991. Communication informants are long-term residents integrated into the neighborhoods and acting as informants about the patterns of communication in the area and the neighborhood QOL.[82]

Communication informants were asked with whom they regularly talk in the community during an average week and what the topics of conversation were. They also were asked how often they frequented various contexts in the community, providing a measure of their "use" of the neighborhood, and how they learn about different things going on in their community. As Table 6.5 shows, communication informants report much less interaction with officials, bureaucrats, and institutional representatives, but much more with neighbors and residents. A similar number interact with people at work and family and friends. Conversations show a similar emphasis on neighborhood issues and problems but considerably more emphasis on small talk and personal topics, as would be expected.

TABLE 6.5
Who Communication Informants Talk With and Topics of Conversation

Who Communication Informants Talk With During An Average Week

Government:	
Officials—council reps., local leaders	4
Bureaucrats & Gov. Offices—area agencies,	
school superintendent	4
Nongovernment organizations—community organizations	1
General Public and others	
Local residents, neighbors	9
People at work, customers, boss, employees	6
Business groups, local merchants	3
Friends and family	4
Local professionals or job roles—clergy	1
Participants in events—scouts	1

Topics of Conversation:

Neighborhood issues and news	6
Specific problems—youth, drugs, housing	4
Institutions and programs (community development organization projects)	1
Current events and politics	2
Job, business, work	4
Other topics—personal, gardening, weather, small talk, family	9

Note. There were 18 informants.

TABLE 6.6
Contexts Frequented by Communication Informants

	Every day	Couple times a week	Once a week	Every couple weeks	Once a month	Every couple months	Less often
			How Often Frequent Context:				
Context:							
Going to local shops, stores, banks	8	6	2	-	1	-	-
Walking down a neighhood street	12	3	-	1	-	-	1
Attending church	-	3	8	1	-	-	3
Over backyard fence or sitting on a porch	6	6	1	-	-	1	2
At meetings of local clubs, orgs	4	2	4	3	1	1	2
In the local library	1	1	1	6	1	3	5
At a local hospital	1	1	1	-	2	-	5
In a fraternal hall or club	-	1	1	1	2	1	7
In a neighborhood restaurant	1	6	-	3	3	2	3
At a corner bar	-	2	2	-	1	2	8
In a local park	1	3	3	1	-	2	7
At a local gym, athletic center or sports event	2	1	2	-	1	2	10
At a local school	1	3	1	-	2	1	8

Note. There were 18 communication informants.

Communication informants also were asked how often they frequented various contexts (see Table 6.6). Informants frequent local shops, stores, and banks and walk down neighborhood streets. They also report considerable involvement at meetings of local clubs and organizations. Informants also go to churches and visit other contexts such as parks relatively often.

Communication informants rely on interpersonal communication (word of mouth, gossip, fliers) and personal observation to learn about their community (see Table 6.7). Informants also show a rather significant contact with government agencies and their council representative as a source of information. Informants also tend to rely, to a considerable extent, on the mass media to learn about what's going on. Rank ordered in terms of importance, word-of-mouth was the most important, followed by mass media, contacts with government agencies and organizations.

Asked to think of a recent situation where everyone seemed to know about something going on in the neighborhood before they did, informants cited incidents or problems, including a rent strike, a racial disturbance, a local fire, a drug bust, and shootings. Only two cited positive events such as local development projects. Consistent with their communication patterns, five heard of the incident from neighbors or personal observation, whereas two heard from a council representative, one saw it in a newspaper and one learned of the inci-

TABLE 6.7
How Communication Informants Learn About Their Community

	Press* Release	Mass Media	Other Contacts by			Going to meet- ings	Word of Mouth
			gov. agencies	busi- ness	org. leaders		
Topics:							
A new development program	1	8	4	4	3	3	5
Some change in social ser-							
vices for residents	1	6	5	-	4	-	6
A local robbery	-	6	4	-	2	-	12
Grand opening of new busi-							
ness in neighborhood	4#	3	1	3#	1	-	8
Council rep's stand							
on city issue	-	9	9	-	-	3	-
Religious festival	1	7	-	-	3	-	8
Ethnic/fraternal							
celebration	1	7	-	-	2	1	7
Going price of homes							
for sale in neigh@	-	5	1	3	-	-	8
Youth/education							
problems@	-	4	6	-	3	-	7
N and % of 186							
citations across	8	55	30	10	18	7	61
all 9 situations:	4%	30%	16%	5%	10%	4%	33%

Note. The 18 informants could cite more than one source.

*The press release refers to personal invitations or notice by mail.

#Three said they would receive invitations from the business, and these are included in each of these figures.

~Included here are observation and seeing signs as well as interpersonal communication.

@One informant said "don't know."

dent at an organizational meeting. Informants said they enjoy talking with almost everyone in their neighborhoods, although a few said they avoid drunks, gossipers, and others.

Informants were asked for their perceptions of communication in the neighborhood and how people got along. Half thought people got along well or very well but they also came up with an assortment of conflicts when asked for examples they had overheard (e.g., conflicts over public issues such as busing, changes in the area, and schools as well as the more frequent personal conflicts over race, rent, barking dogs, and domestic issues). Asked which groups interacted most often and which didn't, informants mirrored editors in citing ethnicity, age, race, and income as barriers. Informants also were asked for their perceptions of the QOL in their neighborhoods, the major problems and efforts to solve them. These are discussed further later.

SUMMARY

Each neighborhood has a unique communication system that reflects the pattern of communication needs distributed among its residents as well as the constraints of geography and social environment. Although no study has attempted to document a neighborhood's communication system through a formal network analysis, case studies have identified some patterns and some descriptive data are available.

Neighborhood communication channels found to be important include neighborhood newspapers and interpersonal communication in both formal (organizational meetings, schools, churches) and informal (over the fence, on the street, in stores) contexts, as well as bulletin boards, handbills, posters, newsletters, and similar "small" channels. Local media reinforced the content of less formal channels in one study.

Personal communication networks provide another picture of how people are linked within neighborhoods. One study of informal ties with friends, neighbors, relatives, and co-workers found that only a small portion of people's networks was within walking distance of respondents' homes or jobs. Furthermore, most people were involved in "private home societies" rather than "street corner societies," reflecting the greater importance of home than neighborhood. Networks reflect a low density—only one third of one's network had ties with each other—and the telephone was the most widely used context for interaction. Another study found a substantial share of one's interpersonal communication in the neighborhood was with family and relatives. Mobility was closely tied to the strength of one's neighborhood communication.

Efforts to map people's personal communication networks have included domain-specific attempts that focus on political communication as well as broader mapping studies examining the frequency of one's interpersonal links across contexts and media use. Two studies examined the number of people talked to "yesterday" in various situations as well as media use. In the first study, the largest number of links—11—was at work, followed by communication with people in the neighborhood and then with people in other public settings. Summary and variability scores were computed and relationships examined. In general, results show that the greater the number of interpersonal links across contexts, the higher one's media use. The use of "neighborhood communication informants" also has been used to characterize neighborhood communication patterns.

7

Neighborhood Newspapers

Leo W. Jeffres
Jae-won Lee

- Grassroots Media
- Goals and Functions of Neighborhood Newspapers
- Neighborhood Newspaper Editors: Their Communication and Involvement in the Community
- News Sources of Neighborhood Residents
- Content of Neighborhood Newspapers
- Comparing Neighborhood Perceptions
- Summary

GRASSROOTS MEDIA

Community newspapers represent "grassroots" organizations that link neighbors to each other while informing residents of what's going on in their neighborhoods. These newspapers are part of the neighborhood communication system (Jeffres, 1994). Clevenger (1977) argued that media can improve communication and increase the speed at which feedback is provided to the system. Neighborhood radio feeds into and is part of community communication networks (Schulman, 1985), and community newspapers provide feedback that allows the neighborhood to solve problems.

Numerous studies have examined the functions and operations of community newspapers. E. Hindman (1998a, 1998b) focused on a neighborhood newspaper's self-perception as an agent of democracy, concluding that the inner-city neighborhood paper tries to develop and encourage community participation. Ward (1980) noted the need for urban residents to get better information about their neighborhoods for participation in policymaking. She noted that citizens and activists have relied on public meetings, rallies, fliers, and telephone networks, as well as neighborhood newspapers, the nonprofit citizen-initiated press. She noted that neighborhood newspapers and newsletters began circulating in numerous cities during the social turbulence of the 1960s.[83] Weissman (1970) concluded that a volunteer-run neighborhood paper played a critical role both within and outside the neighborhood; the paper was a way the council could communicate with the neighborhood and it was a clear symbol of the council to the neighborhood. C. Gaziano (1974) studied a Model Cities newspaper and found high readership, particularly among those with high political interest. Similarly, E. Abbott (1988) examined a small Iowa community of 450 that launched a volunteer newspaper which had lasted a decade and was seen as a model for other small communities too small to support a commercial weekly paper. The paper had high readership, particularly among seniors. Valenty (1976) examined the same paper and two others in the area and concluded they had contributed to creating awareness of neighborhood identity and to participation in problem-solving activities. Conason (1975) reported on a New England regional community media conference attended by 80 people representing diverse papers, where a common view was that working and poor people's issues receive inadequate coverage or do not get a fair hearing.

R. Bryant (1978) described the impact of a community newspaper started in a Glasgow neighborhood in 1967 by a group of radical Christians. A decade later, he said the following:

> for local residents, the main value of a community newspaper is the very fact that the paper is local and produces news and comments which would not appear in a printed form elsewhere. The best community papers attempt to document the social histories of their area and, in a small but significant way, they record many public events and experiences which would otherwise only be preserved in private correspondence and oral history. Because of this locality focus, community newspapers may encourage parochialism, which can be a strength in terms of generating interest but which can also be a weakness in terms of limiting the degree to which the paper's reporting, particularly with reference to social and economic conditions, is related to the wider, structural context of political decision-making. (p. 45)

Lenz-Romeiss (1973) also noted that the local newspaper can be important for local orientations, can be an important transmitter of place-related communication, and can contribute to one's attachment to place.

In summary, the neighborhood press plays a significant role in providing diversity of messages, independent agendas, access to media, and a forum for public affairs. Furthermore, the papers confirm neighborhood identity and establish links within and outside the neighborhood. Neighborhood papers have emerged to fill a gap created by metro media, which do not serve diversity needs (Ward & Gaziano, 1976).

GOALS AND FUNCTIONS OF NEIGHBORHOOD NEWSPAPERS

The functions fulfilled by newspapers and other media are generally summed up in global terms such as keeping the public informed or providing a timely account of current affairs. Lasswell's (1948) classic statement of basic communication functions included surveillance of the environment, correlation of the parts of society in responding to its environment, and transmission of the cultural heritage. C. Wright (1960) added entertainment to the list, and journalists have been citing the set of four functions ever since. McQuail (1994) elaborated on what is involved in these functions and added one in a list of basic ideas about the purposes media serve for society:

1. Information: Providing information about events and conditions in society and the world; indicating relations of power; facilitating innovation, adaptation and progress.
2. Correlation: Explaining, interpreting, and commenting on the meaning of events and information; providing support for established authority and norms; socializing; coordinating separate activities; consensus building; setting orders of priority and signaling relative status.
3. Continuity: Expressing the dominant culture and recognizing subcultures and new cultural developments; forging and maintaining commonality of values.
4. Entertainment: Providing amusement, diversion, the means of relaxation; reducing social tension.
5. Mobilization: Campaigning for societal objectives in the sphere of politics, war, economic development, work and sometimes religion.

Seldom are these functions brought down to the community level, where journalists work and live.[84] Rubin (1994) pointed to the link between traditional notions about media functions and the uses and gratifications literature. The latter emphasizes audience perceptions of how the media serve them. It is a small step toward integrating the two themes by asking journalists how they serve the community.

Most of the research and criticism of newspapers focuses on the commercial press that is the core of U.S. print journalism. Seldom have researchers examined papers beyond the commercial dailies and weeklies; however, a better look at the extent to which newspaper functions are universally accepted by journalists and what influences these functions is found by looking at community papers with different origins and organizations. How are these functions related to the reasons that led to the creation of specific papers?

In the Jeffres et al. (1999) study, editors were asked to rate the importance of a long list of newspaper "goals often attributed to neighborhood and community newspapers." They used a 4-point scale: very important, somewhat important, not very important, or totally unimportant (plus don't know). The list of goals was constructed using the traditional list of functions but expressing them in terms of familiar types of content in most cases. The list was pretested with some community editors of urban papers and items with a uniquely urban focus added.[85]

An analysis of editors' assessments of the importance of different goals and functions yielded eight dimensions: the traditional watchdog function, a civic journalism-activist role,[86] family and personals, ethnics and social services; advertising and entertainment; neighborhood activities and clubs; a people focus; and editorials/no development news. Each of these dimensions can be linked to traditional media functions and are consistent with the literature on mainstream commercial media. The emergence of factors confirming those associated with the mainstream commercial dailies is important because it provides additional evidence of the universality of these goals or functions in the United States.

The 141 community papers represent a diverse lot. Ten papers date to the last century, whereas a couple were less than 1 year old.[87] Editors were asked to select from a list of five descriptions for how their paper began, or to offer another description. Seventy-seven (55%) indicated that an individual or couple interested in journalism and the area began the paper as a personal goal, 10 (7%) indicated that a community group began a newsletter that expanded to serve the neighborhood, 8 (6%) said that a development association or government agency began the paper to reach residents, 15 (11%) indicated that a group of merchants asked an individual to start a paper so they could reach residents, 23 (16%) said that a set of community activists began the paper to support their group's goals, and 8 offered other origins. In nutshell histories of their papers, about 33% said the papers had grown, whereas 25% said the paper was sold and others noted a growth in circulation, changes in finance, readership, and size. Slightly more than 40% of those responding said their publisher was an individual owner, whereas 28% said they were part of a company or chain and 7% were published by development organizations or community groups.

Although almost 66% of the papers are weeklies, 11% are bi-weeklies, 9% dailies, 8% monthlies, and the others have varying frequencies. Some 69% of the papers are distributed free, and the rest either have paid circulation or are purchased at stores. Only 20% of the editors said their papers do their own printing, whereas most do their own layout and send it out for printing. Newspaper size ranges from a few pages to more than 50 pages, with an average of 26 pages. Some 59% of the papers are tabloids and 28% broadsheets, with the remainder letter size or other sizes. Editorial staffs are small for most papers, with 20% reporting no full-time editorial staff, 24% with one staffer, 17% with two and 11% with three. Advertising staff follow a similar pattern, with 29% reporting no full-time employees, 19% with one, 11% with two, and 10% with three.

Examining the urban community press in the 1950s, Janowitz (1952/1967) noted that the "big mass media" are less relevant for guiding community-based activities and he suggested that the effectiveness of the urban community press would continue if it could strengthen its "decentralized roots" and maintain its community focus. His anecdotal evidence of editors' goals and functions in the 1950s and 1960s suggest many of those tapped by items in the current study. The relative importance of individual items is given in Table 7.1, where the local focus is quite clear. Providing news of local festivals and events was ranked as most important, followed by alerting residents to local problems

TABLE 7.1
Relative Importance of Items Tapping Dimensions of Newspaper Goals or Functions

Providing news of local festivals, events	3.73
Alerting residents to local problems, conflicts	3.66
Features on local people	3.56
Covering local schools	3.53
Keeping an eye on local public officials	3.50
Letters to the editor	3.48
Telling residents about local clubs, organizations	3.48
Reporting news about redevelopment projects	3.42
Getting conflict out in the open so the neighborhood can deal with it	3.40
Alerting residents to social services available	3.34
Getting people involved in solving neighborhood problems	3.33
Bring people in the neighborhood together is a goal	3.30
Linking consumers with advertisers	3.24
Discussing political issues in the metro area	3.20
Giving residents a chance to sell via classifieds	3.18
Reporting news of ethnic communities in the neighborhood	3.14
Getting residents pictures in the paper	3.14
Covering crime news	3.10
Investigative reporting	3.10
Providing news about local theaters and entertainment in the neighborhood	3.10
Editorials giving the paper's point of view	3.07
Covering local churches	2.96
Print articles written by local residents	2.94
Trying to develop consensus in the community	2.90
Covering neighborhood sporting events	2.90
Announcing personal items like weddings, births, etc.	2.68
Avoiding problems, focusing on positive things in the neighborhood	2.45

and conflicts, printing features on local people and covering local schools. Keeping an eye on local public officials came next, followed by letters to the editor. Second from the bottom of the list are personal announcements; this is somewhat surprising because tradition says that community journalism focuses more on people and "names do make news." At the very bottom of the list is avoiding problems and focusing on positive things in the neighborhood. Small-town editors and community newspapers often are criticized for being "local boosters" and ignoring problems, so this last-place finish is reassuring for grass-roots press in urban areas.

Next, editors' assessments of the importance of different goals and functions were entered into a factor analysis to see whether the traditional dimensions would emerge across the national sample. As Table 7.2 shows, the "traditional watchdog," or surveillance, is the first function to emerge. Loading positively on this factor were discussions of politics, keeping an eye on public officials, alerting residents to local problems and conflicts, covering crime news, investigative reporting, and printing letters to the editor; in addition, a negative loading was found for avoiding problems and focusing on positive things in the neighborhood. Recently, Stone, O'Donnell, and Banning (1997) found strong public support for the watchdog role, so editors and audiences seem to agree on this important function of papers.

The second dimension was labeled "civic journalism/activist role" and is similar to what has come to be called "public" or "civic journalism," which emphasizes public involvement as a goal.[88] This factor represents an emphasis on bringing people in the neighborhood together, getting people involved in solving local problems, getting conflict out in the open so the neighborhood can deal with it, and trying to develop a consensus in the community. Also loading on this dimension is an effort to print articles written by local residents and avoiding problems while focusing on positive things in the neighborhood. These items include seemingly contradictory goals; thus, editors emphasize both ends of the conflict—consensus dimension to reporting first articulated by Tichenor, Donohue, and Olien (1980). This dimension also captures the mobilization function cited by McQuail (1994).

The third factor was called "family and personals." Here the emphasis is on covering personal items like weddings and births, as well as the chief neighborhood institutions—schools, churches, and neighborhood sports, gener-ally connected either to a recreation center or school in most communities.

The remaining five factors accounting for much smaller amounts of the variance include dimensions representing an emphasis on reporting about "eth-nics and social services," "advertising and entertainment," "neighborhood activ-ities, clubs," a "people focus," and "editorials/no development news." Each of these dimensions can be linked to one or more of the traditional media func-tions, and they are consistent with the literature on mainstream commercial media. Several of the factors suggest an emphasis on what Lemert (1984; Lemert & Ashman, 1983) called "mobilizing information," details and specifics

TABLE 7.2
Dimensions of Newspaper Goals, Functions

Factors: 1-Traditional Watchdog
2-Civic Journalism/Activist Role
3-Family and Personals
4-Ethnics/Social Services
5-Advertising and Entertainment
6-Neigh. Activities, Clubs
7-People Focus
8-Editorials/No Dev. News

	1	2	3	4	5	6	7	8
Keeping an eye on local public officials (WATCHDOG)	.73							
Alerting residents to local problems, conflicts (LOCPROB)	.65							
Covering crime news (CRIME)	.68							
Investigative reporting (INVESTIGATE)	.72							
Letters to the editor (LETTERS)	.39							
Discussing pol. issues in the metro area (POLITICS)	.46							
Avoiding problems, focusing on positive things in the neighborhood (POSITIVE FOCUS)	-.62	.44				-.46		
Print articles written by local residents (LWRITERS)		.57						
Bring people in the neighborhood together is a goal (CENSUS1)		.84						
Getting people involved in solving neighborhood problems (PROBSOLV)		.84						
Getting conflict out in the open so the neighborhood can deal with it (OPEN)		.58						
Trying to develop consensus in the community (CENSUS2)		.78						
Announcing personal items like weddings, births, etc. (PERSONAL)			.73					
Covering local schools (SCHOOLS)			.71					

(continues)

TABLE 7.2 (cont.)

Factors:	1-Traditional Watchdog	5-Advertising and Entertainment
	2-Civic Journalism/Activist Role	6-Neigh. Activities, Clubs
	3-Family and Personals	7-People Focus
	4-Ethnics/Social Services	8-Editorials/No Dev. News

	1	2	3	4	5	6	7	8
Covering local churches (CHURCHES)			.64					
Covering neighborhood sporting events (SPORTS)			.65					
Alerting residents to social services avlb. (SOCSERV)				.68				
Reporting news of ethnic communities in the neighborhood (ETHNICS)				.72				
Telling residents about local clubs, orgs. (CLUBS)				.55		.46		
Giving residents a chance to sell via classifieds (CADS)					.61			
Linking consumers with advertisers (ADS)					.73			
Providing news about local theaters and entertainment in the neighborhood (THEATER)					.65			
Providing news of local festivals, events (FESTIVAL)						.75		
Getting residents' pictures in the paper (PICTURES)						.44	.49	
Features on local people (LPEOPLE)							.82	
Reporting news about redevelopment projects (BUILD)								-.59
Editorials giving the paper's point of view (EDITORIALS)								.65
Percentage of Variance	20.8%	11.8%	10%	5.6%	5.1%	4.1%	4.0%	3.8%

Note. The figures in the table represent loadings on the 8 factors, which are described at the top of the table. All responses were entered into a factor analysis with a varimax rotation. The amount of variance accounted for by each factor is at the bottom of table.

such as phone numbers and addresses that allow readers to take action. Community newspapers are likely to include more of such information than metro dailies.

The factor analysis generated dimensions that seem to represent traditional newspaper functions of the commercial press (e.g., the "Watchdog Role of the Press") as well as the "Activist Role" and an emphasis on "Ethnics and Social Services," which would be more characteristically important of urban papers. However, varying emphases might be expected, depending on the nature of the newspaper. Using factor scores for the importance of the eight dimensions, differences and relationships by newspaper characteristics, structure, and organization were examined.

Origins of community newspapers were grouped into those that demonstrate the paper was begun by an individual entrepreneur or was a commercial effort versus those started by groups or organizations. Differences were found for four of the eight dimensions: editors of papers started by individual entrepreneurs or as a request by local merchants rated three factors as more important—family and personals ($t = 2.04, p < .04$), advertising and entertainment ($t = 2.1, p < .04$), and the people focus ($t = 1.88, p < .06$). Those papers started by groups, activists, or development associations rated serving ethnics and connecting residents to social services higher ($t = 2.67, p < .01$). These newspapers clearly are center-city papers targeting poorer neighborhoods with social problems. There were no differences by origins for the traditional watchdog function, the activist role, focusing on neighborhood activities or the importance of editorials/not focusing on development. Whether a newspaper was part of a chain was related to only one dimension, coverage of family events and personals—which was rated more highly as a goal by editors of chain papers ($t = 3.25, p < .002$). Chain size was related to two dimensions when independents (those not belonging to chains) were coded as 0 and others were arrayed by the size of the chain to which they belonged; this measure was positively correlated with the importance of covering family-oriented events and personals ($r = .37, p < .001$) and to the importance of advertising and entertainment ($r = .20, p < .04$). In a study of newspaper quality and ownership, Lacy and Fico (1990) found that some of the chains with smaller circulation papers produced better papers than would be expected, whereas some groups with larger circulation papers produced lower quality papers than expected. Interestingly, in the urban sample there were no differences in the importance of any goals or functions based on whether there were other papers serving their community (i.e., competition).

The three dimensions accounting for the most variance in the factor analysis were related to age of the newspapers. The older the paper, the more important the watchdog function ($r = .21, p < .04$) and family and personals ($r = .26, p < .01$), and the less important the activist role ($r = -.25, p < .02$). Thus, older papers fit more traditional weekly models, whereas newer ones likely fit a center-city activist model.

Other newspaper characteristics related to the importance of different goals and functions were frequency of publication, circulation, whether the paper was distributed free or had a paid circulation, and the number of pages. Frequency of publication was related to an emphasis on six of the eight dimensions, including correlations that approach statistical significance. Thus, the more frequent the publication, the more important the following dimensions: the watchdog function ($r = .18$, $p > .08$), family and personals ($r = .20$, $p < .04$), advertising and entertainment ($r = .28$, $p < .01$), and editorials/no development emphasis ($r = .24$, $p < .02$). The less frequent the publication, the more important the activist function ($r = -.18$, $p < .08$) and serving ethnics and linking residents to social services ($r = -.35$, $p < .001$). Size of circulation was related to only one dimension, advertising and entertainment ($r = .23$, $p < .03$); Stone and Morrison's (1976) study of small dailies and weeklies found a correlation between local advertising and circulation. This also is consistent with Gladney's (1990) finding that editors of small and large papers share common values even though they evaluate excellence differently. The number of pages was related to the importance of the watchdog role ($r = .19$, $p < .06$), and advertising and entertainment ($r = .36$, $p < .01$); it was negatively related to the importance of the activist role ($r = -.20$, $p < .05$). Whether papers were distributed free or had a paid circulation was related to only one dimension, family and personals, which were emphasized more by papers with paid circulation ($t = 5.33$, $p < .001$).

The nature of the distribution system was related to a couple dimensions. Editors indicated the percentage of their circulation distributed via home delivery, through the U.S. mails, through newsstand sales, or by drops at stores and other locations in the community. Home delivery and newsstand sales were not related to any of the eight dimensions, but the percentage of papers dropped at stores was negatively related to the importance of family and personals ($r = -.25$, $p < .01$) and to neighborhood activities ($r = -.20$, $p < .05$), whereas the percentage of papers mailed to homes and subscribers was positively related to the importance of family and personals ($r = .23$, $p < .02$) and negatively related to the importance of editorials and not emphasizing development ($r = -.20$, $p < .05$).

Both staff size and sources of income were related to dimensions of newspaper functions and goals. Editors gave the number of full-time employees in the editorial and advertising departments. The number of full-time editorial employees was positively related to only the watchdog function ($r = .21$, $p < .04$) and negatively related to the importance of covering neighborhood activities and clubs ($r = -.18$, $p < .07$). The number of full-time advertising staff was positively related to the watchdog function ($r = .21$, $p < .04$) and to the advertising and entertainment function ($r = .23$, $p < .02$) but negatively related to the importance of the activist dimension ($r = -.23$, $p < .02$) and emphasis on ethnics and social services ($r = -.23$, $p < .02$). Editors were asked to estimate the percentage of revenue coming from three sources, advertising, sales and "other sources," the third including organizational support and grants. The higher the percentage of revenue coming from advertising, the more important the advertising and entertainment function ($r = .29$, $p < .01$) and the people focus ($r = .22$, $p < .03$), but there were no relationships with the other dimensions. The greater the percentage of revenue from other sources, the more important the activist role ($r = .22$, $p < .02$). Revenue from sales was unrelated to the importance of any dimension.

As Tichenor and his colleagues (1980) noted, the size of the community served is reflected in the media. Both population and the size of the geographic area served were examined. The size of the population of the community served was correlated with only one dimension of newspaper goals, the importance of advertising and entertainment ($r = .36$, $p < .001$); similarly, the number of zip codes served by the paper was correlated with the same dimension ($r = .21$, $p < .06$).

NEIGHBORHOOD NEWSPAPER EDITORS: THEIR COMMUNICATION AND INVOLVEMENT IN THE COMMUNITY

Journalists use interpersonal communication—the interview, for example—and observation to survey the relevant environment in news gathering. In addition to professional communication patterns, their informal communication network alerts journalists to stories while providing background for future reference and influencing personal values. Newspaper and broadcast journalists rely on authoritative sources and routine channels for much information about hard news stories. Communication patterns also indicate the extent to which journalists are integrated into their environment, whether they are detached and unencumbered or in the thick of things. Northington (1992) discussed the experience of one small newspaper's experience in treating the line between editorial advocacy and community activism (also see Altschull, 1996). C. Gaziano and McGrath (1987) found that newspaper journalists strongly endorsed the concept of knowing many people in the community but most drew the line on involvement in community organizations. In a national survey of more than 1,000 newspaper journalists, Voakes (1999) found that journalists at smaller papers attach more importance to neighborhood news and are more likely to approve of civic journalism practices.

Few scholars have looked at the overall communication patterns of professional encoders in their pertinent environment (except at the "organizational level"). "Small media," often cited as examples of "grassroots journalism," are celebrated in fiction and seen as viable media for small rural communities (E. Abbott, 1988) and urban neighborhoods (Jeffres & Dobos, 1983; Jeffres, Latkovich, & Ceasar, 1983). The community editor is a perfect subject for such study because it is possible to identify a manageable geographic domain within which the communication occurs for both the encoders and the audience decoders. Furthermore, with diversity of purpose and context, there is greater potential for looking at more of the sources of influence cited by Shoemaker and Reese (1991), treating the community newspaper as the unit of analysis. How are journalists' communication patterns related to their perceptions of the environment? And how are those patterns and perceptions related to the characteristics of the neighborhoods being served and patterns of communication within them? And are there differences in routines based on differences in how editors see their papers serving the community (goals, perceived functions, or intended uses and gratifications)? Are there differences in role expectations? Editors with a "democratic-participative" view of their role and their paper might be expected to develop a broader informal communication network in the neighborhood rather than relying on government or institutional resources. Several other relationships deserve attention: editors' communication patterns and content actually appearing in the papers; editors' perceptions of the community QOL and perceptions of community residents.[89]

Jeffres et al. (1991) also conducted interviews with 13 community newspaper editors in Cleveland's central-city neighborhoods and small "first-ring" suburbs at several different points (1985, 1987, 1988, 1989).[90] The interviews sought information on the functions that editors saw their paper performing for the community, interaction patterns within the neighborhood, types of conversations, perceptions of communication within the neighborhood, perceptions of problems within the area, and so on. The interview schedule began with a question that asked editors to take an average week in their neighborhood and tell who they talk with and some of the things they talk about. Responses were categorized by the type of source. As Table 7.3 shows, neighborhood newspaper editors rely on "authoritative" sources for information, although elected officials share the status with neighborhood groups and local merchants or businessmen. Because editors also end up selling advertising, some of this interaction occurs when editors are wearing the business hat rather than the editor's hat. Topics of conversation tend to follow those found with journalists from larger papers—community problems and institutional news coverage—although there's a considerable amount of conversation focusing on current events, politics, and "small talk." This general question was followed by a request to indicate how often editors frequented various neighborhood contexts and the types of conversations that would occur in them.

The contexts ran the gamut, from such professional activities as attending meetings of local groups or visiting schools to contexts that would indicate personal involvement and activity within the neighborhood (attending church, backyard fences, corner bars). As Table 7.4 shows, the contexts frequented most often by neighborhood newspaper editors are stores, shops, and banks, followed by neighborhood streets, neighborhood restaurants, and backyard fences or front porches. These all suggest involvement in the daily life of the community by communicating with a wide range of local residents, not just authoritative figures. In fact, institutional contexts such as local clubs and organizations, local schools, and

TABLE 7.3
Who Editors Talk With and Topics of Conversation

Who Community Editors Talk With During An Average Week:	
Government:	
Elected officials—major, council rep., politicos	6
Bureaucrats & Gov. Offices—fire chief, school supt., city planning office, social agency director	4
Agency Professionals—sports coaches, police detectives	1
Community Development offices	1
Nongovernment organizations—clubs and organization leaders, historical society head, neighborhood groups	7
General Public and others	
Local residents	4
Newspaper staff	5
Business groups, local merchants	7
Friends and family	3
Local professionals or jobs—lawyers, swimming pool attendants	2
Participants in events—swimmers	1
Topics of Conversation:	
Neighborhood Problems (in general or several)	6
Specific problem	
(youth, housing, welfare, prostitution, drugs, crime, fires)	4
Institutions and programs (council news, school news, block grants, social service programs)	2
Current events and politics	4
Newspaper business	6
Other news content (local history, club news, story ideas)	3
Small talk, family	3

Note. There were 13 editors.

fraternal halls are frequented only occasionally by some and seldom by others. Two contexts that appear to be avoided, or frequented outside the neighborhoods being served, are churches and athletic centers, both centers of neighborhood activity for major segments of the neighborhood (e.g., youth sports is one of the few neighborhood-centered activities because busing made schools citywide rather than neighborhood-centered in Cleveland and elsewhere).

Clearly, some contexts are "all work" and "no play," whereas others serve multiple functions for journalists. Thus, all of the conversational topics at meetings of local organizations concerned the clubs or groups, but all conversations at corner bars or over backyard fences were social in nature or mixed. Trips to local shops and stores and conversations at restaurants were more mixed, with half of the discussions focusing on business and half either mixed or purely personal. Individual editors also show tendencies to integrate work and personal concerns in these contexts, with only one editor mentioning only business topics across all contexts. For six editors, business topics dominated

TABLE 7.4
Contexts Frequented by Neighborhood Editors

Context:	Mean*	How Often Frequent Context							Conversations Topics		
		Every day	Couple times a week	Once a week	Every couple weeks	Once a month	Every couple months	Less often	All Work	All Personal	Mixed
Going to local shops, stores, banks	(6.17)	5	6	-	-	1	-	-	5	2	3
Walking down a neighborhood street	(5.5)	7	-	2	-	2	-	1	1	2	3
Attending church	(1.73)	-	-	1	-	1	2	7	1	1	-
Over backyard fence or sitting on a porch	(4.27)	3	3	-	1	-	-	4	-	1	4
At meetings of local clubs, orgs	(3.46)	-	2	1	3	4	1	2	10	-	-
In the local library	(2.58)	-	1	2	-	2	2	5	2	1	-
At local hospital	(2.8)	-	2	1	-	3	-	5	1	2	-
In a fraternal hall or club	(2.27)	-	1	1	1	1	-	7	2	1	-
In a neighborhood restaurant	(5.25)	2	4	1	3	-	-	1	2	2	2
At a corner bar	(2.75)	1	-	1	2	2	1	5	-	3	1
In a local park	(3.50)	2	1	2	1	1	-	5	1	2	1
At a local gym, athletic center or sports event	(2.7)	1	1	1	1	1	-	7	2	-	-
At a local school	(2.8)	-	-	2	3	1	2	4	4	-	-

Note. There were 13 editors.

*The average is based on a scale of 1 to 7, where 1 = less often and 7 = every day.

conversations in more contexts than did personal concerns, whereas three editors showed a balance between the two and one talked about nonwork topics in more contexts. The data are only suggestive, but patterns can emerge to show how journalists interact on personal and work levels in the neighborhoods being served. Those who only talk about business in a few contexts might be expected to also be less involved in the community and to be less familiar with local concerns and views.

Because community newspapers have fewer resources and limited staffs, journalists must depend on their personal networks and communication patterns rather than beat systems for news. Does this alter a documented tendency to rely on authoritative sources or routine channels of information, or are the routine channels merely under the control of less influential individuals? Editors were given nine different items and asked to tell how they would find out about each in their community. The nine items included a new development program, a change in social services provided to local residents, a local robbery, the grand opening of a business in the neighborhood, a councilperson's stand on a current citywide issue, a religious festival, an ethnic or fraternal celebration, the going price of homes for sale in the neighborhood, and youth problems. As Table 7.5 shows, community newspaper editors rely on routine channels and sources similar to their metropolitan counterparts, although it appears that meetings and event coverage are relatively less important. However, they also monitor the larger media and depend on word-of-mouth and interpersonal communication to learn about what's going on. Asked to think of a recent situation where everyone seemed to know about something going on in the neighborhood before they did, editors cited a variety of items, with no consistent pattern (e.g., a new Burger King, a new welfare office, a crime in the area, an ethnic event, and a zoning issue). In two cases, they learned about the situations from the local metro daily, while two learned from a council representative and others from either neighbors or local community leaders.

Editors were asked for their perceptions of communication in the neighborhood and how people got along. Most thought people got along well but they also came up with an assortment of conflicts when asked for examples they had overheard (e.g., conflicts over public issues such as property values, prices, and zoning, as well as personal conflicts over parking spaces, youth turf, race, etc.). Asked which groups interacted most often and which did not, editors cited ethnicity, age, race and income as barriers. Editors also were asked how they thought their local newspaper connects people to each other in the neighborhood. Several cited what Lemert (1984) called "mobilization information" (e.g., times of meetings and information), whereas others mentioned ethnic news or local advertising, informing residents about important issues, and giving residents a sense of community and identity. A few editors mentioned strengthening people's positive views of the neighborhood and reminding folks how they can affect each other.

TABLE 7.5
How Community Editors Learn About Their Community

Topics:	Press Release	Mass media	Other Contacts by			Personal initia- tive*	Going to meet- ings	Word of mouth~
			gov. agencies*	orgs. bus.*	com. leaders			
A new development program	6	1	3	3	2	1	1	2
A change in soc. services for residents	6	1	4*	2	1	2*	2	3
A local robbery	1	3	9#	1	-	-	-	5
Opening of new business in neighborhood	3	3	-	7	-	-	-	3
Council rep's stand on city issue	-	4	10	1	-	-	3	-
Religious festival	-	2	-	12	-	-	-	1
Ethnic/fraternal celebration	2	3	-	8	-	-	-	-
Going price of homes for sale in neighborhood	1	2	5	8^	-	-	-	2
Youth/education problems	-	2	9@	5	-	2	4	-
N and % of 161								
citations across	19	21	40	47	3	5	10	16
all nine situations	12%	13%	25%	29%	2%	3%	6%	10%

Note. The 13 editors could cite more than one source.

*The contacts with agencies and organizations also may involve initiative by journalists here but was not always clear.

#Included here are six contacts with police station, two with crime watch coordinator and one auxiliary police, a mixture of government agencies and community groups

~Included here are observation and seeing signs as well as interpersonal communication.

^Included here are seven contacts with local realtor, one with a neighborhood organization and one with the Board of Realtors.

@Includes three contacts with Board of Education members or superintendent, four with schools, and three with teachers.

Editors also were given 21 different "roles often attributed to neighborhood and community newspapers," where "some are more important than others for different papers." They were asked to indicate how important each role was for their newspaper (using a 4-point scale: *very important, somewhat important, not very important*, or *totally unimportant*). Table 7.6 lists the results. Across all papers, reporting news about neighborhood redevelopment efforts and projects ranks first, although it is followed closely by alerting residents to local problems and conflicts. Third is alerting neighborhood residents to social services available in the area, an important function in urban areas with large concentrations of poor people. Providing news of local festivals and events—a traditional, informational news function—is fourth. Tied for fifth are publishing features on local people and telling residents about local organizations and clubs, both emphasizing the integrative function of the paper and its closeness to the voluntary associations and structured patterns of residents. Some functions that might be expected to rank higher in importance—personal notes about people—fall down the list, perhaps because editors see their papers' efforts in solving community problems and presenting public issues as more important. Some functions that should rank higher with metro media also fall down the list here—investigative reporting (for which most small papers have little time and few resources) and discussing political issues in the area (which did rate a respectable average about midway between somewhat important and not very important). Editors also were asked for their perceptions of the QOL in their neighborhoods, the major problems and efforts to solve them. These are discussed further later.

NEWS SOURCES OF NEIGHBORHOOD RESIDENTS

Neighborhood newspapers have appeared in numerous metropolitan areas in recent years (C. Gaziano, 1974; Ward, 1980; Ward & Gaziano, 1976). Some of the papers reflect efforts of neighborhoods to mobilize their residents for redevelopment, whereas others strive for stronger neighborhood identity and cohesion or fight outside threats. Ward (1980) argued that neighborhood newspapers serve needs for diversity of messages that metro media do not provide to residents of urban neighborhoods. Jeffres et al. (1991) collected 16 sets of quota interviews in nine Cleveland neighborhoods. The data set includes small quota samples of residents in neighborhoods served by community newspapers in the Cleveland area. Some 16 sets of quota interviews were collected in nine Cleveland neighborhoods in 1985, 1987, 1989, and 1991; some neighborhoods were surveyed more than once. Quotas were drawn to assure a balance of male and female respondents, minority groups where they were present, and a range of different ages. All respondents were interviewed in person by journalism students working in the neighborhoods. The surveys of residents include questions

TABLE 7.6
Contexts Frequented by Neighborhood Editors

Context:	Average all editors	All org. papers	All community papers	Dev. orgs.	Other orgs.	Community chain	Community entrep.
Going to local shops, stores, banks	6.17	6.38	5.75	6.33	6.40	7.00	5.33
Walking down a neighborhood street	5.50	5.75	5.00	5.67	5.80	7.00	4.33
Attending church	1.73	1.57	2.00	1.50	1.60	1.00	2.33
Over fence or sitting on a porch	4.27	4.88	2.67	4.00	5.40	1.00	3.50
At meetings of clubs, orgs	3.46	3.38	4.00	2.67	3.80	6.00	3.33
At the local library	2.58	2.12	3.50	1.33	2.60	2.00	4.00
At local hospital	2.80	2.62	3.33	3.00	2.40	1.00	4.50
In a fraternal hall or club	2.27	1.62	4.00	2.00	1.40	5.00	3.50
In a neighborhood restaurant	5.25	4.62	6.50	3.67	5.20	6.00	6.67
At a corner bar	2.75	2.50	3.25	3.00	2.20	4.00	3.00
In a local park	3.50	3.62	3.25	2.00	4.60	6.00	2.33
At a local gym, athletic center or sports event	2.67	2.12	3.75	1.00	2.80	6.00	3.00
At a local school	2.75	2.38	3.50	3.00	2.00	5.00	3.00
(N)	(12)	(8)	(4)	(3)	(5)	(1)	(3)

Note. There were 13 editors, including 3 published by local development corporations (LDCs), 5 by other community organizations, 2 by commercial owners who ran at least two small local newspapers ("chains"), and 3 published by editor-publisher-entrepreneurs (one-person commercial operations). Data in this table were unavailable for one commercial editor and one organizational editor.

about readership of the neighborhood newspaper ("Do you read the _____? How often?"), how people keep up with what's going on in the neighborhood ("How do you keep up with what is going on in this area?"), the frequency of interaction in the area ("How much do people talk to each other in this neighborhood?"), involvement in local groups ("Do you participate in any local group or organizations?"), perceptions of problems and assets of the neighborhood ("What do you think the major problems are around here?" and "What do you like about living in this area?"), who's working to improve the area ("Who would you say is doing the most to improve things in this neighborhood?"), and length of time in the area.

Neighborhood communication patterns are summarized in Table 7.7. Across all neighborhoods, 44% of residents report reading their local neighborhood newspaper, with the figure fluctuating from a low of 16% in the poorest central city area to about 75% in one suburban community and the more middle-class central-city neighborhoods. The most diverse neighborhoods (income, race, ethnicity) fall in the middle, 37% to 44%. There are exceptions to neighborhood stratification by income, however; one bedroom suburb reports a low readership and an old ethnic central-city area reports a high readership. An examination of the papers suggests that newspapers that focus coverage on the community and have a long tradition of serving the area have higher penetrations among residents.

Residents were asked how they keep up with what's going on in their neighborhoods. Where neighborhood newspapers scored the lowest rates of readership, the metro daily and interpersonal channels filled the void. The frequency of interaction varied by the neighborhood, with the greatest among the eastern European ethnic enclave (76% of respondents saying people talk with each other a lot). Participation in organizations varied from a low of 9% in a poor Black central-city neighborhood to a high of 60% in a suburban bedroom community.

CONTENT OF NEIGHBORHOOD NEWSPAPERS

Clearly, newspaper content reflects the community covered. As Corbett (1992) noted, urban papers publish more about wildlife conflict than do rural papers. McCombs (1997) argued that news media generate community consensus by framing issues, giving prominence to community concerns, and focusing community groups on particular issues. He described four visions defining the media's agenda-setting function along a continuum from passive to active—professional detachment, investigative reporting, boosterism, and public journalism. K. Smith (1987) looked at the effects of newspaper coverage on neighborhood and community issue concerns, finding that neighborhood issues received less coverage than those of importance to the entire community. In addition, the newspaper's agenda setting was stronger for perceived community than neigh-

TABLE 7.7
Summary Table of Neighborhood Communication Patterns

Neighborhood Served:	% Reading Neigh. Paper	How keep up with what's going on in neighborhood				Freq. of Com. in Neigh. % a lot^	Part. in Orgs. % Yes
		Neigh. Paper	Metro Paper	TV-Radio	IP Com. People		
First ring suburb	74% (53)	26% (53)	19%	9%	23%	51% (53)	26%
[First, ring, blue collar, integrating suburb]							
Poor central city	16% (75)	— (75)	43%	16%	68%	56% (23)	9% (23)
[Poor, Black, central city neighborhood, low identity, cohesion]							
Poor central city	28% (18)	— (18)	56%	56%	44%	61% (18)	28% (18)
[Poor, black, central city neighborhood, politically active]							
Middle class/blue collar	75% (56)	55% (56)	21%@	5%	86%	64% (56)	48% (56)
[Middle-class/blue-collar area, White, city border with suburbs]							
Diverse, integrated area	40% (312)	—* (392)	26%	20%	46%	36% (392)	22% (392)
[Diverse, integrated area, near city center, parts redeveloping, increasingly Hispanic, with poor Whites, professionals, Asians]							
White, city-center mix	37% (43)	16% (43)	42%	16%	35%	40% (43)	14% (43)
[City-center mix of middle-/lower middle-class, blue-collar residents, aging area, White, increasingly Hispanic]							

Diverse, blue collar	44%	13%	18%	—	32%	48%	41%
	(97)	(97)				(97)	(97)
[Diverse, blue-collar central-city neighborhood with growing Hispanic influence]							
Suburban bedroom community, middle class	28%	—	76%	8%	60%	40%	60%
	(25)	(25)				(25)	(25)
White, Eastern European ethnic community, aging	71%	71%#	17%	5%	85%	76%	44%
	(41)	(41)				(41)	(41)

*The neighborhood newspaper was included with the metro newspaper under "local newspapers" for this area.

^The percentage refers to those who said people in the neighborhood talk to each other a lot or much, in contrast to some, a little or not much.

~This refers to citations of other people, gossip, word of mouth, all forms of interpersonal (IP) communication.

#Two neighborhood newspapers are available in this neighborhood; one was cited by 71% and the other by 34% of the respondents.

@Included here are suburban chain papers circulating in the area.

borhood issues, evidence consistent with the theory that media agenda-setting is more powerful for unobtrusive issues. C. Gaziano (1985) found that the agendas of neighborhood leaders and their definitions of issues was more similar to that of residents, particularly more educated residents, whereas the neighborhood papers' agendas were less related. Jeffres et al. (1991) also did content analyses of a sample of 10 issues of six neighborhood newspapers to ascertain news priorities. As Table 12 in the appendix notes, papers vary greatly in the emphases given different topics. An activist paper serving a diverse area and a Black paper serving a poor area both emphasized calendars of events, the latter focusing broadly on metropolitan-level activities and the former stressing neighborhood organizations and social services available in the area. Development news tops the list for the most middle-class neighborhood served and is third for the ethnic enclave. For three other papers, development topics fall midway on their lists. Crime news, which is a concern across all of the neighborhoods served, is de-emphasized in most papers, falling at the bottom in the neighborhood where crime is worst. In a personal conversation, that editor said he tries to emphasize the "good" things going on, not the "bad."

Religion received little attention in either of the two wealthier neigborhoods served or in the two Black communities, where Black churches are important institutions. However, religion is first or second in the other two papers, largely because of the churches' ties to ethnic groups (Hispanics in the diverse integrated community and eastern European churches in the White ethnic enclave). Sports drop off most of the lists, despite their importance as community centers in the central city. Schools receive relatively more attention in the poorer Black and diverse integrated neighborhoods than in the more middle-class communities; in none of the papers do schools rate as high on the lists as might be expected from residents' concerns.

COMPARING NEIGHBORHOOD PERCEPTIONS

Several theories in mass communication are relevant in the examination of the relationship between editors' perceptions of the neighborhood, informants' and residents' perceptions of the area, and emphases in media content.[91] Editors' perceptions of problems should be reflected in the content emphasized by the newspaper, and that content—when decoded by audiences—should have some "effect" on perceptions by informants and residents. The first relationship may appear obvious, but a host of constraints intervene between the paper's goals, what an editor sees and what finally appears in the paper. News values, news-gathering routines and strategies employed, resources available, and perceptions of the audience and its needs all are factors. Table 12 in the appendix also provides a comparison between editors' assessments of the papers' functions and the content actually appearing in the papers. For each of the four newspapers, several of the *very important* functions cited by editors are almost directly translated into the top content categories of their papers (e.g., providing news of festivals and telling residents about organizations match the top ranked content area—calendar of events, etc.). With a sample of only four papers, little beyond inspection is possible, unfortunately.

The second relationship is that identified in the agenda-setting literature, image formation, and cognitive effects. Again, media must compete with other influences (personal observation, interpersonal communication, metro media, uses and gratifications that sustain media behavior patterns, and audience values).

Table 13 in the appendix lays out the public's perceptions of neighborhood problems, chief assets, and who's doing the most to improve things in the area. Clearly, major problems are found across central city neighborhoods—crime, unemployment, government services, schools and youth, and neighborhood development. People also cite similar items as chief assets of their neighborhoods, beginning with the people themselves and their friendliness. And, as real estate agents often say, the most important three things about a neighborhood are "location, location, location." Despite economic constraints and other problems associated with density and poverty, residents like the central locations of their neighborhoods. Perceptions of who's trying to improve things vary widely. "No one" is the clear winner or runner up in several neighborhoods, suggesting either a level of cynicism, accurate perceptions that little forward-looking activity is taking place, or beliefs that those "responsible" are ineffective. Local neighborhood organizations and groups are identified by significant percentages in only four neighborhoods, including the ethnic enclave, a diverse blue-collar neighborhood with a strong community association bearing the area's name, a first-ring integrating suburb and the most diverse neighborhood in the city, which has a long tradition of activism and community organizations. Both of the poor, Black central-city neighborhoods identify the city council representative as a key player, as does the strong blue-collar neighborhood represented in part by the city council president. Thus, objective characteristics of the neighborhoods and political and social activity are reflected in public perceptions.

How similar are perceptions of editors, informants and neighborhood residents? All were asked to identify major problems of the neighborhood. As Table 14 in the appendix illustrates, although there certainly are differences, the similarities among the three are quite apparent. Thus, when the schools or crime appear on the public agenda, they also are likely to be found on the list of editors and informants. However, there also are glaring differences. Although the editor of an integrating suburb identified racism and racial problems (which have received some attention in the metro media), racism was either ignored in the public survey or included by citing the "schools," which have been a focal point for racial issues. And the poor Black central-city neighborhood where almost half identified crime as a major problem was served by a paper whose editor said he tried to focus on positive things, leaving crime for the weekly

Black newspaper serving the entire metropolitan area. Indeed, the content analysis shows that crime falls far down the list in terms of space devoted to various topics in this paper.

The middle link here is media content. Because patterns are being inspected rather than relationships tested, the limits are obvious. However, neighborhood problems cited most frequently (crime, schools, development) also appear in the top half of content categories emphasized by two of the three newspapers for which survey data are available. Also, the same two editor's perceptions of problems are reflected in higher rankings of the pertinent content categories (schools, crime, poverty, economic development).

Jeffres et al. (1991) noted there are few efforts that look at larger communication patterns of encoders, probably because of their residence in media organizations. Thus, the tendency is to examine journalists' activities as existing within organizations and to view the community as a constraint rather than a legitimate "context" within which communication occurs. Considerable literature does look at how journalists "frame" news or employ community news values (e.g., localizing stories), but little attention is paid to the actual communication patterns of journalists within the neighborhoods themselves.

Jeffres et al. (1991) argued that the "community context" is important for understanding subsequent encoding activities, and there is a need to look beyond merely characterizing journalists for their political outlooks or background variables. They suggest conceptualizing the journalists/media professional's symbolic activity as existing in several communication systems. When the "other person" is in the same media organization, the activity is part of that system. When the other person is in the neighborhood or pertinent environment being served, the activity is part of that system, and so forth. Clearly, it is possible for a complete overlap, where one's family runs the newspaper, the journalist lives in the neighborhood, and the individual participates in a fully integrated community life as a workaholic. At the metropolitan level, further differentiations are needed (e.g., the "beat" may represent the pertinent environment being served). However, for the community context and the community newspaper, it is possible to examine the extent to which an individual's symbolic activity is parceled out among the neighborhood communication system (connecting residents to each other outside their families), the larger urban system (connecting neighborhoods and their residents to other neighborhoods and residents), and the larger national or international system (connecting residents to the rest of the country and, eventually, the world).

In characterizing the journalist's communication behavior, both the motivations that direct the behavior and relationships with a diverse environment should be noted. The research into journalists' role perceptions suggests looking at motivations not just for specific news-gathering activity (e.g., routine channels and use of authoritative sources) but also those directing general surveillance activities (implicitly, all communication). To what extent are journalists prisoners of habit and routine, seeking confirmation and engaging in communication relationships that are comfortable rather than looking for the unusual and seeking diversity or risk? Probably only the young idealist seeks the experience of talking with new "types" of people and learning about "new" domains of life. However, there is considerable distance between that individual and the ritualistic elder who avoids anything or anyone with whom he or she is not familiar. The literature on journalists' integration into community life (through membership in organizations) suggests looking at communication "diversity" across contexts and roles. To what extent do community journalists exhibit a "participative communication pattern," interacting with people representing diverse roles in and across contexts? For example, a story about a labor strike may focus on labor and/or management. While completing an actual assignment, the reporter may communicate with both; however, across one's "life," does the journalist communicate with people from many different roles and do the interactions focus only on the role-relevant behavior or extend further. Quite different perspectives emerge when reporters know both chief executive officers and bag ladies and have chatted about the price of eggs with both. Of course, if the journalist has had conversations with both, he or she is more likely to have discussed the stock market with the former and the uncertainties of social services with the latter. When the communication outside of assignments represents diversity and reach, the reporter is better prepared to ask questions and frame issues "objectively," asking questions and arranging information from perspectives of the audience and nonparticipants as well as those directly involved. Looking at the San Francisco Bay area, Silverman (1992) advanced the concept of the public style of neighboring, suggesting that mutual obligation of differences rather than friendship allows urbanites sharing a neighborhood space to live together and maintain privacy in diverse neighborhoods. This situation tends to break down when the population grows too diverse.

Several "ideal types" are suggested, but it should be noted that the types refer to people's communication across interpersonal communication "situations"; within the dyad, an individual may be characterized as exhibiting any one of the many "styles" or engaging in all the diverse "communicative sequences" studied by interpersonal communication scholars. The relevant context here is the "community":

1. **The Renaissance Communicator**: This journalist seeks new types of individuals, new contexts, and new topics for interaction. Although likely to be young, there's no need for an age limit and personality may be just as important. This style most likely requires a continuing interest in people and ideas and a willingness to display vulnerability (by interacting on topics where one is ignorant, with people who don't know you or "your type," and in contexts where the rules are unclear). The match of this type with the editorial role is a natural for the young idealist out to "experience life" and seeking diversity.

2. **The Task-Oriented Communicator** This individual engages in communication for instrumental purposes and avoids those conversations that may further the relationship but do not lead to apparent goals. This individual is not receptive to conversations initiated by others and tends to avoid "unproductive" contexts and the interactions associated with them. This individual also tends to convert the social into a work context. The match of this type with the editorial role is represented by the workaholic who always talks business and takes work into the home, the restaurant, the bar, the waiting room.

3. **The Administrative Communicator**: This individual seeks the authoritative voice in almost every communicative situation and looks for "who's in charge," whether from a need for the best expertise or the wish to avoid uninformed chit-chat. Thus, this individual would look for the parent in a family, the manager in the store, the minister in the church, the CEO in the firm. The match of this type with the editorial role is consistent with those inclined as "professionals" to seek authoritative voices and institutional sources.

A variety of factors would promote individuals as candidates for one style or another, from personality factors to individual differences (achievement factors such as income and education and ascriptive factors such as gender and ethnicity). Life-cycle changes also would be a factor, as an individual seeking diversity in youth sought comfortable relationships and the predictable later in life.

Clearly, the nature of the community should interact with individual characteristics and communication style. Few renaissance communicators should be found in homogeneous neighborhoods where people interacted little, there was virtually no street life or voluntary associations with opportunities for exchanges, and informal socializing was limited. Thus, there also is a need to examine characteristics of the community and the community communication patterns as well as those of the journalist. Following the sequence, particular communication patterns of journalists should be a "better fit" between particular neighborhoods and newspaper audiences (e.g., a diverse community should have a diverse communication system and a renaissance communicator is more likely to capture that diversity and meet audience needs than someone whose communication pattern is more task-oriented).

A relationship between the communicator style of the journalist and the newspaper's functions also should be expected (e.g., an administrative communicator is less likely to be found at an activist paper in a diverse community). With small community newspapers, the stated goals and functions of the paper are likely to be good indicators of the communicator style followed by its reporters.

Clearly, there is considerable potential in studying community media as units of analysis and in examining the communication patterns of journalists and the neighborhoods they serve. Future studies with larger numbers of neighborhood newspapers will allow researchers to look at differences in the types of newspapers that populate U.S. urban centers. This research also can show to what extent editors' perceptions of the community and their audiences are related to the functions they see their papers fulfilling. By studying relationships among variables at the community level, it is possible to learn how to better study those at other levels where diversity on many dimensions is more restricted.

SUMMARY

Community newspapers represent "grassroots media" that link neighbors to each other while informing residents of what's going on in their neighborhoods. They are part of the neighborhood communication system. Various studies and observers have found that neighborhood papers encourage community participation, create community identification, serve as a forum for public affairs, increase public knowledge of their community, and allow the community to solve problems.

In general, the same functions that media fulfill for society at large—information, correlation, continuity, entertainment, and mobilization—operate at the community level, but seldom are these functions applied at that level. In a national study of grassroots journalism, newspaper editors rated the importance of different goals and functions; an assessment yielded eight dimensions that were linked to traditional media functions and are consistent with the literature on mainstream commercial media (e.g., the traditional watchdog function), providing evidence of the universality of these functions in the United States. The importance of various functions was related to newspaper characteristics and their origins (e.g., papers started by groups or development associations rated serving ethnics and connecting residents to social services higher, whereas papers started by individual entrepreneurs emphasized advertising and entertainment more).

Editors of neighborhood papers tend to rely on authoritative sources much like their counterparts at commercial dailies, but their patterns of neighborhood activity suggest a high level of involvement in the daily life of the community by communicating with a wide range of local residents. Community journalists have fewer resources and depend on personal networks and communication patterns for news rather than beat systems. Their perceptions of what's important reflect neighborhood concerns; interviews with center-city neighborhood newspaper editors showed that neighborhood redevelopment efforts and projects ranks first in importance, followed by alerting residents to local problems and conflicts.

Residents of neighborhoods rely on their community papers to find out what's going on in their areas. A series of small samples of center-city and first-ring suburban neighborhood residents in one major urban area found that newspaper readership was considerable, averaging 37% to 44% in the more diverse neighborhoods. When available, neighborhood papers were cited as more important than other media channels for keeping up with what's going on in the community. However, interpersonal channels were more important sources most of the time, particularly in the poorest neighborhoods.

As would be expected, newspaper content reflects the community covered; a content analysis of a set of urban neighborhood papers showed a clear match between the neighborhood environment and the papers' news and other features. And, as theories in mass communication would predict, there was a positive relationship between what editors think is important and what appears in the paper. The "community context" is important for understanding how editors view their own roles; several "ideal types" were suggested for characterizing how journalists communicate and operate within the neighborhood—the renaissance communicator, the task-oriented communicator and the administrative communicator.

8

Neighborhoods, Networks, and Systems

Leo W. Jeffres
Kimberly Neuendorf
Larry Erbert

OVERVIEW OF THE TWO APPROACHES:
NETWORK THEORY AND SYSTEMS ANALYSIS

Network theory and systems analysis each provides an opportunity for viewing neighborhoods as units themselves. Each of these approaches also is useful whether there is interest in generalizing to communication or urban sociology, or in integrating phenomena across the two disciplines.

In network theory, relationships and patterns of relationships, rather than individuals, are examined. For sociologists and urban scholars, this often refers to relationships between people or roles in neighborhoods—the notion of "weak ties" is an example of links between people built on contacts that are more casual rather than those that refer to enduring historical relationships such as close friendships or family. For communication scholars, networks refer to communication relationships that often use the dyad as a building block for constructing larger patterns of symbolic activity in the neighborhood context; thus, patterns of information flow and communication roles that link segments/groups into larger networks can be examined. The two overlap because relationships between people can refer not only to familial, friendship, or work relations but also to encoding and decoding activity patterned to establish and strengthen relationships. Unfortunately, most of the empirical network research and conceptualizing—particularly in communication—has occurred in organizational contexts and infrequently in geographic neighborhoods. Within communication, networks are seen as a level of analysis (see Chaffee & Berger, 1987).

In systems theory, neighborhoods are seen as integrated wholes, units of complexity that can be studied for their interrelationships. As Laszlo (1996) noted, in the systems view, nature is a sphere of complex and delicate organization as systems "communicate" with other systems and jointly form larger suprasystems. The task is to identify the patterns and forms that make order out of neighborhoods and link them into cities. However, there are different approaches to systems analysis, and they will be applied to neighborhood communication systems as well as neighborhood social systems.

NETWORK CONCEPTS

The Network Metaphor

The network as a concept is steeped in old analogies, from the "spider's web" to "six degrees of separation."[92] To even the casual observer, the network as metaphor has some utility in describing patterns of links and relationships among people, as well as organizations, electronic configurations, and even nonhumans.[93] For current purposes, it is the relationships among people and their communication that is the focus here, and the question is to what extent "network" concepts are useful in describing human activity in neighborhoods and cities.

Key Concepts

Networks are defined in a variety of ways, which represent different emphases and purposes—as networks of objects, as networks tracing the flow of information or influence, as patterns of interaction or relationships. In any case, network analysis includes as a minimum a set of *objects,* or *actors* (sometimes called nodes), and a *set of relationships* defined *in some domain* or *context.* The objects may be people, businesses, organizations,[94] computers, neighborhoods, or other units. Once these elements are identified, a host of other concepts come into play in describing the networks and participation within them.

In both social networks and communication networks, the nodes generally are people, and it is the nature of the relationship or linkage between them that requires attention.[95] "A relation is not an intrinsic characteristic of either party taken in isolation but is an emergent property of the connection or linkage between units of observation" (Knoke & Kuklinski, 1982, p. 10).[96] Measures of relationships capture aspects of social systems that cannot be measured by simply summing up the characteristics of individual members. Thus, for example, the network of relationships and the pattern of communication within a neighborhood would not be captured in a summary of individual reports of relationships or symbolic activity.

Relationships are the building blocks of network analysis, and a network is often defined as a specific type of relation linking a defined set of persons, objects, or events (see Mitchell, 1969). Different types of relations identify different networks, even when imposed on the identical set of elements. Thus, for example, within a neighborhood there may be an advice-giving network, which is different from the "crime-fighting network," which is different from the formal authority network. The set of persons, events, or objects on which a network is defined are often called actors or nodes.[97] As Burt and Schott (1985) noted, "the content of relationships is a problem for network analysis" (p. 288). The problem is illustrated in the distinction between naturally occurring relations and analytical relations; the first refers to those in which people are actually involved, whereas the second refers to those identified for a specific network analysis. Thus, when one solicits advice from a neighbor, that communication occurs in the context that includes talks over the fence, over lunch, at meetings, and so forth. The naturally occurring relationship actually is a bundle of different elements.[98]

Although a network may refer only to those linkages that actually occur in the designated context, network analysis also must take into account relations that do not exist among the actors.[99] Thus, within neighborhoods, the density of communication linkages reflects both those that exist and those that don't but "could." Considering social networks, Knoke and Kuklinski (1982) discussed some of the basic types of network structures and research design elements, including: unit of analysis-individual, family,[100] organization, group, and so on; the form of relations—the properties of the connections between pairs of actors (dyads) that exist independently of specific contents (e.g., strength of the link); relational content (e.g., whether the relationship refers to kinship, is one intended to exchange goods, services, information; or reflects sentiment relations, etc.);[101] and levels of analysis (egocentric network—each node's relation with all the others; dyads—all pairs of nodes, triads, and complete networks). Network analysis has been used in sociology and anthropology to uncover the social structure of a total system through the identification of significant positions within a given network of relations that link the system's actors (Knoke & Kuklinski, 1982).[102] In a review of network research, Rogers (1987) noted that such research has been scientifically imbalanced. He noted that some scholars equate network analysis with structural analysis, where "structure is the arrangement of elements in a system and the set of relationships that connect these parts together" (p. 291). There also are as many kinds of structure as there are social scientists: social, political, economic, communication, and semantic.

Characteristics of Networks and Characteristics of Individual Participation in Networks

Clearly, once the network has been identified in terms of elements, relationships, and domain, there are almost an infinite number of concepts that describe characteristics of networks, as well as of an individual's participation within networks. Among the concepts that Knoke and Kuklinski (1982) and others used to describe characteristics of a social network are *network cohesion, network density*,[103] *network multiplicity* (extent to which actors are in more than one network, e.g., advice-giving, money-lending, etc.), and *actor multiplexity* (portion of an actor's ties with all other actors in the system).

However, it also is possible to consider measures of individuals (whether people, groups, or countries) and how they fit into a network, including a measure of one's "centrality" in the network, of one's prestige within the network, of the extent to which other actors show deference to him or her in their relationship, of one's influence in the network (e.g., total number of actors who directly or indirectly send messages to an individual),[104] and so on. For example, Kang and Choi (1999) noted the central structural position of countries such as the United States, the United Kingdom and Japan in international news distribution in cyberspace. Other concepts describe the distance between members of a network. Tutzauer (1993) noted that network analysis has been criticized for providing only a static picture of social relations when it is often the dynamical aspects of networks that are of interest; thus, concepts that describe changes in network patterns and account for those changes are needed.

Communication Networks

Communication research employing the network metaphor has been concentrated in organizations,[105] although it has been employed across a variety of contexts, including groups[106] and the international arena.[107] For example, researchers have looked at formal and informal communication networks in organizations[108] (Bolton & Dewatripont, 1994;[109] MacDonald, 1976[110]), as well as interorganizational networks in public relations (Danowski, Barnett, & Friedland, 1987; Jang, 1997). As Kincaid (1993) noted:

> The network metaphor is an appealing way to think about human communication because it enables us to visualize the structure of relationships formed by communication while at the same time providing us with a rich descriptive vocabulary.[111] Terms such as ties, links,[112] nodes, connectedness, distance, openness,[113] centrality,[114] and cohesion are useful ways to think about structure; flow, rate of transmission and volume are readily applied to processes within communication networks.[115] The network approach also provides a more concrete way to think about the rather abstract concepts of systems theory and social systems in general. And finally, network analysis of social systems is appealing because it lends itself to precise, quantitative measures of structure to accompany the graphic visualization made possible by network analysis. (p. 112)

He added that researchers have concentrated on improving these tools rather than improving theories with those tools. A second factor hindering theoretical development has been an emphasis on static network structure rather than dynamic network processes.[116]

Patterson's (1995) study of communication network activity among the young and elderly suggests that family contact increases with age while communication and solidarity with friends declines. A project to create a neighborhood-oriented communication system in a small midwestern town relied on personal computers installed in homes of all 500 participating families (Trachtman, 1991). The system was expected to improve parent–teacher–school communication, but 350 families elected to cancel the service eventually and the program was cancelled, largely because of technical inadequacies, the availability of faster, more efficient, and desirable communication media, no institutional mandate to use the system and lack of commitment to the system by local opinion leaders.

Communities and Neighborhoods as Networks

A neighborhood can be viewed as a set of overlapping networks. One network consists of residents linked in terms of social relationships—family, friend, acquaintance, neighbor, work colleague, fellow parishioner, and so forth.

Another network consists of residents as encoders and decoders (i.e., a communication network in which residents are linked through sending and receiving messages). And, by specifying the nature of the relationship, it is possible to turn these more encompassing networks into sets of overlapping networks; thus, the social network could be limited to describe paths of influence or economic links, and the communication network could be limited to the political domain. In addition, the shape and characteristics of the social and communication networks are related, but not isomorphic.[117] For example, in his list of propositions about communication networks in communities, Wigand (1977) said that an individual's integration into the network is positively related to one's knowledge, in this case, about urban environmental issues.[118] Moving beyond the problematic boundaries of neighborhoods to the entire community rapidly increases the number of overlapping networks.[119] M. Davis (1997) noted that some evidence supports the view that computer-mediated communication can sustain interpersonal links that already exist but questions whether such networks can create a sense of community in people otherwise separated by time, space, context, or culture. Newby and Bishop (1996) examined Prairienet and concluded that the community network was serving its purpose—providing information access and serving as a community resource in creating a network. Shade (1999) noted that electronic community networking in Canada is tied to support for Canadian content and cultural sovereignty.

Laudeman (1995) noted that communities have patterns of information flow that are similar to those of organizations but they tend to be much less hierarchical, centralized, and structured than traditional organizations. Although organizational social networks function to integrate their members, help them grow and prosper through recruitment, socialization, and social control processes, community information systems should parallel the structure of communities and support their processes. Badran (1992) found that the physical characteristics of a neighborhood shopping center discouraged communication with too-narrow sidewalks, landscaping that was not integrated, and similar factors.

Bulmer (1985) noted that network analysis may be used in a variety of ways to study neighboring (e.g., to examine the strength of weak ties; ties are weaker with neighbors than with kin generally). The strength of a tie is a combination of the amount of time, emotional intensity, intimacy, and reciprocal services that characterize it (Granovetter, 1973). Bulmer (1985) hypothesized that weak ties are indispensable to individuals' opportunities and to their integration into communities. "Strong ties, breeding local cohesion, lead to overall fragmentation. Weak ties are not generative of alienation" (p. 435). Bulmer (1985) said, "network analysis also provides a means to study reciprocity. . . . An approach through network analysis meshes well with the use of exchange theory" (p. 436).

Looking at the urban context in general, Dervin (1977) provided a taxonomy of citizen information needs in cities: about self, about the urban environment, about how to do something, about problems, about institutions. She then looked at linkages between citizens and information sources, between citizens and solutions, between sources and information needs, and so on. Dervin (1975) made the point that "an information system is not a communication system. The former collects, stores, retrieves, and delivers information. The latter, when it is invented, would help people inform themselves, create their own order, establish their own understandings, and cope with their own accidents" (p. 13). She added that "most of the important questions seem unanswered. How do people inform and instruct themselves? How do they create answers? What strategies do people use in life-facing and how do they implement these strategies? How do they make their connections? What role does information play?" (p. 13).

EMPIRICAL NETWORK RESEARCH

Community and Individual Networks

As Donnelly and Majka (1996) noted, changes in the economic role of the center city and patterns of migration and suburbanization have significantly altered urban neighborhoods. Neighborhoods have lost population as economic and social problems have increased. According to some scenarios, this turnover in population, the lower SES of urban residents, and increasing racial and ethnic diversity of residents have undermined the ties among residents and limited their ability to address problems affecting the neighborhood (Bursik & Grasmick, 1993; Bursik & Webb, 1982; Wacquint & Wilson, 1989). Thus, there is the expectation that neighborhood social networks are less dense and patterns of communication "weaker" as links deteriorate along with ties within the neighborhood.

Donnelly and Majka (1996) examined the relationship between such changes and neighborhood cohesion, including neighboring and friendship patterns, organizational involvement, and residential commitment in a study of the Five Oaks neighborhood of Dayton at two points, 1984 and 1990. During that period, the poverty rate climbed, the percentage of residents who were African American grew from more than one fourth to almost half, and crime grew significantly. Their research showed that outdoor socializing among neighbors remained constant from 1984 to 1990, but causal and invited visiting among neighbors over a 3-month period declined 10%. There was a small increase in the percentage of residents who reported getting some kind of help from neighbors, and the index of informal connections within the neighborhood (a composite of helping and neighbor interaction variables) did not change significantly. The percentage indicating most of their friends lived in the neighborhood dropped only slightly. Involvement in neighborhood associations and church organizations declined but involvement in school-related groups was stable. Perceptions of racial diversity as a positive feature of the neighborhood grew from 39% to 55%.

Wellman and Leighton (1979) proposed using a network approach to the question of how to separate the study of communities from the study of neighborhoods. Looking at National Election Studies data collected in 1980, Eulau and Rothenberg (1986) examined interpersonal relations in social networks, with a focus on political behavior. They looked at context as a set of circles within circles, beginning with the family in the center and moving outward to neighborhood, workplace, groups, and city government. They noted that, "Conversation about politics with friends may bring home to a person that his or her views are not in agreement with those of the friends," and people may either conform and succumb to social influence or avoid conflict. How does this occur? In their study, the networks constructed are limited to neighbors, to see whether the neighborhood was a politically salient context and for whom: "To discover whether place of residence is the 'socially' significant environment in people's lives, and whether this environment influences political behavior, we adopted the conception of a person's life space" (p. 136). For some people, the residential neighborhood is the focal point of their daily lives—these folks are called *day dwellers*. For others, most time is spent outside the neighborhood during the day, and these people are called *night dwellers*. In the study, residents were asked where they engage in life's routine activities—working, shopping, relaxing, and worshiping. Results showed that jobs pull people out of their neighborhoods (only 20% work in their neighborhoods), while shopping and the pursuit of leisure were neighborhood-centered (61% did most shopping in the neighborhood, 20% worked there, 50% worshiped there, and 60% relaxed there). They constructed an additive life-space scale to show how people vary in the extent to which they were involved in their neighborhood.

Relating people's political activities and personal contacts with life-space context, they found that a number of social variables were positively correlated with a neighborhood focus (day vs. night dwelling life space measure), including the number of years of residence in the neighborhood, commitment to the area, knowing one's neighbors, and frequency and intimacy of contact with neighbors. However, discussing politics with neighbors, knowing their voting intentions and partisan affiliation were not correlated with the life space measure. Thus, they concluded that the neighborhood as a geographic unit does not appear to be a salient environment for political behavior, but neighbors constitute a social network that has an independent impact on partisan affect for political parties and voting preferences: "Thus, although the neighborhood appears to be of minor importance as a political environment, social relations among particular neighbors result in an interpersonal context that has an impact on political behavior" (p. 130).

Another study examined residents' friendship networks and interpersonal communication skills. Parks (1977) found that perceived similarity among members of close friendship networks and the level of interpersonal communication skills were negatively related to anomia (characterized by a discrepancy between individual goals and the socially dictated or available means of obtaining them), or alienation. Residential mobility (number of moves between and within cities in past 5 years) was positively associated with anomia. And the level of communication network integration (connectedness) was not related to anomia but was negatively associated with level of perceived communication effort.

Marsden (1987) used data from the 1985 General Social Survey to examine interpersonal networks in which Americans discuss "important matters." Respondents were asked for the names of people with whom they had discussed important matters in the past 6 months, whether these issues were family, financial, health, political, recreation, or other things. Respondents were left to decide what was considered important. They also were asked to describe relations between the first five names mentioned (e.g., whether they were close friends, strangers, etc.), and how often respondents communicated with each. Individual characteristics of people identified also were obtained. Network density was measured by finding out how well the respondents' "alters" (those in his or her network), considered in pairs, knew each other; if none knew each other, the density measure would be 0 and if all knew each other, 1. A similar measure of heterogeneity on age, education, race/ethnicity, and sex also was obtained.

Results showed that network size ranges from none to more than six, with one quarter of respondents having networks of zero or one and few respondents indicating they had more than six discussion contacts. The mean was 3. Networks drew heavily on kinship, with an average of 1.5 kin (slightly more than 1.4 nonkin) cited. Some 30% of interpersonal networks consisted only of persons with some family relation to respondents, whereas 20% contained no family members. "This appears comparable to the level of kin composition found in previous surveys of large populations including network items based on intense name generators" (Marsden, 1987, p. 126).

The alters tended to be fairly densely linked, with a mean network density of .61, compared with .44 reported by Fischer (1982) in a regional sample and .33 reported by Wellman (1979) in an urban sample. Some 22% of the networks consist of alters who are all "especially close" to one another, whereas 5% consist of alters who are mutual strangers (network density of 0). Network density rises with age, whereas heterogeneity in race/ethnicity and gender fall; younger people have more diverse networks. These differences remain when kin/nonkin composition is controlled.

Networks tend to be homogeneous compared to the population, especially in terms of race/ethnicity, but there is variation, with more diversity on age and education. Only 8% of respondents cited alters with any racial/ethnic diversity, whereas 22% of networks were composed of only one gender. Age diversity occurs because of the high kin composition of networks and ties that bridge generations, many crossing-gender to spouses, siblings, parents, and children; at the same time, kin-dominated networks reduce race/ethnic diversity. "If networks were composed only of nonkin, they would be substantially less heterogeneous" (p. 126).

Network structure (diversity, density) differs by subgroups defined by age and education. Overall network size drops with age at an increasing rate, with people over age 65 having a mean network size of slightly more than 2; citation of kin falls with age, with the proportion of alters who are kin relatively large for both younger and older respondents and smallest for the middle-aged.

Education was the personal characteristic most clearly influencing differences in network structure; network range grows with education, so that those with college degrees have networks 1.8 times larger than those who did not finish high school. More educated people also cite more nonkin and more kin as well. Alters in the networks of more educated people are less likely to know each other and density declines from a mean of .71 among those who did not finish high school to .54 among those with at least a college degree. Whites had the largest networks (mean size of 3.1), Blacks the smallest (mean of 2.25), and Hispanics and others in between. Gender diversity was highest in Whites' networks.

> Race/ethnic differences in race/ethnic diversity are worthy of special comment, since they are consistent with Blau's (1977) proposition about group size and heterogeneity. The mean index of qualitative variation in the race/ethnicity of alters is 0.03 among whites, who constitute 83% of the GSS [General Social Survey] respondents. It rises to 0.13 for blacks (10 percent of the respondents), to 0.22 for Hispanics (5 percent of the respondents, and further to 0.24 among others (1.5 percent of the respondents). These differences remain, for the most part, when proportion kin is controlled. The structural constraints of group size identified by Blau are visible even in the highly limited levels of intergroup contact measured in the interpersonal environments of the GSS respondents. (Marsden, 1987, p. 129)

Network structure did not differ greatly between men and women; the only significant difference was that women's networks contained more kin and fewer nonkin than did men's.

Results showed that network range was greater in more urbanized places, although size-of-place differences in overall network size were not statistically significant. "Persons in larger places did cite more nonkin and fewer kin, in both absolute and relative terms. Network density falls with size of place, while race/ethnic heterogeneity rises. These differences persisted when controlled for proportion of kin" (Marsden, 1987).[120]

Scheufele et al. (2000) looked at the heterogeneity of a person's discussion network, finding a relationship with interest in local politics and neighborhood affairs as well as awareness of a major local issue and attitudes toward that issue. Alba (1978) found a relationship between the ethnic homogeneity of one's network of primary relations and attitudes toward free speech and child-rearing. O'Connell (1984) looked at exchange in three social relationships—kinship, friendship, and the marketplace.

Berg and McQuinn (1989) found that loneliness was correlated with self-disclosure and network density for both men and women in a study of social support networks of college students.[121] Van Tilburg (1992) found that the size of an individual's support network stayed the same after retirement although relationships with colleagues declined and those with unemployed individuals grew. Loneliness was related to network size[122] and network multiplexity for men but not for women. The importance of social support networks for ill people and for their caregivers also has been examined (Braithwaite, Waldron, & Finn, 1999; Ikkink & van Tilburg, 1998; Lehman & Hemphill, 1990; Morgan, 1986; Morgan & March, 1992; Revenson & Majerovitz, 1990). Nussbaum (1983) found that a network of relational closeness among seniors was positively related to life satisfaction.

Families and Relationships

Dyads that include married couples and other relationships have been the focus of numerous communication network studies (e.g., Banks, Altendorf, Greene, & Cody, 1987; Gottlieb, 1985; Hansson, Jones, & Fletcher, 1990; Leslie, 1989; Trinke & Bartholomew, 1997; Veiel, Crisand, Stroszeck-Somschor, & Herrle, 1991). H. Kim and Stiff (1991) found that an individual's involvement in a partner's social network was a good predictor of the couple's relational development, whereas Surra (1987) found different individual, dyadic, and social network influences on courtship patterns (also see Newcomb, 1986). Eggert and Parks (1987) looked at the impact of communication network development and adolescents' friendships and romantic attachments. Tardy and Hale (1998) examined health-related conversations in informal networks, relying on diffusion theory in a network analysis study. Albrecht and Hall (1991) also focus on innovation networks, arguing that an examination of network communication patterns reveals a core group characterized by strong linkages and high social, personal, and work communication.

Other Networks

Looking at organizations, Marshall and Stohl (1993) argued that involvement and empowerment in the communication system affects worker satisfaction, whereas network position in educational organizations has been linked to job stress and burnout (Ray, 1991) and the nature of one's communication network predicts employee turnover (Feeley & Barnett, 1997). Pilotta, Widman, and Jasko (1988) argued that organizations take on some of the qualities of cultural systems in establishing a communication network. Johnson, Meyer, Berkowitz, Ethington, and Miller (1997) argued that more research is needed comparing the impact of formal and informal structures and communication environment on organizational innovativeness. Kramer (1996) found peer communication and network multiplexity related to employee uncertainty and adjustment during job transfers, whereas Rohrle and Hellmann (1989) looked at the impact of unemployment on social networks and social support.

J. Carey (1998) argued that the Internet should be understood as the first instance of a global communication system, one that threatens national communication systems.[123] K. Kim and Barnett (1996) looked at the international network linking countries via news flow, finding domination by Western industrialized nations. Scholars also are linked in networks, including communication (Barnett & Danowski, 1992; W. White, 1999). Maitland (1998) suggested focusing on culture to explain differences in the diffusion of the Internet and interactive networks around the globe. Wellman et al. (1996) argued that evidence shows computer-supported social networks can sustain strong, intermediate, and weak ties that provide information and social support in both broad-based and specialized relationships; however, little attention is given to neighborhoods or geographic-based communities outside of work and organizations.

Corman and Scott (1994) noted the need to link perceived and observed communication networks. Davison (1972) argued that survey research can be seen as one component of the social communication network. Carley and Kaufer (1993) developed the notion of "semantic connectivity" in semantic networks, using such network concepts as density and consensus.

Consequences of Networks

Network analysis often is combined with other behavioral consequences outside the defining domain. For example, as Homans (1950) noted, the structure of informal friendships and conflict in formal work groups can affect both group and individual productivity rates in ways not predictable from such personal attributes as age, experience, intelligence, and the like. Also, the structure of communication among medical practitioners can affect the speed of diffusion of medical innovations (Coleman, Katz, & Menzel, 1966). Gaunt (1998) looked at five community projects, finding social networks important in assessing project effectiveness. Homel et al. (1987) found that two aspects of parents' networks displayed strong effects on their children—a network of regularly seen dependable friends and parents' affiliation with formal organizations. The network of dependable friends was related to a child's happiness, negative emotions, school adjustment and social skills, as well as the child's friendship network. Formal group affiliations were related to school adjustment, and social skills. Both networks were associated with the child's perception of his or her happiness. O'Sullivan (1995) analyzed the Public Electronic Network in Santa Monica, California, concluding that such interactive computer networks facilitate pluralistic political participation.

> If the concept of process is taken seriously, then communication theory should focus on changes in the state of a system which lead to some outcome. Kincaid (1987, 1988) proposed the "convergence" of belief, attitudes, and behavior among members of a social system who share the same information as the primary process and outcome of human communication. Empirical evidence of the relationship between communication network structure, specifically connectedness or cohesion, and convergence of attitude and behavior was reported by Rogers and Kincaid (1981) in their study of the adoption of family planning in Korean villages. (Kincaid, 1993, p. 112)

Kincaid (1993) used data from his study with Rogers (Rogers & Kincaid, 1981) to look at the relationship between network communication and family planning, finding that information about the topic was highly correlated to the measures of network centrality: degree, closeness, betweenness, and entropy.

Kincaid posited, "as communication and the number of network links among initially disconnected cliques increases, members of the network as a whole would gradually converge toward a state of greater cultural homogeneity" (a dynamic model, p. 125). "Knowledge of the network structure can be used to modify that hypothesis [the more often family planning is discussed among one's peers, the more rapid would be the collective change, depending on the attitudes expressed n the network]. High network centrality characterized by a dominant leader would enhance resistance to change if it is opposed by those in the central positions of the network, or, conversely, high network centrality would accelerate change if the central nodes favor the change" (p. 131).

How innovations diffuse in a community is tied to the nature of the communication network. Weenig and Midden (1991, 1997; Weenig, 1993) looked at how communication networks influence the diffusion process in two Dutch neighborhoods where a community-based communication program was implemented to promote the adoption of energy conservation measures. It was expected that information diffusion would be related to the number of network ties, whereas program effects would be related to the strength of network ties.

Weenig and Midden's (1991) research focused on the concept of communication tie,[124] and the strength of ties was expected to be important because people are motivated to agree with the opinions of strong ties more than with weak ties, and people who are kin or friends are usually regarded as more trustworthy sources of information. Also, studies on group behavior have consistently shown that pressures toward uniformity in attitude and behavior are stronger in more cohesive groups (e.g., Cartwright, 1968). Thus, they expected that the speed and scope of information diffusion in a community will be related to the number of existing ties.

However, strong ties tend to cluster into interlocking networks (see also Feld, 1981), which usually form subgroups (or cliques) in the larger communication network. Granovetter (1973) argued that communication ties between subgroups tend to be weak and, therefore, weak ties may be even more useful to the purpose of information diffusion than strong ties because weak ties prevent information from remaining inside clique boundaries. Thus, new information from outside a clique, such as information about a program's existence, is likely to enter a subgroup via weak ties (i.e., weak ties serve as information bridges between cliques of strong ties). Subsequent research supported this notion (e.g., Friedkin, 1980; Weimann, 1983). Within a clique, however, strong ties appear to be more important for the flow of in-group information (Friedkin, 1982).

Based on these notions, Weenig and Midden (1991) hypothesized that the process of information diffusion (i.e., awareness of program) would be positively related to one's number of ties with community members, regardless of their strength, as well as the availability of a direct tie with the information source. Adoption decisions were expected to be related to the strength of network ties rather than to their number.

The study measured the number of strong ties by adding the number of kin to the number of close friends in the neighborhood. The number of total ties was ascertained with this question, "With how many people in this neighborhood do you speak regularly, by which I mean more than saying just 'hello' to each other?" The number of strong ties was subtracted from this figure to produce the number of weak ties.

Results supported the main hypothesis that information diffusion would be related to the number of communication ties, not to the strength of ties, while adoption decisions was related to the strength of ties. Also, program awareness was positively related to the number of weak ties but unrelated to the number of strong ties. Thus, even in small communities like the neighborhoods investigated, new information originating from outside the community diffuses through weak rather than strong ties.

Another interesting approach to communities is found in the work of Galaskiewicz and Krohn (1984), who looked at community structure as a network of interorganizational links, in which groups exchanged money, information and moral support. Galaskiewicz (1985) also noted the importance of proximity in personal networks of a set of bureaucratic professionals. Comparing communication networks of two different businesses, Papa (1990) argued that three network factors—diversity, size, and activity—are significant predictors of the speed with which new technology increases productivity. In extending the relationship to the community context, it is possible to ask whether the same network factors would predict a similar relationship between the introduction of community Web sites/technology and grassroots problem solving at the neighborhood level.

The network connecting residents to their environment should have consequences for their assessments and knowledge of the community in which they live. Using data from one of the two surveys reported in chapter 6, Jeffres, Neuendorf, and Erbert looked at the relationship between people's personal communication networks and measures of community knowledge and perceptions of the QOL. They viewed each person as living at the center of a communication network composed of links that—together with personal observation and experience—define sources from which one learns about the environment. They hypothesized that the stronger one's communication links, the greater one's level of community knowledge. A parallel hypothesis would relate communication links to QOL assessments, but the logic for such a relationship is not compelling. People very aware of their environment may differ greatly in their QOL assessments because of differences in values and the fortunate or unfortunate circumstances in which they find themselves. Thus, they asked the following research question: "What is the relationship between the strength of one's communication links and one's QOL assessments?" Because the pattern of one's communication links fits into a matrix of influences that also affect what is learned about the environment, they asked to what extent social categories and other individual differences in personal sources of identification, communication needs, routines and leisure can affect what one gets out of communication activity.[125]

Their focus was on the strength and pattern of communication links, but the traditional "competition" between interpersonal and mass communication also gets some attention. Generally, in diffusion research mass media have proven superior at conveying information, whereas interpersonal channels have been more effective in persuasion. Thus, one might expect media to be more important influences on community knowledge and interpersonal channels more influential for QOL assessments.

They conducted a study that focused on community knowledge and assessments as the dependent variables in a model that mapped people's patterns of communication links and incorporated the following variables: demographics, communication needs, communication routines, sources and strengths of identification, and patterns of public leisure activity—viewed as an opportunity for personal observation of the environment. The variables are arrayed in Fig. 8.1

The variables in Fig. 8.1 are arrayed to describe influences. Social categories affect both communication needs and the importance attached to different aspects of people's lives; thus, for example, older people attach more importance to religion and neighborhood. And people who have different needs for communication (as senders and receivers) will have different routines and patterns of links.

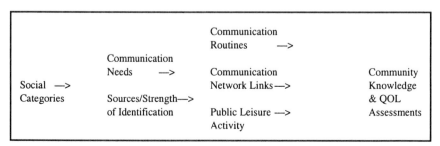

FIG. 8.1. Relationships among variables.

In the model, "public leisure activity" is included as a representation of the third source of information—personal observation and behavior. People learn about the environment through the media, through face-to-face communication with other people, and through observation and experience in the environment. Although it is a less-than-perfect concept representing this third source of influence, public leisure does represent a strong option for learning about the community and it is often seen as competition to the media (coach potatoes vs. active participants or spectators). The communication links, the longer established pattern of communication routines, and the observation-based source of knowledge—public leisure are seen as directly affecting the dependent variables, level of community knowledge, and QOL assessments. The model captures contextual factors and relationships between variables that traditionally have been portrayed as prior influences or mitigating factors in studies of media effects (see Jeffres, 1997) and of QOL assessments (see Jeffres, Neuendorf, & Atkin, 2000).

A survey of a midwest metropolitan area was conducted in early 1996 using traditional random-digit dialing and a CATI system. The study included items mapping people's communication links as well as the other variables in Fig. 8.1. There were 377 adults age 18 or older interviewed. The variables were operationalized as follows.

Communication Links. In operationalizing communication links, items used give an indication of the strength of each link, whether measured by number of individuals talked to or the volume of mass communication activity measured by frequency or hours. *Person-to-person communication links* were obtained with a series of requests for how many people respondents talked with "yesterday," starting with "people in your household, including spouse, children, or others." Subsequent items asked for the number of people talked with in the following categories: in one's neighborhood, at one's job, elsewhere in the city, locally by phone, and outside the area by phone.

Mass communication links were measured using the traditional items. Because some mass communication activity is so infrequent, respondents were asked to gage their behavior over longer time spans (e.g., items solicited the amount of television watched yesterday but the number of books read over the past 6 months). Measures included the following: TV viewing (number of hours watched yesterday and the number usually watched), radio listening (number of hours listened yesterday), newspaper reading (number of days last week read a newspaper), magazine reading (number of different magazines read regularly), book reading (number read in past 6 months), video viewing (number watched in past month, whether borrowed or rented), and film viewing (number times went out to see a film in a theater in past month). Some of the mass communication links are measured over longer time spans because they are such infrequent behaviors. Certainly, an accurate diary system spanning a longer period of time would be more accurate. Next items were summed for a total "interpersonal" (face-to-face plus phone and fax) linkage score and a total "mass communication" score. Because the mass communication items were measured on different scales, those scores were standardized first. Measures of variability within the two types of communication linkages, mass and interpersonal communication, were computed.

> **Communication Needs**: Respondents were asked to use 0-10 scales to indicate how much they agreed or disagreed with each of a series of statements tapping the need to send and receive messages across both mass and interpersonal roles; 0 means one *completely disagreed*, 10 means one *completely agreed* and 5 was *neutral*.[126]
>
> **Communication Routines**: Respondents were told, "today may be an unusual day. Using the same 0-10 scale, where 0 means the statement *doesn't apply to you at all*, 10 means the statement is *very accurate* and 5 is *neutral*, please consider how the following describe you." Then respondents were given a set of items tapping communication routines or patterns.[127]

In addition to measures of communication activity, the survey included respondents' sources of personal identity, QOL assessments, and community knowledge.

Importance of Sources of Personal Identity. No measures of personality were included but several items captured the importance of different sources of personal identity—where people look for meaning in their lives. This captures individual differences in values and lifestyles. A set of items asked respondents to indicate the importance of different aspects of their life—family, job, ethnicity, community (neighborhood and the metro area), hobbies-leisure activities, and religion, using 0-10 scales.

Community Knowledge. The study occurred during a year marking the founding of the metropolitan area. Thus, the media and community events provided considerable information about the history of the area. Nine questions tapped knowledge of the metro area including items about people, places, and things from the past to the present, including, for example, the location of a center-city neighborhood, the area's largest private employer, the name of the founder of the city, and when the area's population peaked.

Quality of Life. The QOL literature provides us with standard measures of how respondents assess different aspects of their life and the environment in which they live (see Andrews, 1986; Andrews & Withey, 1976; Campbell, 1981; Campbell, Converse & Rodgers, 1976). Respondents were asked to rate the QOL across such domains as the nation, the metro area, neighborhood, job, and family. Respondents used 0-10 scales to rate the community in which they live, where 0 is the *worst place to live*, and 10 is the *best place to live* and 5 is *neutral*. Similarly, respondents used the same 0-10 scale to assess their neighborhood, how things are going in the nation, how things are going at work, and how things are going in their family.

Social Categories. The standard measures of social categories also were used in the survey to measure education level, household income, gender, age, and household size.

They hypothesized that one's community knowledge would be related to the strength of one's communication links and to QOL assessments. To examine this relationship, several summary variables were constructed. Because media-use variables were measured using different scales, they were standardized before summary scores were computed. Table 8.1 shows the bivariate correlations between the communication variables and dependent variables. The summary measure of communication links is not correlated with community knowledge, so that hypothesis is not supported. Looking at breakdowns shows that the summary links score is correlated only with the assessment of one's job but none of the other domain assessments. In general, none of the media measures are correlated in any consistent pattern with QOL assessments, although print media links are positively related with neighborhood and national assessments and audiovisual media links are negatively associated with neighborhood assessments. The strength of interpersonal communication links is positively associated with the summary QOL assessment as well as assessments of job and family life; a negative correlation is found for assessment with how things are going in the country today.

Table 8.1 also gives correlations between individual measures of interpersonal and mass communication links, where there is further confirmation of where TV and video have negative relationships with both community knowledge and QOL assessments; one could argue that people use the entertainment media as escape from more difficult circumstances and turn to newspapers for instrumental purposes. However, reading daily newspapers appears to produce positive QOL assessments across almost all domains of life; either people who are satisfied with life turn to the print media to learn about their environment or reading the paper produces a more favorable assessment of life. Access to the Internet also is positively associated with the summary QOL assessment, as well as the judgment about how things are going in the country. These relationships hold up when social categories are held constant.

Several individual interpersonal communication variables also are correlated with community knowledge and assessment. The former is negatively associated with the number of people one talked to at home yesterday. The more people one talks to at work or on the telephone, the stronger one's overall QOL assessment and the stronger one's job satisfaction, and the relationships are confirmed when social categories are held constant. Apparently, being around people enhances one's assessment of life.

Another research question asked whether individual differences reduce the hypothesized relationships. Table 8.1 also gives partial correlations between knowledge and communication links while controlling for education, income, and gender. There is only a small reduction in the strength of relationships.

The bivariate correlations tell us little about processes suggested in Fig. 8.1. Next, relationships between the blocks of variables in the model were examined. Blocks of variables earlier in the model are seen as influencing subsequent blocks. Results showed that the six demographic predictors explain significant amounts of variance for 8 of the 12 measures of communication needs, as well as the summary needs score. Also, social categories explain a significant amount of variance for 5 of the 9 measures of identity (city, neighborhood, family, and religion) and 3 of the 5 measures of communication routines (see Table 8.2).

Next, relationships were examined between communication links and 6 social categories, the importance of 9 different sources of identity and 12 communication needs. Results show that communication needs explain additional variance in the summary score for interpersonal links beyond that already accounted for by social categories and sources of identity. Communication needs also are significant predictors for three of the six types of interpersonal links. Neither personal identity nor social category variables are as important in predicting the strength of interpersonal links (see Table 8.3). Communication needs are not significant predictors of the summary score for mass communication links once social categories and sources of identity are in the equation. In fact, communication needs are significant predictors only for TV viewing. Social categories are the most important predictors (see Table 8.4).

Relationships involving communication routines and participation in public leisure activities were examined (see Table 8.5). Communication needs explain significant amounts of variance beyond that accounted for by social categories and sources of identity for the summary measures of routines and public leisure activity, as well as three of the five individual measures of communication routines. Identity measures are significant predictors of the summary score for communication routines, whereas social categories are not significant predictors; the reverse is found for the index of public leisure activity, where social categories are significant but sources of identity are not.

Community knowledge ranged from 0 to 9 and included current and historical information about people, places and things. Answers to several of the items were reported in one or more stories in the media in the period just prior to the survey. Table 8.6 shows the significance of the full set of predictors of community knowledge, entered in a stepwise regression. Social categories are significant, reflecting the impact of education in particular. Sources of identity fail to explain additional variance, as do communication needs or interpersonal communication links. However, the 10 mass communication links explain significant amounts of variance, and the variance explained by communication routines approaches significance.

TABLE 8.1
Relationships Between Communication Variables and Community Knowledge and Assessments

	Community Knowledge Score	Summary QOL Assessment	QOL Assessments by Domain				
			Qmetro Area	Qneighborhood	Qjob	Qfamily Life	Qnation
Summary/All Com. Links[a]	.05 (.02)	.12* (.09*)	-.06 (-.07)	-.03 (-.04)	.12* (.10*)	.07 (.006)	-.04 (-.07)
Summary/Interp. Links[b]	-.03 (-.04)	.11* (.11*)	-.03(-.03)	-.01(-.01)	.14* (.14*)	.09#(.08#)	-.11*(-.12*)
Summary/Media Links[c]	.08 (.05)	.03 (.00)	-.07(-.08#)	-.01 (-.02)	.03 (.02)	.00 (.01)	.02 (-.01)
Summary/Media Links+Tech[d]	.10*(.07)	.06 (.03)	-.05 (-.06)	-.03 (-.04)	.03 (.01)	.01 (.01)	.04 (.02)
Summary/Print Media[d]	.23***(.17**)	.07 (-.02)	-.01 (-.04)	.10* (.06)	.02 (-.02)	.02 (.00)	.09# (.05)
Radio-TV-Film-Video[e]	-.10*(-.09#)	-.02 (.01)	-.09# (.08#)	-.12* (-.10*)	.03 (.05)	-.02 (-.01)	-.05 (-.05)
Specific Audio/Video Media:							
TV yesterday	-.02 (.07)	-.17* (-.08#)	-.05 (-.03)	-.15* (-.10*)	-.01 (.03)	-.06 (-.03)	-.11*(-.07*)
TV usually	-.09#(.02)	-.21**(-.10*)	-.05 (-.03)	-.07 (-.02)	-.09 (-.04)	-.06 (-.04)	-.11*(-.05)
Radio listening	.03 (.05)	.02 (.03)	-.05 (-.06)	.08 (.08)	.03 (.04)	.06 (.05)	-.04 (-.03)
Video viewing	-.15**(-.19**)	.06 (.05)	-.05 (-.05)	-.08 (-.08)	.03 (.02)	-.02 (-.01)	.05 (.03)
Film viewing outside home	-.07 (-.10*)	.05 (.03)	-.03 (-.03)	-.09#(-.10*)	.01 (.00)	-.02 (-.03)	.01 (-.02)
Cable TV subs.	.15** (.14*)	.08 (.05)	.01 (.01)	-.04 (-.05)	-.04 (-.06)	.05 (.04)	.03 (.00)
Specific Print Media:							
Newspaper reading	.29** (.23***)	.19**(.11*)	.07 (.05)	.19**(.16**)	.14*(.11*)	.12*(.10*)	.13*(.09#)
Magazine reading	.09 (.03)	.02 (-.05)	-.04 (-.05)	-.03 (-.05)	-.01 (-.04)	-.09#(-.10*)	.08 (.04)
Books reading	.07 (.06)	-.07 (-.10*)	-.06 (-.07)	.04 (.02)	-.09 (-.10*)	.01 (.00)	-.04 (-.04)
Internet access	.06 (-.05)	.26***(.17**)	.06 (.03)	.04 (-.01)	.12* (.07)	.06 (.05)	.17**(.12*)
Specific Interpersonal Links							
No. talk to at home	-.13* (-.12*)	-.04 (-.03)	-.06 (-.05)	-.12*(-.11*)	.06 (.07)	.00 (.00)	-.10*(-.10*)

No. talk to in neighborhood	-.04 (-.03)	.03 (.05)	.00 (.01)	.00 (.00)	.11#(.12*)	.05 (.06)	-.04 (-.03)
No. talk to at work	.01 (-.02)	.18**(.16*)	.01 (.00)	.00 (-.01)	.13*(.11*)	.07 (.06)	-.03 (-.05)
No. talk to elsewhere/city	.04 (.02)	.02 (.00)	-.03 (-.03)	-.04 (-.04)	-.04 (.05)	.09#(.09#)	-.05 (-.07)
No. talk locally by phone	.02 (.02)	.08 (.09*)	-.07 (-.08#)	.07 (.07)	.11*(.12*)	.02 (.01)	-.08 (.08#)
No. talk long-distance by phone	.00 (-.02)	.12* (.10*)	.02 (.02)	.07 (.06)	.12*(.11*)	.06 (.05)	-.09#(-.10*)

Note. The first figure represents the bivariate correlation between the communication links and knowledge/assessment variables. The second represents the partial correlation controlling for education level, household income and gender. #p < .10; *p < .05; **p < .01; ***p < .001.

aThis includes all communication variables as standardized scores (α =.45).

bThis includes the standardized scores on the number of people talked to in six contexts, at home, in the neighborhood, at work, elsewhere in the city, by phone locally, and by phone long distance (α =.62).

cThis includes standardized scores on media use for the amount of time spent watching TV yesterday, the amount of time spent listening to the radio yesterday, the number of days one read a newspaper in the past week, the number of magazines read regularly, and the number of books read in the past 6 months, the number of videos—borrowed or rented—watched in the past month, and the number of times one has gone out to see films in a theater in the past month (α =.21).

dThis includes the standardized scores on media use plus cable subscription and Internet access (α =.31).

eThis includes the standardized scores on print media use, including newspaper reading, magazine reading, and book reading (α =.32).

fThis includes standardized scores of four audiovisual media use variables, listening to the radio, watching TV, going out to see films, and watching purchased or rented videos.

TABLE 8.2
Predicting Communication Needs, Communication Routines, and Importance of Sources of Identification From Social Categories

Dependent Variable	Multiple R	Multiple R^2	F	Sig.
Communication Needs				
Summary Score for Communication Needs	.29	.084	4.88	.0001
CMU4 Talk with strangers	.17	.027	1.49	n.s.
CMU5 Talk with different people	.21	.045	2.54	.02
CMU18 Wish talk more with neighbors	.19	.038	2.10	.05
CMU19 Leave house to talk	.21	.042	2.36	.03
CMU20 Value solitude	.18	.031	1.71	n.s.
CMU11 Would send messages to everyone	.24	.056	3.13	.01
CMU14 Wish were newspaper columnist	.31	.095	5.63	.0001
CMU17 Need to express myself	.16	.025	1.36	n.s.
CMU13 Would like 500 TV channels	.34	.117	7.06	.0001
CMU Enjoy intl., natl. news	.22	.049	2.77	.02
CMU8 Wish more neighborhood news	.21	.045	2.53	.02
Importance of Sources of Identification				
Summary Score across Sources of Identity	.39	.148	8.27	.0001
Importance of city/metro area	.53	.280	18.5	.0001
Importance of neighborhood	.18	.032	1.56	n.s.
Would miss neighborhood	.33	.111	6.01	.0001
Would hate to move	.22	.050	2.49	.03
Importance of job	.19	.038	1.87	.09 n.s.
Importance of ethnicity	.17	.028	1.38	n.s.
Importance of family	.38	.146	8.16	.0001
Importance of hobbies	.17	.028	1.35	n.s.
Importance of religion	.38	.141	7.8	.0001
Communication Routines				
Summary Score for Com. Routines	.18	.031	1.67	n.s.
CMU2 Talk with lot of people at work	.14	.020	1.11	n.s.
CMU3 Talk in family	.34	.118	7.12	.0001
CMU6 Talk w/people from same area	.21	.043	2.40	.03
CMU15 Talk about stuff w/friends	.23	.052	2.91	.01
CMU16 Clubs good place to find people	.12	.015	.81	n.s.

TABLE 8.3

Predicting Interpersonal Communication Links From Communication Needs, Importance of Sources of Identity, and Social Categories

Dependent Variable	Predictor Variables	Multiple R	Multiple R²	R Sq. Change	F Change	Sig. Change	F for Equation	Sig.
Summary Score for Interpersonal Links	6 social categories	.19	.034		1.66	n.s.		
	9 ID variables	.28	.077	.04	1.39	n.s.		
	12 com. needs	.40	.161	.084	2.17	.02	1.84	.01
No. talk with at home	6 social categories	.40	.162		9.01	.0001		
	9 ID variables	.42	.180	.02	.66	n.s.		
	12 com. needs	.46	.213	.033	.91	n.s.	2.69	.0001
No. talk with in neighborhood	6 social categories	.23	.052		2.54	.02		
	9 ID variables	.31	.099	.047	1.57	n.s.		
	12 com. needs	.38	.142	.044	1.10	n.s.	1.59	.04
No. talk with at job	6 social categories	.19	.035		1.69	n.s.		
	9 ID variables	.28	.076	.041	1.32	n.s.		
	12 com. needs	.41	.168	.092	2.38	.01	1.93	.01
No. talk with elsewhere in city	6 social categories	.12	.014		.67	n.s.		
	9 ID variables	.22	.046	.032	1.01	n.s.		
	12 com. needs	.34	.118	.072	1.75	.05	1.29	n.s.
No. talk with by phone locally	6 social categories	.11	.013		.62	n.s.		
	9 ID variables	.21	.044	.031	.97	n.s.		
	12 com. needs	.34	.117	.072	1.77	.05	1.27	n.s.

TABLE 8.4
Predicting Mass Communication Links From Communication Needs, Importance of Sources of Identity, and Social Categories

Dependent Variable	Predictor Variables	Multiple R	Multiple R^2	R Sq. Change	F Change	Sig. Change	F for Equation	Sig.
Summary Score for Mass Com. Links	6 social categories	.26	.067	.067	3.28	.01		
	9 ID variables	.28	.077	.010	.31	n.s.		
	12 com. needs	.36	.127	.050	1.20	n.s.	1.36	n.s.
Time spent watching TV yesterday	6 social categories	.30	.089	.089	4.48	.001		
	9 ID variables	.33	.110	.020	.67	n.s.		
	12 com. needs	.39	.153	.043	1.06	n.s.	1.69	.02
Time spent watching TV usually	6 social categories	.41	.165	.165	9.01	.001		
	9 ID variables	.42	.175	.010	.36	n.s.		
	12 com. needs	.51	.257	.082	2.34	.01	3.24	001
Time spent listening to radio	6 social categories	.19	.035	.035	1.66	n.s.		
	9 ID variables	.33	.107	.072	2.39	.02		
	12 com. needs	.36	.128	.020	.49	n.s.	1.37	n.s.
No. days read newspaper in past week	6 social categories	.41	.165	.165	9.02	.001		
	9 ID variables	.46	.217	.052	1.94	.05		
	12 com. needs	.51	.258	.042	1.18	n.s.	3.26	001
No. magazines read regularly	6 social categories	.21	.044	.044	2.10	.054		
	9 ID variables	.26	.067	.023	.70	n.s.		
	12 com. needs	.36	.133	.067	1.61	.09	1.43	.08

		R	R^2	R^2 change	F	p	F	p
No. books read in past 6 months	6 social categories	.34	.114		5.89	.001		
	9 ID variables	.38	.148	.034	1.16	n.s.	1.98	.01
	12 com. needs	.42	.174	.026	.67	n.s.		
No. videos watched in past month	6 social categories	.31	.098		4.94	.001		
	9 ID variables	.36	.132	.035	1.19	n.s.	1.98	.01
	12 com. needs	.42	.174	.042	1.06	n.s.		
No. films seen in theater in past month	6 social categories	.31	.093		4.70	.001		
	9 ID variables	.35	.122	.029	.97	n.s.	2.20	.001
	12 com. needs	.44	.190	.068	1.77	.054		
Subscribe to cable TV	6 social categories	.15	.023		1.08	n.s.		
	9 ID variables	.24	.057	.034	1.07	n.s.	1.25	n.s.
	12 com. needs	.34	.118	.061	1.45	n.s.		
Internet access	6 social categories	.47	.220		12.9	.001		
	9 ID variables	.50	.245	.024	.95	n.s.	3.87	.001
	12 com. needs	.54	.292	.047	1.41	n.s.		

TABLE 8.5
Predicting Communication Routines and Public Leisure Activity From Communication Needs, Importance of Sources of Identity, and Social Categories

Dependent Variable	Predictor Variables	Multiple R	Multiple R^2	R Sq. Change	F Change	Sig. Change	F for Equation	Sig.
Summary Score for communication routines	6 social categories	.15	.022		1.02	n.s.	2.38	.01
	9 ID variables	.34	.118	.096	3.23	.001	3.57	.001
	12 com. needs	.52	.274	.156	4.57	.001		
CMU2 talk at work	6 social categories	.22	.05		2.41	.03		
	9 ID variables	.30	.092	.042	1.38	n.s.		
	12 com. needs	.39	.154	.062	1.57	.10	1.72	.02
CMU3 talk in family	6 social categories	.27	.072		3.57	.01		
	9 ID variables	.34	.114	.042	1.41	n.s.		
	12 com. needs	.41	.167	.053	1.35	n.s.	1.89	.01
CMU6 talk with people in same part of town	6 social categories	.18	.031		1.48	n.s.		
	9 ID variables	.29	.082	.051	1.64	.10		
	12 com. needs	.54	.295	.213	6.42	.001	3.95	.001
CMU15 talk with friends	6 social categories	.20	.039		1.85	.09		
	9 ID variables	.36	.130	.092	3.13	.01		
	12 com. needs	.57	.319	.189	5.89	.001	4.43	.001
CMU16 clubs good place to find people to talk with	6 social categories	.16	.027		1.27	n.s.		
	9 ID variables	.27	.075	.048	1.54	n.s.		
	12 com. needs	.49	.236	.161	4.48	.001	2.92	.001
Summary score for public leisure activity	6 social categories	.32	.100	013	5.18	.001		
	9 ID variables	.34	.112.		.44	n.s.		
	12 com. needs	.44	.194	.081	2.16	.01	2.30	.001

The equation predicting the summary measure of QOL assessments shows that social categories and sources of identity are significant predictors, with the variance explained by mass communication links approaching significance (see Table 8.6). None of the other blocks are significant. Next, individual QOL assessments were examined. Social categories and the importance of different sources of identification explain significant portions of variance for most of the five assessments of the QOL. Communication needs are significant predictors only for assessments of the QOL in the metro area, whereas public leisure activity is a significant predictor only for "how things are going in your family" (Qfamily). Mass communication links are significant predictors of the perceived quality of neighborhoods and the variance explained for "how things are going at work" (Qjob) approaches significance.

The importance of mass communication links to learning about one's community is affirmed by this study, whose results are consistent with the traditional view that media are more powerful in producing cognitive effects. The results occur even when social categories, the importance of different sources of identity and meaning in one's life, communication needs, and interpersonal communication links have been taken into account. Clearly, the network of links reflected in an individual's media use patterns is more than a mere reflection of life style and individual differences. This could be interpreted as an extension of Gerbner's notion that people who watch an extensive amount of television come to adopt television's view of the world (Gerbner, 1972, 1990; Gerbner & Gross, 1976; Signorielli & Morgan, 1990). The accumulation of images across media links could have the same impact.

However, the sources of meaning and identity in one's life are more important as predictors of QOL assessments. As Table 8.6 shows, the nine identity measures explain significant amounts of variance in all five individual QOL assessments as well as the summary scale. Clearly, the interrelationships among this set of variables needs to be examined across populations and with different dependent measures tapping people's perceptions.

A SYSTEMS VIEW

Systems theory has become a useful approach for integrating "strands of organized complexity" (Laszlo, 1996, p. 8).[128] Addressing scholars and researchers in general but particularly scientists, Laszlo noted that too often specialty barriers mean that "knowledge, instead of being pursued in depth and integrated in breadth, is pursued in depth in isolation" (p. 2). Although specialists in the various disciplines and subareas of disciplines concentrate on detail and disregard the wider structure, scientists employing the systems perspective concentrate on structure at all levels of magnitude and complexity, and fit detail into its general framework. They discern relationships and situations (Laszlo, 1996).

TABLE 8.6
Predicting Community Knowledge and Assessments

Dependent Variable	Predictor Variables	Multiple R	Mul. R^2	R.Sq.Ch	F Ch.	Sig.Ch.	F for Eq.	Sig.
Community Knowledge Scale	**6 social categories**	.46	.207		10.46	**.001**		
	9 ID variables	.49	.243	.036	1.23	n.s.		
	12 com. needs	.52	.270	.028	.69	n.s.		
	6 interpersonal com. links	.53	.280	.010	.47	n.s.		
	10 mass com. links	.61	.375	.100	3.11	**.001**		
	5 communication routines	.64	.407	.032	2.12	**.06**		
	public leisure score	.64	.407	.000	.06	n.s.	**2.77**	**.001**
Summary Score for Quality of Life Assessments	**6 social categories**	.35	.121		5.55	**.001**		
	9 ID variables	.61	.368	.247	10.08	**.001**		
	12 com. needs	.63	.396	.028	.85	n.s.		
	6 interpersonal com. links	.64	.410	.014	.86	n.s.		
	10 mass com. links	.68	.455	.045	1.67	**.09**		
	5 communication routines	.69	.469	.014	1.07	n.s.		
	public leisure score	.69	.471	.002	.62	n.s.	**3.60**	**.001**
Qmetro Area	**6 social categories**	.28	.081		3.52	**.01**		
	9 ID variables	.51	.263	.182	6.37	**.001**		
	12 com. needs	.57	.330	.068	1.85	**.05**		
	6 interpersonal com. links	.58	.343	.012	.67	n.s.		
	10 mass com. links	.60	.362	.019	.62	n.s.		
	5 communication routines	.62	.379	.016	1.05	n.s.		
	public leisure score	.62	.382	.004	1.23	n.s.	**2.50**	**.001**

	R	R²	R² change	F	sig	Overall F	Overall sig
Qneighborhood							
6 social categories	.30	.090		3.95	**.001**	**3.28**	**.001**
9 ID variables	.55	.304	.215	7.96	**.001**		
12 com. needs	.59	.352	.047	1.34	n.s.		
6 interpersonal com. links	.61	.377	.026	1.47	n.s.		
10 mass com. links	.66	.429	.052	1.86	**.05**		
5 communication routines	.67	.448	.018	1.33	n.s.		
public leisure score	.67	.448	.000	.00	n.s.		
Qjob							
6 social categories	.17	.029		1.22	n.s.	**1.70**	**.01**
9 ID variables	.40	.156	.126	3.86	**.001**		
12 com. needs	.44	.191	.035	.79	n.s.		
6 interpersonal com. links	.47	.219	.028	1.26	n.s.		
10 mass com. links	.53	.279	.060	1.69	**.08**		
5 communication routines	.54	.290	.012	.65	n.s.		
public leisure score	.54	.296	.001	1.63	n.s.		
Qfamily life							
6 social categories	.21	.044		1.85	**.09**	**1.88**	**.01**
9 ID variables	.44	.196	.152	4.88	**.001**		
12 com. needs	.49	.236	.040	.96	n.s.		
6 interpersonal com. links	.50	.246	.010	.48	n.s.		
10 mass com. links	.54	.286	.040	1.14	n.s.		
5 communication routines	.56	.308	.022	1.27	n.s.		
public leisure score	.56	.318	.010	2.89	**.09**		
Qnation							
6 social categories	.28	.081		3.56	**.01**	**1.80**	**.01**
9 ID variables	.40	.158	.076	2.33	**.02**		
12 com. needs	.47	.217	.060	1.40	n.s.		
6 interpersonal com. links	.50	.254	.037	1.75	n.s.		
10 mass com. links	.53	.279	.026	.72	n.s.		
5 communication routines	.55	.306	.027	1.53	n.s.		
public leisure score	.56	.308	.002	.53	n.s.		

The urban context is an excellent candidate for the systems perspective. Urban scholars integrate physical ecology with social structures and theories of planning and social action.[129] As Laszlo (1996) noted, "The systems view perceives connections and communications [sic] between people, and between people and nature, and emphasizes community and integrity in both the natural and the human world" (p. 11). What is generally missing is the emphasis on neighborhoods as systems, and communication, when present, is little more than a single variable rather than a complex system in its own right.[130]

Systems theory is more than merely relying on classification of relevant observations or part-whole relationships.[131] Laszlo (1996) offered four propositions of organizational invariance that answer what characteristics an object must have to be considered a natural system:

1. Natural systems are wholes with irreducible properties (e.g., wholes are not the simple sum of their parts, as are heaps and aggregates).
2. Natural systems maintain themselves in a changing environment.[132]
3. Natural systems create themselves in response to self-creativity in other systems.[133]
4. Natural systems are coordinating interfaces in nature's "holarchy," with simple systems at the bottom and a few complex systems at the top, and intermediate systems to link them.[134]

In contemporary systemic thinking, the human being is a natural entity inhabiting several interrelated worlds—as a biological organism, as a social role carrier, as a conscious personality integrating and coordinating the biological and the social worlds.[135] Laszlo (1996) noted the following:

> Ultimately the strands of communication straddle the space-time region within which the primary systems have come together, and those of its layers which provide conditions favorable to such structuration become organized as systems in their own right. We reach the level of the "global" (ecological, and on Earth also sociocultural) "Gaia system." (p. 63)

Laszlo also noted:

> In the world of organized complexity the arrow of time does not determine which pathway is taken by individual systems, only in which direction their paths converge. The general irreversibilities of organization include the progressive differentiation of existing systems, the merging of smaller systems within large units without loss of individuality, and the increased level of communication among systems on their own hierarchical level. . . . Relatively isolated and simple clans and tribes are incorporated in larger, more complex communities with an increase in communication among the incorporated units. The larger communities enter into communication

among themselves, and jointly constitute still more embracing societies—nations, state, and empires. In our day we are approaching the outer limits of international communication and system-building. Further development, being unable to proceed extensively, will take effect intensively. Increasing communication among a finite number of national and multinational systems can only result in greater mutual determination among them. As the ratio of noise to signal is reduced through wider channels of effective international communication, the world will become more and more like a single unit. (pp. 83-84)

According to Laszlo:

We are faced with the following variables: increasing communication—hence determination—on the macrolevel of sociocultural systems, great differentiation among individual aptitudes and potentials, and the value of individual human fulfillment. Our humanistic goal is to enhance individual fulfillment in an increasingly deterministic multilevel society composed of greatly differentiated individuals. Fortunately, this is a feasible endeavor. Like all complex natural systems, human institutions and societies function best when they are spontaneous expressions of the freely chosen activities of their interrelated members. Such a society is the norm against which we must measure existing forms of social structure. (p. 87)

Systems sciences are important, he added, because they locate humans within the multiple structures of nature and enable them to make constructive use of their capacities.[136]

The principles of systems theory are quite abstract and can be applied in various ways by different theorists. It is probably more appropriate to think of systems theory as a loosely organized set of principles that can be used to help understand complex phenomena, whether one is talking about social systems or communication systems. The key principle of systems theory is the characterization of a whole that functions by virtue of the interdependence of its parts, that is, defining the system self; thus, one defines the system not as a set of components (individuals or roles) but as a set of interdependent relationships of components. The classic phrase, "the whole is greater than the sum of its parts" (often called the principle of nonsummativity), reflects this thinking. A set of components or group of people without relationships is an aggregate (i.e., all the people watching television during prime time do not constitute a system but a group of neighbors tied by proximity, problems, and patterns of communication may be).

Relationships among the components can be described in terms of such concepts as function, structure, and evolution. Structural relationships imply a spatial relationship in some views of communication systems (e.g., see Fisher, 1978) or status/organization in social systems (see Eisenstadt, 1985). Functional relationships deal with purposes or uses and, sometimes have been used to infer support or time. In interpersonal systems, Fisher (1978) viewed functional relationships as implying a time-oriented relationship among components that are events (e.g., information giver or energizer). In mass communication, uses and gratifications theory is viewed as a functional explanation of people's media behaviors at the individual level (i.e., one's media-use pattern persists because of the uses to which it is put and the gratifications derived); at a social systems level, media are often viewed as agents of social control, functioning in support of power and system maintenance (see Demers, 1996b, for a discussion of mass media and social systems theory). Evolution refers to how a system evolves or changes.

The organic metaphor often is cited to describe how a system operates through time (Martindale, 1988), for example, systems strive for equilibrium, a notion sometimes paired conversely with the concept of equifinality. This is one application of systems theory that has generated criticism over the decades, for example, if systems strive to maintain order, or equilibrium, there's an inherent conservative bias and a tendency to ignore social change; however, other models focusing on process emphasize that social systems are fluid, changing and dynamic. The notion of equifinality is applied in systems classified as open, which interact with their environment. In these cases, the same final state may be reached from different initial conditions (e.g., neighborhoods starting from different initial conditions can arrive at the same destination, such as a unified community). Social systems, including neighborhoods, are open systems, with permeable boundaries that often are problematic to observers.

As pluralism theory suggests, the size of a system affects its characteristics. Thus, as a system grows and becomes more complex, there is increasing differentiation. In social systems, this is sometimes described in terms of the distribution of power. The notion also can be applied to communication systems (e.g., the pattern of communication in larger neighborhoods shows increased differentiation in the channels used and the specialization of communication roles). The challenge is to see how systems theory helps researchers to describe neighborhoods as they evolve and change over time in larger, dynamic urban environments. Part of this challenge is to see whether the same approach helps researchers understand the nature of neighborhood communication systems, and the relationship between neighborhoods as both social and communication systems.

In communication, systems theory has been applied to various units of analysis, including communication systems in general (Librero, 1993), families (Folwell, Chung, Nussbaum, Bethea, & Grant, 1997; O'Connor, Hetherington, & Clingempeel, 1997; Yerby, 1995), groups (Contractor & Seibold, 1993), sports (Creedon, 1993), social interaction (Barbee & Cunningham, 1995; Frandsen & Millis, 1993), argumentation and debate (Lichtman, 1986; Madsen, 1989), organizations (Barker & Tompkins, 1994; Belanger, Lafrance, & Taylor, 1990; McMillan & Northern, 1995; van Every & Taylor, 1998), mass media (McQuail & the Euromedia Research Group, 1990; Turow, 1992), communities (Demers, 1998; Tichenor et al., 1980), and ethnic groups (Y. Kim, 1994).

INTEGRATING NETWORK THEORY
AND SYSTEMS THEORY

Much of the literature employing network analysis in urban settings also views the community as a social system, and many studies utilizing the systems perspective in studying communities also draw on concepts from network analysis. But seldom are the two perspectives integrated beyond stating assumptions that the system has a network and the network exists within a social system.

Several factors may be responsible, and both research purpose and disciplinary traditions are central. Research that begins with network analysis may define the unit of analysis a priori (e.g., the neighborhood or community) or the conceptualization of the network itself may define the system. Within communication, the network is a level of analysis (see Chaffee & Berger, 1987), and network concepts can be used to define social units such as neighborhoods. Within sociology, economics, and urban studies, geographic units themselves are useful in examining social systems, with network concepts drawn in later as variables.

The general outlines of the two perspectives earlier provide clues for integrating the two. Specification of the domain is crucial because both systems theory and network analysis have been applied to a variety of units—groups, organizations, communities, and nations. In addition, the individual and dyads such as couples have been treated as systems and their involvement in networks used as variables.

First, the domains for application need to be identified, then systems and network theory need to be applied to each domain, and finally the relationships among them must be stated. Table 8.7 provides some basic descriptions in identifying the domains, which largely represent the application of concepts from the pertinent disciplines—sociology and urban studies, communication, political science, and economics. Although the focus here is on the first two, neighborhoods as social units and as a communication context, political and economic issues are certainly important and are included to a limited extent.

The domains serve as the units for applying each of the two major theories to be integrated. Table 8.7 again provides descriptions of each unit as a system within domain. In addition to the basic descriptions of social systems, communication systems, political systems, and economic systems, some indication is given of constituent components (e.g., subsystems) and of relationships in the other direction (e.g., neighborhood economic systems are highly dependent on the larger urban economic system in most cases and, although neighborhood residents are decoders/audiences, most of the encoders/message construction occurs outside the neighborhood).

Each domain also is characterized as a neighborhood network. Here, the focus is on the social and communication networks examined earlier in this book. At a basic level, the social network is a pattern of social relationships represented by kinship and friendship ties. Similarly, the communication network is composed of links through which residents exchange messages and meanings.

TABLE 8.7
Issues for Integrating Network Theory and Systems Theory

Identify Domains for Application
    Domains:
       neighborhood as a social unit
       neigborhood as a communication context
       neighborhood as a political unit
       neighborhood as an economic unit

Characterize Units for Systems Theory by Domain
    Systems:
    neighborhood as a social system (part of larger urban social system, which is part of larger social systems).
         neighborhood social system itself is composed of component systems and institutions described along various lines.
    neighborhood as a communication system (part of larger urban communication system, which is part of larger communication systems)
         neighborhood communication system can be conceptualized as being composed of interpersonal and mass communication subsystems, which can be broken down further into dyads and media and described along other lines.
    neighborhood as a political system (part of larger urban political system, which is part of larger political systems)
         neighborhood political system can be viewed as being composed of roles, patterns representing the exercise of power, from institutional bases, other sources.
    neighborhood as an economic system (part of larger urban economic system, which is part of a regional economic system, etc.)
         neighborhood economy can be viewed as having the same components as the larger urban economy, with residents performing economic roles while seeking resources and acting as both producers and consumers.

Characterize Units for Network Theory by Domain
    Networks:
    neighborhood social network—represented as a pattern of relationships (e.g., kinship, friendship).
    neighborhood communication network—represented as a pattern of encoder–decoder links via interpersonal and mass communication.
    neighborhood political network—represented as a pattern showing paths of influence through relationships in the community.
    neighborhood economic network—represented as a pattern of consumer–producer relationships.

Although both systems theory and network theory have generated a wealth of hypotheses and empirical evidence (e.g., the literature and research on pluralism examined earlier), potential relationships between them—across and within domains—are examined. First, what is the relationship between social systems and social networks, between communication systems and communication networks, and so on? Second, what is the relationship between social systems and communication systems, between social networks and communication networks? In a variation on the second point, what is the relationship between social systems and communication networks, and between social networks and communication systems?

This is not a novel undertaking. As later chapters on mobilization and communication show, the relationship between communication networks and efforts to mobilize social systems has proven useful in studies that also have drawn on other pertinent communication theories (e.g., diffusion theory) and on theories of social action. However, efforts to utilize both network and systems concepts generally are conducted with the intent to generalize to the problem-solving literature and social systems in general rather than to neighborhoods in particular. The current effort to integrate systems and networks theories is carried out as an attempt to see what questions should be raised in studying the neighborhood as a domain.

What are the concepts that help link the two theories? From systems theory, the notions of an open system, functional relationships, and equifinality, among others, are borrowed. Neighborhoods as either social or communication systems are open systems, and in any open system the same state may be reached from different initial conditions and in different ways—equifinality (see Buckley, 1967, 1968; Demerath & Peterson, 1967; Laszlo, 1996; von Bertalanfry, 1968, for discussions of basic systems theory concepts). If the neighborhood is treated as a dynamic, evolving entity, then it is possible to examine how states of a communication system and states of a social system are related through time, particularly in response to external forces and other systems. In social systems theory, changes in migration, fertility, and mortality are major influences. Technology is a parallel influence for communication systems. In both cases, the nature and structure of the neighborhood system is affected (e.g., an influx of professionals in a "redeveloping neighborhood" alters the pattern of relationships, and the appearance of a community newspaper or development of a neighborhood Web site changes the neighborhood communication system). Of course, any of the human systems—social, communication, political, or economic—can be impacted by physical factors, whether the origins are man-made or in mother nature, from major fires to ecological disasters.

Systems theory represents a reorientation in science from looking for simple relationships to dealing with isomorphisms of structure and similarity across specialties and fields. The goal is to achieve a higher level of generality, and, in this instance, the level of generality is the neighborhood, where similarities and parallels can be identified. As Rogers (1987) and others noted, there is not a single structure, or pattern, but many patterns—social, communication, economic, and political, for example. Thus, it is possible to look for isomorphisms across social and communication structures. This is also a point at which network theory should be considered, because it offers concepts of structure beyond those employed in systems theory. Indeed, the literature covered earlier in this book showed relationships between communication patterns and patterns of social relationships, even if network concepts weren't invoked explicitly. For example, a "dense" network of social relationships (kinship, strong friendships, intimates) would be expected to occur concurrently with a "dense" interpersonal communication network (e.g., high information centrality and consensus).

However, the search for "isomorphisms" can be somewhat sterile if they are not linked to problem solving across time and to concepts that refer to other human behaviors and variables that may be crucial for the survival of neighborhoods. This includes public opinion—perceptions and opinions about one's community—and community involvement—extent to which residents utilize their neighborhood or are involved in its defense or advancement. Thus, a dense communication network should be functional for mobilizing residents against immediate external threats.

Most of the descriptive literature, as described earlier in this book, is static, but neighborhoods are dynamic, evolving entities that face problems and uncertain futures. Social science theories are most useful when they show the constraints faced and the opportunities for intervention in problem solving. This book began with the notion that neighborhoods still are relevant and offer an option to people seeking community. One of the studies examined earlier showed that people vary considerably in the extent to which they look for meaning in their lives through neighborhoods, work, ethnic heritage, and other sources. This has implications for both systems theory and network theory in their application toward neighborhoods.

How can the integration of network theory and systems theory inform efforts to understand how neighborhoods survive and evolve as entities? As open systems, neighborhoods are generated when a sufficient (but problematic) number of people settle in a geographic area and incur a measure of interdependence. The defining characteristics of both the social system and the communication system are generated in the process of settling. Thus, based on the status and ascriptive characteristics of residents (either "given"—through kinship—or "developing"—friendship formation), social structures emerge. Similarly, given the needs for communication and enhancing or inhibiting factors of proximity and purpose, patterns of symbolic activity develop and evolve. Clearly, it is possible to identify how factors of the social structure influence the development of the communication system (as Blau, 1977, noted, similarities promote communication), and how the nature of the communication system affects aspects of the social structure (friendships and, in some cases, kinship, evolve through communication). However, once set in motion, neither the social system nor the communication system (or political or economic systems) is "determined" by the other. The task of social and behavioral sciences is to explain how these systems of organized complexity are related.

A schema for studying neighborhoods employing systems and network theories together with other concepts is found in Table 8.8. The schema can be used to generate hypotheses stating relationships in comparisons of neighborhoods with each other and across time.

TABLE 8.8
Schema for Studying Neighborhoods Across Time

Variables Conceptualizing Links Between Residents and Their Neighborhoods

Level of people's attachment to community

*Mean level of attachment to community is a measure of affect.

Basis of people's attachment to community—linked to patterns of needs fulfilled by neighborhoods and other sources of fulfillment.

*Needs are represented by Maslow's hierarchy, with safety at the bottom and affiliation and self actualization at the top. Neighborhoods vary in their ability to fulfill each of these needs, and people vary in the extent to which they seek fulfillment in neighborhoods versus other contexts. At the neighborhood level, the degree to which the neighborhood fulfills residents' needs is a useful measure of the successful match at a point in time.

Extent to which community is relevant in people's search for "meaning" in their lives.

*People may look for meaning, or assign portions of their identity, to achievements at work, to family, to leisure activities, to ethnicity and gender, to neighborhood, to churches and religion, and to other sources. The extent to which neighborhoods are relevant and fulfilling sources of meaning and identity for their residents is a useful measure of whether neighborhoods still count in modern societies.

*At the community level, not only is the mean level of significance of neighborhood as a source of meaning and identity important, but how it fits into the diverse patterns of meaning sought by residents is also important (e.g., an upscale neighborhood populated by intact families who locate most of their meaning in jobs and families and seek little more than safety, education, and real estate appreciation in their neighborhood may represent a "good" fit between meanings sought by residents and opportunities offered by the neighborhood).

*This is the site at which to locate the "search for community," a concept that must be linked at some point to the need for affiliation, as well as other needs.

Forces, Factors "Threatening" Viability of Neighborhood

Rapid change in community diversity—ethnicity, life cycle, status—that threatens neighborhood cohesion.

Demands by larger systems (metropolitan area, region, state, nation) **that threaten ability of neighborhood to fulfill residents' needs and meaning** as developed above (e.g., loss of jobs, increase in crime by nonresidents).

Stages and States of Neighborhood Systems

Stages of neighborhood development—Hoover and Vernon (1962) suggested that neighborhoods follow a series of stages generally marked by progressive decreases in social status after the early development from low density, rural uses to dense urban uses.

*A more complex view of neighborhood stages needs to be developed to pick up where the earlier stages stop, characterizing changes in functions fulfilled, stability of populations in terms of life cycle, ascriptive and achievement-oriented factors, and stages defined by other domains—economics and politics. Neighborhoods generally

(continues)

TABLE 8.8 (cont).

Stages and States of Neighborhood Systems

are defined in economic terms of growth and development, or by social changes linked to such factors, but it also is possible to describe neighborhoods in terms of how institutionally complete they are and how this evolves. Systems theory says that such systems increase in differentiation and complexity, but also know that some neighborhoods in decline show signs approximating a randomness, with fewer institutions, less structure. To some extent, neighborhood stages reflect external threats and periods of stability.

States of neighborhood social systems—Again, although systems theory says that systems tend toward increased complexity, clearly there are many examples of neighborhoods moving from periods of homogeneity (in terms of social relations as well as ascriptive, achievement-oriented, and life-cycle factors) to growing diversity and back to homogeneity. How are these states of the social system related to other factors, to states of the communication system, to factors describing links between residents and their neighborhoods?

States of neighborhood communication system—No attempts have been made to describe neighborhood communication systems as they evolve through time. However, like social systems, such systems can be envisioned as moving through patterns representing more or less complexity, weaker and stronger connections. In addition, neighborhoods can be viewed in terms of their reliance on interpersonal versus mass communication, the variety of channels available, the extent to which residents' personal communication patterns are located solely within the neighborhood, and so forth.

States of neighborhood political system—Although generally measured and conceptualized in terms of such factors as population, the number of different groups and social characteristics, the structural pluralism model conceptually is political in that it is based on and emphasizes the distribution of power in a social system. The literature has viewed communities as differing along a pluralism dimension, making level of pluralism equivalent to states of the system. However, it is possible to conceptualize the distribution of power as being more complex and multidimensional (e.g., the extent to which power is based on economic interests versus political legitimacy or other sources).

States of Neighborhood Networks

States of neighborhood social networks—The neighborhood social network might be expected to evolve in a manner that parallels changes in neighborhood diversity—in terms of life cycle, ascriptive, and achievement-oriented factors.

States of neighborhood communication networks—Neighborhood communication networks vary in terms of the variety of network concepts examined earlier—their density, information centrality, and so on. However, although systems may become increasingly complex, there is no reason to a priori state that a neighborhood communication network always tends toward complexity. Empirical evidence needs to be gathered to see how neighborhood communication networks evolve through time and the extent to which they are stable on various dimensions.

SUMMARY

Network theory and systems analysis each provides an opportunity for viewing neighborhoods as units themselves. In network theory, relationships and patterns of relationships are examined rather than individuals. In sociology, this refers to relationships between people; in communication, networks refer to communication relationships that often use the dyad as a building block for constructing larger patterns of symbolic activity in the neighborhood context. The two overlap because relationships between people can refer not only to familial, friendship or work relations but also to encoding and decoding activity patterned to establish and strengthen relationships. In systems theory, neighborhoods are viewed as integrated wholes, units of complexity that can be studied for their interrelationships.

This chapter reviewed network concepts, from the network metaphor to key concepts—objects or actors and a set of relationships in some domain or context—and characteristics of networks and individuals participating in them. Communication research employing the network perspective has been concentrated in organizations but a neighborhood can be conceived as a set of two overlapping networks, one consisting of residents linked in terms of social relationships, and one of residents as encoders and decoders.

Empirical network research suggests that neighborhood social networks are less dense and patterns of communication "weaker" as links deteriorate along with ties within the neighborhood. These are linked to neighborhood cohesion, neighboring and friendship patterns and residential commitment. Network characteristics also are linked to patterns of diffusion of innovations and the diffusion of information. Studies cast at the individual level but focusing on neighborhoods have examined the strength of people's communication links—both mass and interpersonal—and their relationship to community knowledge and community assessments. Results showed that an overall index tapping strength of links across interpersonal and mass communication channels and contexts was related to an overall QOL assessment index. Community knowledge was related only to the strength of mass communication links, whereas the strength of interpersonal links was positively correlated with an assessment of the QOL.

Systems theory has become a useful approach for integrating "strands of organized complexity." In contemporary thinking, the human is a natural entity inhabiting several interrelated worlds—as a biological organism, as a social role carrier, as a conscious personality, as a communicator who both encodes and decodes messages. Much of the literature employing network analysis in urban settings also views the community as a social system but seldom are the two perspectives integrated beyond stating assumptions that the system has a network and the network exists within a social system. This chapter offered a template for that task, including a blueprint of issues for integrating network theory and systems theory (identification of domains for application; characterization of units for systems theory by domain; characterization of units for network theory by domain) and a schema for studying neighborhoods across time (identifying variables conceptualizing links between residents and their neighborhoods; identifying forces and factors "threatening" the viability of neighborhoods; identifying stages and states of neighborhood systems; and identifying states of neighborhood networks).

9

Neighborhood Development and Social Change

- Neighborhoods and Governance
- Neighborhood Planning
- Neighborhoods as Development Units
- Neighborhood Participation as Social Action
- Neighborhood Quality of Life
- Summary

Urban debate often has focused on what cities "should" do or what they "should" be. And these arguments play a part in efforts to reconstruct city neighborhoods and solve social problems. As D. Hill (1988) noted:

> Dewey and Park criticized the big American city because its impersonal crowds and constantly shifting social structures leave the individual without the intimate territorial community support necessary for emotional health and democratic political participation. [Jane] Jacobs [1961] counters that territorial neighborhoods with centers and boundaries are impossible and undesirable in dynamic high-density cities. Family life and friendships based on work and interests form the basis for real city intimacy, while the basic units of the territorial community are the streets and sidewalks of individual blocks and street corners. She argues that the social instability of the modern city comes about because the city is separated spatially into stagnant ethnic, class, status, and age sections. That separation forces people to continually change living and working places throughout their lives.

> If a person could be born, work, prosper and age without having to leave
> the same diverse street and area, city social relations would become proper-
> ly stable and enriched. (p. 306)[137]

Notions of neighborhood and community are intermingled in the
development literature, so the two are integrated in the discussion. Summers
(1986) noted the distinction between those arguing for efforts to bring about
development in the community, for example, economic growth, improved social
services, and those focusing on development of the community, a distinction
also noted by H. Kaufman (1959).

> Treated in this way, community is essentially a territorial setting where
> social processes take place which may enhance the lives of at least some of
> the people who reside there or which may improve a locality's standing rel-
> ative to other localities. However, it is altogether possible that the process
> of achieving development in the community may produce development of
> the community. (Summers, 1986, p. 356)[138]

The notion of community development is closely linked to social
action in general, to resource mobilization, and to other perspectives on how
human activity occurs or is shaped to effect change. Drawing on research in
urban and rural areas in both industrial and developing countries, Checkoway
(1995) identified six strategies of community change: mass mobilization (creating change by amassing individuals around issues), social action (creating
change by building powerful organizations at the community level), citizen participation, public advocacy (the process of representing group interests in leg-
islative, administrative, and other established institutional areas), popular education (creating change by raising critical consciousness about common concerns), and local services development (process in which people provide their
own services at the community level). In the urban context, professional practitioners utilize the strategy that has the greatest likelihood of success and of
community empowerment.[139]

This chapter examines community development in the neighborhood
and how communication fits into longer term notions of neighborhood development, neighborhood involvement, and the QOL achieved. Chapter 10 focuses
explicitly on how communication fits into more directed, shorter term efforts to
mobilize resources for neighborhood development.

NEIGHBORHOODS AND GOVERNANCE

Aristotle and Plato viewed the state as the institution designed to realize the
final end of man, the good life (Long, 1975). Thus, the state was the human
organization to whose purpose all others were subordinate. What is the "pur-

pose" or function of the city and its neighborhoods in this conception? As Long noted, "the importance of ethos to the American city lies in the importance of the city's capacity to govern and the relation of that capacity to local legitimacy" (p. 43). However, R. Warren (1978) showed how the vertical institutions of the nation state and national markets have eroded the functions of horizontal institutions such as the city. Others also have noted that the city as currently constituted is relatively powerless to affect the lives of most residents, although it may enrich lives of a few (Dahl, 1961).

Long (1975) noted the view that the "vertical institutions of the nation state, public and private do not suffice to insure a viable local normative order and this fact is far from trivial" (p. 44). Long added that city neighborhoods have shown a quite impressive capacity to mobilize the resources of their inhabitants to make changes affecting the quality of their lives. Since the 1970s, this statement about neighborhood versus city power affecting residents' QOL might be questioned, but it does raise questions about what the neighborhood as a unit might do. Turner (1999) also noted that policymakers and urban planners often assume that low-income residents are pessimistic about improving their lives and are unlikely to organize. There also is a general belief that local citizens lack the problem-solving capacities to change their communities and the civic infrastructure to support their efforts.

The neighborhood is a platform for the exercise of power, but it often emerges as an important platform only when problems emerge at that level.[140] Eulau and Rothenberg (1986) looked at national election studies data to identify the impact of neighborhood as a geographical unit. They concluded that the neighborhood was not a "perceptually salient environment for political behavior" but the interpersonal context of neighborhood social networks had an independent impact on partisan affect for the parties and candidates, as well as voting preferences. Gans (1964) offered the view that people's lives are not influenced significantly by the physical neighborhood and the important aspects of life occur within the family, peer group, and on the job. Although this may be true for increasingly large numbers of people, the neighborhood also remains a source of identity and vehicle in the search for "community," particularly for newcomers to urban areas and singles. Furthermore, when problems occur at the local level, it is neighborhood units that often are mobilized by residents, and that process leads to a claim on council representatives and the governance process. Doyle and Luckenbill (1993) examined survey data collected from residents of eight Chicago and six Atlanta, Georgia neighborhoods in 1979-1980, finding that the best predictors of contacting officials were getting together with neighbors to solve a problems and membership in a block club. Thus, neighborhood participation through the block club was a key to involvement in social action. Income had no effect on the likelihood of contacting officials and education had only a weak and inconsistent effect.

NEIGHBORHOOD PLANNING

Neighborhood planning did not arise directly from the social activism of the 1960s and has roots that extend much further, perhaps 100 years (Silver, 1985). The formative phase (1880-1920) involved spreading the ideas of the neighborhood as a rallying point for social reform, followed by social science study of the neighborhood as a planning unit from 1920 to 1960. Revisionism was brought to the neighborhood movement and its constituency expanded in the 1960s and 1970s.

Reviewing the history of neighborhood planning, Checkoway (1985) noted that neighborhood-planning organizations cannot be expected to save urban areas from decline, and national policy and intervention are required.

> Neighborhood planning is a process through which people develop plans, programs, or services at the neighborhood level. Practitioners work in either public or private settings and in several substantive service or functional fields. They mix and phase methods and skills to develop community-based resources and to activate citizens to participate in decisions that affect their lives. Neighborhood planning is not a form of mandated participation in plans originated elsewhere or of outside advocacy for local groups, but a process through which people strengthen themselves as they strengthen their communities. (p. 472)

NEIGHBORHOODS AS DEVELOPMENT UNITS

Locating development in the neighborhoods can be both a top-down and a bottom-up phenomenon, a distinction that often gets embroiled in ideological positions. In urban centers, waiting for bottom-up development is a chancy proposition when center-city neighborhoods must compete with more attractive suburban areas; thus, city administrations long ago turned to neighborhood-based but politically accountable development organizations to lead planning and resource mobilization, particularly in the economic area but also through development of residential organizations or links with those already in existence.[141] At the same time, stressing ties with private groups is at the center of other efforts. A Republican senator is quoted as saying that community-based development fit the George Bush administration's program because it works from the bottom up, and is "the antithesis of big government programs that run from the top down; it involves people taking responsibility for their own communities and lives; it has strong support from the private sector."[142]

The institution most often associated with long-term development in neighborhoods is the community development corporation (CDC), a governmental unit charged with residential, business and social problem solving. Two sets of community studies (Rabrenovic, 1995; Ramsay, 1996) stress the importance of community and the impact of neighborhood associations. Looking at the post-World War II decline of Albany and Schenectady, New York, Ramsay (1996) described how the agricultural town of Princess Anne, Maryland and the fishing community of Crisfield, Maryland blocked economic development to stop changes in their ways of life. Rabrenovic (1995) also noted that the mobilization of Schenectady, New York residents in the face of rising crime, worsening local services, and high unemployment shows that even poor and socially fragmented neighborhoods have resources and that their residents can mobilize to address local problems. T. Robinson (1996) noted how CDCs act as agents of urban regeneration in an analysis of a San Francisco neighborhood.

To effect long-term change within neighborhoods, CDCs must involve residents and other stakeholders and this requires the establishment of effective communication patterns, including interpersonal and organizational links as well as mass media. Birru (1991) conducted experiments in two diverse inner-city communities undergoing economic development programs, finding that CDCs were vehicles for disseminating communication resources needed to engage communities in economic development. Also, communication led to more community participation, which in turn fostered community economic development. Thus, effective communication was a critical element for economic development. Wang (1995) looked at five such neighborhood organizations on the west side of Chicago and their relationship with the media, using participant observation, content analysis, and in-depth interviews. Despite the focus of the metropolitan press on urban problems, Wang found much positive news conveyed in news reports on residents' response to social problems with self-help actions. Results also showed that the community organizations had positive images but their neighborhoods negative media images. Results also contradicted the perceptions of community leaders that they could attract media attention only with confrontational tactics.[143]

Improved communication among influentials as well as within neighborhoods and the public is a theme running through comments of many observers concerned with neighborhood development. James E. Kunde, then urban affairs program director of the Kettering Foundation, said that urban leaders must use the media more. He described media as power in influencing public opinion but poor performers in sustaining dialogue (A. Kaufman, 1985). Franz and Warren (1987) noted that the growing professionalization of neighborhood action in the United States ran parallel to the formation of elaborate national networks of communication. Korte (1988) conducted a longitudinal study comparing two neighborhoods, one for which a neighborhood directory was produced and a second, control neighborhood without a directory. Results showed a small increase in the level of general help exchange in the neighborhood with the directory, where 14% of the residents used the directory to seek assistance from a neighbor or to offer assistance to a neighbor. There were no changes in the level of acquaintance among neighbors or satisfaction with neighbors or the neighborhood.

NEIGHBORHOOD PARTICIPATION AS SOCIAL ACTION

Although CDCs provide a link to the larger city government—and indirectly to state and federal resources—voluntary associations that reflect in part the neighborhood networks discussed earlier also are keys to development efforts. R. Jensen and Hammerback (2000) pointed out that communication scholars should broaden their interest beyond community mobilizing traditions (see chap. 11) to look at the community organizing tradition. The former often focuses on large-scale events designed largely for short-term support of social causes (e.g., marches used in the civil rights movement), whereas the latter emphasizes long-term development of leadership in the community (R. Jensen & Hammerback, 1998).

Voluntary neighborhood associations are as varied as their purpose. Some are improvement or protective associations. Although the decline-of-community thesis has seen considerable attention from urban sociologists, most empirical evidence has been cross-sectional, not longitudinal. An exception is a study by Lee, Oropesa, Metch, and Guest (1984); in a comparison of 1929 and 1979 characteristics of neighborhood organizations in the Seattle area, they found that groups met more often in 1929 and offered more opportunities for participating outside of formal meetings (e.g., parties); there also was a clear trend toward a more exclusively political emphasis among groups, and less social emphasis. In 1979, organizations were less restrictive on membership (e.g., 1929 groups were more likely to use property ownership to limit membership). However, they found that neighborhood groups at both times experienced difficulty in maintaining extensive involvement by residents.

Maintaining and increasing residents' involvement in neighborhood organizations is a long-standing problem. R. E. Park (1925/1967) proposed that social solidarity positively affects local involvement because neighborhood interaction fosters a sense of attachment to the neighborhood and increases awareness of common interest that, in turn, are foundations of neighborhood organization. Thus, stronger ties and stronger communication patterns among residents should increase organizational involvement. In another study of the Seattle area, Oropesa (1992b) surveyed some 1,642 residents, finding 19% belonged to neighborhood improvement associations, with 38% of them actively participating in group activities for an hour during the previous month.[144] Results showed that informal interaction among neighbors increased the likelihood of membership, but the relationship was curvilinear so that those with close friends and few friends in the area showed lower levels of membership. Similarly, community satisfaction showed a similar relationship, so that moderately satisfied residents were least likely to be association members. Thus, Oropesa (1992b) concluded that residents who engage in neighboring and who have some friends in the area are the best candidates for active participation in associations that strive to improve their neighborhoods.

Olsen, Perlstadt, Fonseca, and Hogan (1989) noted that the problem of promoting citizen participation in voluntary neighborhood associations is an example of collective action where a few participate and everyone in the neighborhood benefits. They reviewed a series of strategies for encouraging participation: neighborhood cohesion, community satisfaction, public concern, effective organization, community problems, political mobilization, status interest, and demographic characteristics. In a study of three East Lansing, Michigan neighborhoods in 1985, they found that 50% of those surveyed were unaware of the neighborhood association, whereas 8% were aware but uninvolved, 13% read the association newsletter, 11% belonged and paid dues, 9% attended meetings, and 10% served on committees or as officers. Six of the eight strategies provided significant predictors of participation; community satisfaction and public concern were discarded. The three strongest sets were neighborhood assimilation (interest in neighborhood, number of neighbors known, neighborhood a good place to live, length of residency, neighbors are friends, attend neighborhood gatherings), SES (home ownership, household income, education, occupational status, employment status), and political activities (attending meetings of public bodies, political actions in a club, writing letters to paper, officials, contacting officials, agencies). In a path model, SES affects neighborhood assimilation and political activities (which have a reciprocal arrow between them), which then affect neighborhood association participation. SES also makes a direct contribution.

Haeberle (1987) looked at citizen participation in neighborhood associations in Birmingham, Alabama, via a unique type of political activity that is similar to open public hearings extended from city hall to the neighborhood. The Birmingham Citizen Participation Plan (CPP) was created to improve communication between city residents and city government; the agenda for the forum was determined by the public. Looking at attendance by neighborhood, he found that the strongest predictors were environmental variables—population size, median rent, and age of housing. As the size of stock of older housing in a neighborhood increases, so does the participation; age was taken as an indicator that helps produce a community identity. The larger the neighborhood, the lower the level of participation. Socioeconomic variables (household income, level of education, percentage Black, and median age of residents) were poor predictors of neighborhood participation in CPP and none reached statistical significance.

Seeking to identify what influences the effectiveness of neighborhood organizations in a Seattle-Bellevue, Washington study, Oropesa (1989) found that the groups emphasized a diverse set of problems—from land use and services, to safety and neighborhood decline. Only groups under the control of neighborhood residents were included in the study. Neighborhood poverty was negatively related to overall success of the groups, but results suggest that this stems largely from a difficulty in recruiting skilled leaders rather than monetary resources or size of membership. They noted that professionals possess the communication and analytic skills to develop effective strategies leading to success.

If neighborhood organizations are tapped as mechanisms for delivering urban services or influencing their delivery, how representative are they of the public at large? Swindell (2000) collected data from both residents and volunteer-led neighborhood organizations throughout Indianapolis, Indiana; he found that organizations in neighborhoods with stable populations were better able to represent the residents' most important concerns.[145] Those groups that met more often—giving members more opportunities to voice their concerns and discuss issues—were more representative of neighborhood concerns.

NEIGHBORHOOD QUALITY OF LIFE

Research into QOL began in the early 1960s when concern arose over the secondary effects on U.S. society of national programs (Andrews, 1986; Schuessler & Fisher, 1985).[146] Quality of life measures and concepts were more frequently used as indicators of the success of efforts to solve problems or the need to take actions. Scholars followed the policy questions and researchers examined people's perceptions and assessments of the quality of life, as well as the dimensions of such global variables. Much of the QOL research focuses on the relationship between people's physical and social environment and measures of QOL, including the neighborhood. Campbell (1981) noted, "correspondence between our objective conditions and our subjective experience is very imperfect. If we try to explain the population's sense of well-being on the basis of objective circumstances, we will leave unaccounted for most of what we are trying to explain" (pp. 2, 4; also see Diener & Suh, 1997). Reporting on a lengthy program of research into the QOL, Campbell (1981) focused on the "mental well-being" of the American people, relying on a definition that is "entirely subjective, known directly to the individual person and known to others only through that person's behavior or verbal report" (pp. 13-14). This subjective QOL concept is further subdivided into global measures and those limited to particular domains (e.g., satisfaction with family life, work life, or community life).

In general, satisfaction with one's life as a whole (a global perceived QOL) is additive, reflecting the sum of one's satisfaction across various domains (Andrews & Withey, 1976; Inglehart & Rabier, 1986; Shen & Lai, 1998). Atkinson (1982) looked at satisfaction with job, finances, housing, and health and found most QOL measures were stable among people whose lives were stable. Atkinson concluded that his analysis of both domain and global QOL indicators should "dispel several doubts about the utility of subjective social indicators," which were shown to be stable in unchanging conditions and sensitive to change when it occurred.[147] Numerous studies over the past 20 years have related personal status and values to QOL. Indicators that have been related to QOL include age,[148] adequacy of income and satisfaction with standard of living,[149] occupation,[150] gender,[151] education,[152] marital status,[153] urban-rural,[154] ethnicity,[155] health,[156] physical appearance,[157] and nationality.[158] Personal values, goals, and perspectives shown to be related to QOL include personal needs,[159] internal states,[160] material and postmaterial values,[161] and religious commitment.[162]

The QOL literature offers a link between people and their neighborhoods. Mandell (1974) found that business executives and cultural elites decision to leave an area or remain in it was strongly predicted by their perceptions of QOL. Looking at national data, J. Robinson (1973) noted that neighborhood satisfaction is affected by residents' perceptions of how well kept up the neighborhood is. St. John and Cosby (1995) found that neighborhood satisfaction was greatest among life-cycle stages where residents' expectations and current conditions were most similar. "That there are life cycle differences in standards of comparison for assessing neighborhood quality is consistent with evidence that the elderly tend to be more satisfied with their life situations, including their residential environments, than younger people or than objective conditions would seem to merit" (St. John & Cosby, 1995, pp. 147-148). Looking at two groups of low-income, single-parent women participating in a rental subsidy program, Cook (1988) found that suburban respondents were significantly more satisfied with their neighborhood than their urban counterparts. Housing and location characteristics and residential attachment were more important to suburban than urban respondents. Neighborhood safety was important to both groups.

Nachmias and Palen (1986) looked at the relationship between neighborhood stability and revitalization in a Milwaukee neighborhood. They measured individual characteristics (time in neighborhood, age, education, income, and race), participation in the neighborhood social network (frequency socialize in neighborhood and number of relatives who live in the neighborhood), and neighborhood perceptions (20 items on neighborhood satisfaction and expected improvement in neighborhood). In one model using background and social network variables to predict home improvement and renovation activity, both socializing and number of relatives were positive predictors along with length of residence, age, education, and income. See Harris (1996) for community development experiences to enhance the QOL in low-income urban neighborhoods. Numerous scholars and other observers have looked at objective QOL indicators for U.S. cities and metropolitan areas (Garoogian, 1999; Lieske, 1990; Liu, 1978, 1979; Savageau & D'Agostino, 2000), U.S. suburbs (Willis, 1993), U.S. counties,[163] U.S. states (Meltzer, 1998), and world cities (Kurian, 1997; Marlin, Ness, & Collins, 1986), and the same can be done for neighborhoods (Gould, 1986).[164]

Fitzsimmons and Ferb (1977) looked at 10 communities, measuring citizens' attitudes toward 15 life areas that included education, health, employment on dimensions of importance, influence, equal opportunity, and satisfaction. Residents gave high importance and equality ratings (4 on a 5-point scale), a moderate 3.2 satisfaction rating, and a 2.9 influence rating. Communities also differed in their assessments among the life areas (e.g., importance of religious life ranged from 3.2 to 4.7 and communication from 3.4 to 4.1), although some life areas showed little variation (e.g., family life went from 4.6 to 4.8 and health from 3.8 to 4.3). Cluster analysis was used to see how the life areas grouped within each dimension; on assessments of importance, religion and family went together, as did education and employment. Two subclusters consisting first of government and law/justice and second of transportation and communication were grouped with economic base for a larger cluster. In terms of influence, community residents again grouped family and religious life together, and added recreation to the communication–transportation combo. Housing, an economic base and employment formed an economic cluster, whereas government, law and justice, welfare, health, and social services grouped together in another. Environment and education were located separately in the space. In terms of satisfaction, two of the clusters from influence are replicated: religious and family life; and transportation, communication, and recreation. The life areas of economic base and housing join with environment for another cluster. Education and employment form a separate cluster. And a larger cluster of the remaining breaks down into health and two subclusters: government, law and justice; and welfare and social services.

The QOL literature should be of interest to not only urban studies scholars but also communication scholars; however, there have been few attempts to examine how media and other communication variables affect people's QOL perceptions. Clearly, the mass media provide an abundance of images about the environment (at all levels and across domains) that people use to make comparisons and assessments about the quality of their lives, including how things are going at work or in the neighborhood, community, and country. Jeffres and Dobos (1993a, 1995) conducted three studies in the 1980s that found mass media use positively correlated with perceptions of the QOL in a U.S. metropolitan area.

Jeffres, Neuendorf, and Atkin (2000) reported on a research program that has been tracking people's perceptions of the quality of life in the metropolitan Cleveland, Ohio area for many years. The key global measure of people's perceptions of QOL in the metropolitan area and the measure of quality of life in the neighborhood were obtained in all six surveys, conducted as the NorthCoast Poll from 1992 to 1999. Each survey was presented as a general public poll of current issues and topics. Respondents were selected through traditional random-digit-dialing methods and interviewed using a CATI system.[165] A variety of QOL measures was tapped across the studies, but all six surveys asked respondents to rank the Cleveland area on a 0-10 scale, where 0 represents the worst place to live and 10 represents the best place to live; this was called Perceived Metro QOL. In four of the surveys, respondents used the same 0-10 scale to rank the neighborhood they live in (Perceived Neighborhood QOL).[166] The QOL measures used were those found most commonly in the classic QOL studies (e.g., Andrews, 1986; Andrews & Withey, 1976; Campbell, 1981; Campbell et al., 1976). Media use was tapped with the usual measures, which asked respondents how much time they spent watching TV yesterday, listening to the radio yesterday; how many days in the past week they had read a newspaper, the number of books read in the past 6 months, the number of times they had gone out to see a film at a theater in the past month, the number of magazines read regularly, and the number of videos watched in the past month—either rented, borrowed or purchased.[167] All measures of media use were standardized and indices created summing across the variables for level of mass media use, level of print media use, and radio-TV-film-video use. In the 1999 survey, several measures of communication technologies were added, including frequency one used e-mail in the past week, whether one has ever been on the Internet, the amount of time spent on the Internet in the past week, whether one has Internet access at home and at work, whether one has visited a local/community Web site, and three attitude items that tapped affect toward the internet (Internet attitude).[168] In addition, the Internet access and use items were standardized and summed up for an Internet use/access index. Measures of social categories, including formal education, household income, gender, race, and age, also were tapped.

An examination of the relationship between QOL assessments and use of the individual media showed that perceived neighborhood QOL and perceived metro QOL each is positively correlated with how often people read the daily newspaper but only spotty relationships are found for the other media. When media use indices are compiled, print media usage is positively related to the same two QOL indicators. All of these relationships generally persist when social categories (education, income, and gender) are controlled. Neither of the metro or neighborhood QOL assessments is correlated with the measures of communication technology, with a couple exceptions. After controlling for social categories—gender, race, age, education, and household income—perceived neighborhood QOL is positively related to frequency of e-mail use and Internet use.[169]

SUMMARY

Urban debate often focuses on what cities should do or what they should be. Thus, notions of neighborhood and community are intermingled in the development literature. The notion of community development is closely linked to numerous concepts—to social action, to resource mobilization, and to other perspectives on how human activity occurs or is shaped to effect change. This chapter examined community development in the neighborhood and how communication fits into longer notions of neighborhood development, neighborhood involvement, and the QOL achieved.

Neighborhoods are minor characters relative to the city as a whole as a platform for the exercise of power, but neighborhoods have shown an impressive capacity to mobilize resources of residents to make changes affecting the quality of their lives. Neighborhood planning extends back a century or more, but its current form gained currency in the 1960s. The institution most often associated with long-term development in neighborhoods is the CDC, which has been the subject of considerable research. CDCs often have positive images even when their neighborhoods have negative images. Improved communication among influentials as well as within neighborhoods and the public is a theme running through comments of observers concerned with neighborhood development.

In addition to CDCs, voluntary neighborhood associations are closely tied to neighborhood development. Maintaining and increasing residents' involvement is a long-standing problem. Informal interaction among neighbors increases the likelihood of such membership. Data also show that organizations in neighborhoods with stable populations are better able to represent residents' most important concerns.

The QOL literature offers a link between people and their neighborhood. In general, satisfaction with one's life as a whole is additive, reflecting the sum of one's satisfaction across various domains. One of these domains is the neighborhood environment. Neighborhood satisfaction is affected by residents' perceptions of how well kept up the neighborhood is; that satisfaction is greatest among life-cycle stages where residents' expectations and current conditions were most similar. Neighborhood stability and revitalization were linked in one study, with demographics and network variables predicting home improvement and renovation activity. Studies examining residents' perceptions of the QOL in their neighborhood and metro area found both were related to how often people read the daily newspaper.

10

Communication, Mobilization, and Social Action in Neighborhoods

- General Mobilization Theory
- Mobilization at the Community Level
- Communication Campaigns in the Community
- Diffusion and Networks
- Summary

Change at the community level, as noted earlier, is associated with a variety of theories, perspectives, and research traditions in sociology and urban studies, including collective action, social change, social movements, and resource mobilization.[170] Within communication, several additional theories and research traditions are pertinent—communication campaigns, development—generally employed in Third World contexts, and the diffusion literature.

GENERAL MOBILIZATION THEORY

Useem (1998) pointed out that mobilization theory replaced breakdown theory, once the dominant theory in the study of collective action, in the 1970s, when the latter could not account for contemporaneous events.[171] Resource mobilization posits that collective action stems from groups vying for political position and advantages (see Tilly, 1978). In this view, existing organizations, formal and informal, facilitate collective action by providing resources, by educating participants in civic cooperation and public mindedness and by enhancing interpersonal bonds.[172]

Pichardo (1988) argued that resource mobilization theory has had positive effects on the study of social movements and has generated a host of empirical and theoretical studies but it is also beset by internal disagreements that center around two models. The "professional organizer model" (McCarthy & Zald, 1973) and the "political process model" (McAdam, 1982) differ along a single dimension, the character of the involvement of elite groups in formation and maintenance of social movements. Resource mobilization theory stresses the technical aspects of social movement formation, finding people's shared grievances, interests, and aspirations less problematic than their ability to act on them collectively. Rather than asking why people want social change, the question shifts to asking how they can organize, pool resources, and wield them effectively.[173] Essentially, the theory seeks a rational basis for participation in such movements, which is viewed as a political process. Focus shifts from the rational nature of participation to the problems faced by organizers (see Giugni, 1998).

However, if a social movement is the product of groups organizing for social change, how are impoverished communities able to obtain scarce resources and create organizational structures? The professional organizer model posits the involvement of external groups and agents—from the middle class and influentials, who have the leadership skills and resources required. The political process model stresses the internal capacity of the minority community to generate organizations and limits the activities of elites to a supporting role that serves their own self-interests. Disagreements between these models concern the involvement by influentials in terms of resources, motivation, and the political environment. Pichardo (1988) argued that the two models can be reconciled by viewing elite involvement also as politically motivated to retain or gain power rather than viewing it as altruistic.[174] Furthermore, the professional organized model may be better suited in situations where the movements do not have a natural social base.

Social movements generally target not only powerholders but also the general public, and thus, public opinion must be taken into account in studies of social movements (Giugni, 1998). Consequently, communication variables become crucial as the link to either public, whether through standing interpersonal networks, formal contacts such as letters, or through the mass media. Communication is the vehicle through which organizers cement relationships within the movement, solicit new members, negotiate with influentials, and generate support external to the community. Calhoun (1998) said that previous protest movements have shown mass media facilitate popular mobilization but that they also make it easy for relatively ephemeral protest activity to outstrip organizational roots.

MOBILIZATION AT THE COMMUNITY LEVEL

Most of the social mobilization research is pitched at a higher level, in a general social context (e.g., racial unrest, war protests) or at the metropolitan community level, rather than in the neighborhood. Similarly, most of the communication research also is located at these levels, whether we're talking about communication campaigns, diffusion or development.

Schuftan (1996) characterized social mobilization as community development that gets people actively involved in the process—from assessment to analysis and action. It includes mobilizing resources, making concrete demands, networking, building coalitions, and consolidating sustainable social movements. Discussing the economic development of Montreal and other North American cities in the past couple decades, Klein, Fontan, and Tremblay (1998) suggested that community mobilization is creating a bottom-up socioeconomic development. Stoecker (1995) described how a neighborhood protest movement in East Toledo, Ohio changed over time to a development movement. The effects of community mobilization may differ by level (e.g., benefit activists through expanded friendship networks, build watchdog organizations that persist even if their social protest fails). In their evaluation of a substance abuse prevention project in local communities in Baltimore, Maryland, Peyrot and Fenzel (1994) concluded it is appropriate to view community organization as a network of neighborhood organizations, which serve as a mechanism for diffusing information and mobilizing residents. Information-gathering establishes communication channels that can be strengthened and developed further and that are used in forming mini-coalitions that strengthen community organization and mobilize prevention efforts.

Neighborhood residents, like people in general, mobilize around problems. When there are few problems, apathy reins and there is no need to engage in social action. Gotham (1999) examined the emergence of an anti-expressway movement in Kansas City, Missouri during the 1960s and 1970, challenging traditional urban analyses contending that an intimate bond of community identity must exist for individuals to engage in neighborhood collective action and political mobilization. He argued that community identity can be a political strategy used by neighborhood coalitions and civil rights groups to contest policies and mobilize constituents.

The nature of mobilization and the extent to which strategies can be implemented across neighborhoods is a significant, empirical question (see Thompson, Corbett, Bracht, & Pechacek, 1993). Grassroots participation also varies across cultures (e.g., Togeby, 1993, found major differences in the Nordic countries, with participation highest in Sweden and lowest in Finland, with Denmark, Norway and Iceland falling in between). Markowitz (1992) found that Soviet Jews who immigrated to the West during the 1970s have not established viable voluntary organizations, based on observations in New York City's Brighton Beach neighborhood in the mid-1980s.

Jeffres and Dobos (1984) posited a path model of communication and mobilization tested in a survey of urban neighborhoods. The model begins with perceptual frames (fear of decline and fear of gentrification), measures of commitment (time in area, intention to move, and home ownership), and social status (education and income); see Fig. 10.1. These predict to communication mea-

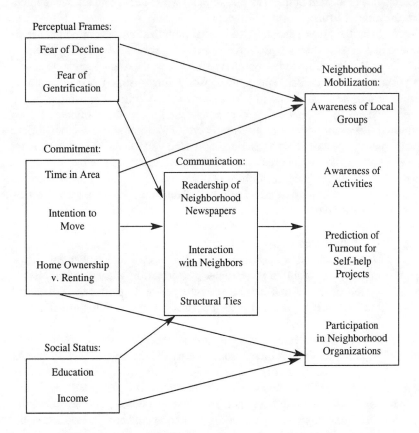

FIG. 10.1. Model of communication and mobilization.

sures (readership of neighborhood newspapers and interaction with neighbors) and structural ties, which are seen as affecting neighborhood mobilization in terms of four exogenous variables: awareness of local groups, awareness of activities, prediction of turnout for self-help projects, and participation in neighborhood organizations. Results showed that the key communication variable for awareness of local groups and their activities was readership of neighborhood newspapers. This is consistent with the diffusion literature, which shows media as playing a more significant role in awareness stages of campaigns. Neither of the other two communication and structural links was related to the dependent variable, and the only other measure related to awareness of groups was education. In a third model that predicted participation in neighborhood organizations, only the perceptual frames—fear of decline and gentrification—were significant predictors, pointing to the importance of motivation for organizational involvement. None of the communication or structural ties were significant mediators. In the fourth model, the block of communication and structural ties again was a significant predictor of predicted turnout for self-help projects, as was social status. Time in the area was a positive predictor and intention to move a negative predictor, both in direct paths.

COMMUNICATION CAMPAIGNS IN THE COMMUNITY

The importance of using both mass media and interpersonal networks in communication campaigns is well noted. Schooler, Flora, and Farquhar (1993) found complex interactions among media messages, interpersonal discussion, and individuals' knowledge, attitudes, and behavior in the Stanford five-city risk-reduction project. Attention to media messages increased residents' discussion of the campaign topic. Media messages covered smoking cessation and prevention, nutrition, blood pressure, weight control, exercise, and general heart health. Of the campaign messages, 60% were TV shows and spots, 30% newspaper and newsletter messages, 5% radio messages, and 5% other printed materials such as booklets. They propose a health education program that begins with media alerting people of the topic and making them aware of facts and prevention behaviors and other educational materials. This leads to increased perceived self-efficacy among residents, who initiate behavior changes as a trial, many not completely successful, and that leads to more interpersonal discussion and information seeking through the media. As a result, the behavior changes are more successful and self-efficacy greater. Treno and Holder (1997) noted the importance of media advocacy in community mobilization for implementation of prevention programs.

Emphasis on prevention in public health campaigns has become a focus of recent communication campaigns. McAlister et al. (2000) reported on a quasi-experimental HIV prevention project that used community newsletters distributed in selected communities, finding that the campaigns reached 40% to 80% of the intended audiences. Exposure to campaign messages was associated with theoretical cognitive determinants of behavior change and with risk-reduction behavior in communities otherwise not being effectively reached by HIV prevention messages; targeted attitudes and behaviors included condom use with main and nonmain partners and injection hygiene. The campaign utilized a "dual-link communication technique" (Bandura, 1986) found effective in other studies, with media communication being used to present peer models for behavior change and interpersonal channels being used to provide peer support and reinforcement for imitating the models.

Oropesa (1992a) looked at the mobilization of human resources in 62 neighborhood associations in Seattle, finding that newsletters and the value of residential property promoted membership and discouraged participation. The negative effect of newsletters was particularly evident for representative democracies in wealthy areas.

DIFFUSION AND NETWORKS

Diffusion is a key communication theory that describes a generally top-down view of how ideas and innovations spread through a social system, which can be a neighborhood. Diffusion theory has many roots and has been more widely used than almost any other model or theory in communication. The summaries of diffusion research by Rogers (1962/1995) are widely available.

Rogers initially laid out diffusion as a series of steps, from awareness to interest, to evaluation, trial, and eventual adoption. Thus, to use a neighborhood example, a community group trying to reduce crime through a lighting campaign would try to make residents aware of the innovation, interest them in participating, provide opportunities for evaluating the innovation and trying it out to the extent feasible, and eventually obtain adoption. Later, Rogers suggested the linear model of steps was too rigid in its application to all innovations, but it's still instructive in illustrating the process.

Research showed that mass communication channels were more important at the awareness stage, while interpersonal channels were more significant in later stages. Rogers also added a confirmation function in later models. Although criticized for being a "top-down" model, later iterations of diffusion theory took into account grassroots initiatives in the process (see the development literature, e.g., Rogers, 1976a, 1976b; Schramm & Lerner, 1976).

The diffusion model is useful in the neighborhood context, because community organizers and community leaders—internal or external—act as change agents within the diffusion process. Thus, a development corporation representative might use the diffusion model to get neighborhood businesses to adopt a storefront renovation program. Or a block club or improvement association might use the model to diffuse known crime-fighting techniques. In a survey of residents of three center-city neighborhoods, Jeffres and Dobos (1983) asked how they would learn about two spot news events—a local fire and a neighborhood shooting, the meeting of a local organization and a free paint program. Interpersonal, organizational, neighborhood media, mass media, and leaflets were major sources cited in the study. The key sources of diffusion about the critical news events were actual observation (44% for the fire) and interpersonal communication via neighbors and friends in the area (39% for the fire and 42% for the shooting). News of the meeting would diffuse largely through leaflets left in the door at home (68%) or from interpersonal channels (10%). News of the free paint program, a classic example of an innovation one would expect to be the subject of such a study, would diffuse through a variety of channels, including leaflets (33%), neighbors and friends (30%), groups or organizations (11%), and newspapers (9%). Women and younger residents were more likely to learn about the paint program through the neighborhood paper, whereas higher income people were more likely to cite the metro mass media. Neighborhood ties also were linked to the diffusion channel. Those most integrated into the neighborhood were more likely to learn about the paint program through leaflets or neighbors and organizations.

Clearly, the literature on social movements and resource mobilization can be integrated, to the extent that we're discussing community dissatisfaction with a situation and potential solutions.[175] When there is community consensus on the problem, some of the ingredients crucial in social movement and collective action literatures are of less importance, and the professional organizer model of social mobilization—with its emphasis on "how"—is elevated as a source of ideas. But, when people disagree on solutions to problems, the political process model returns to the discussion. In either case, an analysis of the specific neighborhood context and problem can draw applications from both.

Any analysis of how innovations diffuse into a neighborhood, or any other social system, would not treat the community as an "aggregate," and, thus, the structure of relationships and, more importantly, the communication network, become significant connections between the literatures on community mobilization and diffusion. Valente (1995) noted that the communication network determines how quickly innovations—ideas, opinions, and products— spread among individuals in a social system, and the timing for each individual's adoption.[176]

Diffusion, like collective behavior models, can be applied to a wide range of social change processes, from mundane daily activities to adopting complex computer innovations. Collective behavior examples include such processes as riots, revolutions, and community actions that are often political in nature, whereas innovations that generally are the focus of communication scholars employing the diffusion model are such things as crime prevention steps, using condoms to avoid AIDS, or using a new computer software program. As innovations diffuse into a community, adoption decisions often entail some risk and uncertainty. In collective behavior, people can rely more easily on some vague perception of what's normative behavior; risk is usually considerably lower because consequences of engaging in the behavior are considerably less. Also, the probabilities for two courses of action are better known for collective behavior than when the individual resident faces the adoption decision alone. When there's risk and uncertainty, residents are more likely to rely on the behavior of immediate others rather than on some perception as to what the social norm is (i.e., people turn to their neighbors and peers to gain more information and reassurance about potential adoption decisions; Valente, 1995).

Thus, a neighborhood or community communication network is important for adoption decisions. Valente (1995) identified two types of network diffusion models: relational models and structural models (Burt, 1987; Rice, 1993).[177] Relational network diffusion occurs when interpersonal influence flows through direct ties (e.g., the classical model of opinion leadership). Structural network diffusion occurs when interpersonal influence is a function of one's position in his or her social structure.

Valente (1995) analyzed six data sets with both network and diffusion measures. In relational diffusion networks, direct contacts between individuals influence the spread of an innovation. Four types of models based on types of contacts are presented: opinion leadership,[178] group membership,[179] personal and network density,[180] and personal network exposure.[181] All four posit that one's direct contacts influence his or her decision to adopt or not adopt an innovation.[182] The relational models demonstrate that innovativeness is influenced by the direct ties through which an individual sends and/or receives. If an individual receives many ties he or she is likely to adopt an innovation early because he or she is perceived as the system's opinion leader. "An individual's direct ties also determine his or her group membership and although the present research showed little direct effect of group membership on adoption behavior, in the extreme case of network isolation, isolates were found to be later adopters" (Valente, 1995, pp. 46-47).

Although relational models emphasize how an individual's direct contacts determine his or her adoption behavior, structural models consider the whole network. Thus, "the network influence on adoption for any individual cannot be determined by his or her nominations alone but must be considered in light of who everyone else in the network nominated" (Valente, 1995, p. 47).[183] According to structural models of diffusion, the rate and character of diffusion are determined by structural characteristics of the social system within which diffusion occurs. As network analysis increased in sophistication, so too did network models of diffusion. The first and perhaps most influential of network models of diffusion that emerged in the 1960s and 1970s was Granovetter's (1973, 1982) strength of weak ties,[184] which says that weak ties—people loosely connected to others in the network—are necessary for diffusion to occur across subgroups within a system (Valente, 1995, p. 49). Weak ties connect otherwise disconnected groups and act as a bridge for diffusion of innovations in a community context. Weak ties enable the innovation to be passed from one group within a network to another via someone who's either a member of both or someone acting as a bridge between networks. Weak ties accelerate the rate of diffusion.

Structural models employ a variety of concepts that locate an individual within a communication network. For example, centrality concepts include "centrality betweenness," the degree to which an individual lies between other individuals on their paths to one another. "Centrality closeness" measures the extent to which an individual is near other individuals in the network. Someone with high centrality closeness reaches others in the network more quickly and through fewer intermediaries than do those with lower centrality scores. Both betweenness and closeness are linked to greater likelihood to receive information and influence concerning innovations. "Positional equivalence" refers to the degree two individuals are similar in their relations to all others in the network. Diffusion of innovations theory argues that people monitor the behavior of their near peers and are influenced by those similar to themselves (i.e., modeling behavior). However, in his secondary data analysis, Valente (1995) did not find influence of network position on adoption behavior. "Structural equivalence" refers to the degree that two individuals have the same relations with the same others (i.e., the degree that two people occupy the same position in the social system). Those occupying the same position monitor each other's behavior and may adopt innovations at about the same time. Another concept is "threshold." This views people as having varying thresholds for adoption of an innovation. Earlier adoption occurs for those individuals with lower thresholds. Granovetter (1978) defined an individual's threshold as the proportion of the group he would have to see join before he would do so.

Some concepts represent characteristics of the network as a whole, not the individuals within the network. Thus, "network centrality" refers to the degree that the links are concentrated in one or a group of individuals. A centralized network contains a few members who are the locus of contacts, whereas connections are spread among many members in a decentralized network. Diffusion occurs faster in centralized networks because it spreads more rapidly once it's adopted by a central member. In decentralized networks, it takes longer for innovations to reach everyone in the network. Valente noted there is empirical support for the relationship.

SUMMARY

Change at the community level is associated with a variety of theories in sociology and urban studies—collective action, social change, social movements, and resource mobilization—and in communication—communication campaigns, diffusion, and development. Resource mobilization theory posits that collective action stems from groups vying for political position and advantage. Thus, in the neighborhood context, such organizations facilitate collective action by providing resources, by educating residents and enhancing interpersonal bonds. Research has stressed the technical aspects of social movement formation, focusing on professional organizing and political processes.

Neighborhood residents, like people in general, mobilize around problems. One study tested a path model of communication and mobilization across several urban neighborhoods. The model began with perceptual frames (fear of neighborhood decline or gentrification), measures of neighborhood commitment and social status; these predict to communication measures (e.g., use of neighborhood newspapers and interaction with neighbors), and structural ties, which affect neighborhood mobilization in terms of four exogenous variables—awareness of local groups, awareness of activities, prediction of turnout for self-help projects, and participation in neighborhood organizations.

The importance of using both mass media and interpersonal networks in communication campaigns is well noted. Neighborhood newsletters were significant in one study of neighborhood associations. Diffusion is a key communication theory that is useful in the neighborhood context because community organizers and leaders act as change agents within the diffusion process. In one study at the neighborhood level, interpersonal channels, communication within organizations, neighborhood media, mass media and leaflets were key sources of information about neighborhood projects and events. The neighborhood communication network is important for adoption decisions, and two models have been used to examine the significance of neighborhood networks for diffusion—the relational model—which focuses on direct contacts between residents—and the structural model, where interpersonal influence is a function of one's position in the social structure.

11

Urban Communication Systems, Neighborhoods, and Communication: Summary and Conclusions

This book began with a discussion of three key concepts—communication, community and neighborhoods,[185] and it ends with an assessment of what we know about their interrelationships and prospects for understanding future development. Ultimately, the significance of urban neighborhoods will depend on the extent to which they help people in their search for meaning in life. Thus, neighborhoods continue to be options, often minor ones, for people seeking meaning in their family, in friendships, in achievements and relationships in the workplace, in religious and philosophical beliefs, in ethnic and ascriptively defined heritage, in hobbies, interests and lifestyles providing fulfillment, and in neighborhoods and the larger community. Each of these offers a source for identity and fulfillment, and they often overlap each other, providing added strength to tightly integrated lives. Thus, some people live in intact, extended families in an institutionally complete homogeneous neighborhood that mirrors their ethnic heritage (e.g., "street corner societies") and offers a full range of opportunities for fulfilling one's personal and leisure interests. Each "circle" overlaps the others and the strength of the pattern is reinforced by communication patterns and relationships that both reflect and add to the strength.

However, today a relatively small percentage of Americans in urban areas fits such a description. Most work in one place, live in another and socialize in yet another. And both jobs and homesteads are more tentative as patterns of mobility and forces of the economy reduce one's tenure in any one location. The pattern of urban sprawl suggests that more and more people will live in

lives pulled apart by circumstances and other needs. In this scenario, some of
the work examined in this book will require further investigation to see whether
older findings persist or require development of new theories to capture and
describe significant relationships.

The first chapter examined the continuing significance of neighborhoods despite changes in technology, family patterns, and mobility associated
with employment. The neighborhood concept itself was distinguished from the
larger notion of "community" and personal ties, as well as the more precise
"academic" concepts that refer to more limited turf—natural community, the
community of limited viability, the organizationally dependent community,
social bloc, and residential area. A "neighborhood" has both social and physical
components as well as a pattern of interaction and ties and a common identification and experience.

The history of the neighborhood concept is a continuing story that
needs an author. This will require attention to not only the central city but also
to rings of suburbs facing their own problems and prospects. Old distinctions
based on such concepts as "bedroom communities" and "planned communities"
fail to capture the dynamic nature of changes in neighborhoods and their ability
to maintain and attract populations. The relationship between neighborhoods
and the larger community needs particular attention, with an integration across
disciplines that includes not only urban studies and sociology but also political
science, economics, communication, business, anthropology, ecology, and others. For example, would an inventory of neighborhoods in America's urban
areas show that more institutionally complete neighborhoods have a greater
chance of maintaining their viability across time, or do neighborhoods that
"specialize" show an ability to regenerate themselves quickly—and how do
these overlap with patterns of relationships and communication? Scholars from
many disciplines need to bring their concepts to the table and focus attention on
neighborhoods.

The second chapter examined the relationship between urbanism, pluralism, and communication, focusing on the relationship between size, social
structure, and communication. The impact of social structure on communication
processes is expressed in both the "linear hypothesis" (that size leads to diversity and differentiation) and "pluralism theory" (that communication networks,
mass and interpersonal, are constrained by the social structure-distribution of
power in a society). The key factors in the linear hypothesis exert their influence through social relationships, the notion being that common characteristics
of community are necessary for social bonds and warm relationships. Research
linking social relations with urbanism have examined neighboring behaviors,
community attachment, and community attitudes; so ethnic diversity encourages
social interaction among people from different backgrounds, urban residents
socialize more than less urban people and community attachment is lowest in
more urban areas but mobility and friendship ties are more important than
urbanism for one's integration into a community. Size and social structure

affect some variables that operationalize social relationships but not the full range of variables tapping neighboring, attachment, and attitudes. Much of the pluralism literature focuses on individual communities that are not part of urban areas. Because most Americans and most people in the world live in large metropolitan areas, the literature that focuses on differences within these areas should be expanded. In this case, size isn't likely to be the crucial variable, but other aspects of urbanism (e.g., density and distance from the core) might. Furthermore, pluralism in an urban context is a quite different matter; not only is the distribution of power within a community potentially important but the level of "power" in the neighborhood relative to the larger community is probably equally important.

Chapter 3 examined the empirical evidence between communication and community linkages, a multidimensional concept associated with such notions as community integration and community ties, the latter defined to include structural ties such as owning a home, social network ties such as the number of friends and relatives and interaction with them, participation in local groups, cognitive ties, personal identification with the neighborhood and affective ties with an area. Media use and newspaper reading in particular have been closely related to measures of community ties and integration, but evidence also supports a positive correlation between interpersonal communication variables and community integration. Measures of urbanism also have been linked to communication variables (e.g., interpersonal sources are more important in the central city). If, as the evidence suggests, a straightforward reflection hypothesis is too simple, then the relationship between community characteristics and communication phenomena should be treated as more complicated.

The growing diversity in America's urban areas should be captured in measures that can be linked to the performance of neighborhood media as well as diversity, strength, and content of interpersonal communication patterns. As one study suggests, perhaps it is diversity in terms of race, ethnicity, lifestyles, and personal goals that is more important than the power associated with economics and social status. Although community is generally viewed as being built on commonality, Rothenbuhler (2000) suggested that community can be seen as an "effort to construct a container of differences" and researchers should also look at how communication addresses differences that make up the community. This is a particularly apt point to make for diverse urban neighborhoods, where commonality is likely to be found in the problems facing residents rather than their common backgrounds, shared styles of communication or family relationships. He concluded that "community is more a matter of effort and faith than behavior, cause and effect" (p. 174). Some of the research in this books translates "faith and effort" as products of residents' finding meaning in neighborhoods rather than other domains of one's life.

The consequences of communication for neighborhoods were the subject of the fourth chapter. Given rather meager evidence for the linear hypothesis, size and social structure should not be expected to account for all the variability of communication patterns in communities. Over time, influence should flow in both directions as dense communication networks help community residents fight off threats and solve problems. Neighborhoods are formed through communication and their viability over time is likely to depend on maintenance of particular patterns of communication, but the empirical evidence is limited and there are almost no studies coinciding with the emergence of new neighborhood patterns. Several studies link both mass and interpersonal communication variables to sense of community.

Chapter 5 examined social relationships and communication. Although the two are closely linked, they are not the same thing. The pattern of one's social relationships in the community is not automatically "reflected" in a specific pattern of communication. With mobility, people's relationships have become tied less to proximity than to communication. Neighborhood relationships and communication are linked to neighborhood attachment expressed as use of local facilities, belonging to organizations, and feelings of attachment. Studies provide much evidence for the interrelationships among media use, measures of community involvement, and measures of community attachments.

Neighborhood communication patterns were the focus of chapter 6. Each neighborhood has a unique communication system that reflects the pattern of communication needs distributed among its residents as well as the constraints of geography and social environment. No studies have documented a neighborhood's communication system through a formal network analysis but case studies have identified some patterns. Neighborhood communication channels found to be important include both neighborhood newspapers and interpersonal interaction through organizations, institutions, and informal contexts. Personal communication networks provide another picture of how people are linked within neighborhoods.

Neighborhood newspapers were the subject of chapter 7. This "grassroots" medium links neighbors to each other while informing them of what's going on in their neighborhood. Various studies have found that neighborhood newspapers encourage community participation, create community identification, serve as a forum for public affairs, increase public knowledge of their community, and allow the community to mobilize and solve problems.

Network theory and systems analysis each provides an opportunity for viewing neighborhoods as units themselves. This was explored in chapter 8. Network theory looks at relationships and patterns of relationships rather than individuals; in sociology this refers to relationships between people, whereas in communication networks refer to communication relationships that often use the dyad as a building block for constructing larger patterns of symbolic activity in the neighborhood context. The two naturally overlap. Evidence shows neighborhood social networks are less dense and patterns of communication "weaker" as neighborhood ties are reduced. These are linked to neighborhood cohesion, neighboring, friendship patterns and residential commitment. Network characteristics are linked to patterns of diffusion of innovations and diffusion of information. The strength of interpersonal and mass communication links also was related to an overall QOL assessment index in one study. Much of the literature using network analysis also employs systems theory, but seldom are the two integrated. This chapter offered a template for that task, including a blueprint of issues for integrating network theory and systems theory.

Although many observers dismiss neighborhoods as relatively unimportant, they are at the center of any debate over what cities should do or should be. Neighborhoods are key players in discussions about urban redevelopment. Chapter 9 focused on neighborhood development and social change, whereas chapter 10 examined the relationship between communication and mobilization. In the urban studies literature, neighborhood development has been associated with the CDC. Improved communication among influentials as well as within neighborhoods and the public is a theme running through comments of observers concerned with neighborhood development. One study found support for a path model of communication and mobilization across several urban neighborhoods. The importance of using both mass media and interpersonal networks in communication campaigns and social action is well documented.

Recent literature calls into question whether the level of civic involvement initially documented by de Tocqueville will survive the pressures of modern life (Stolle, 1998; Stolle & Rochon, 1998). More research is needed that examines the types of neighborhood involvement, patterns of communication, and social change. Furthermore, can the Internet help sustain links between organizations and residents with severe time constraints? The QOL literature offers another link between people and their neighborhood. Cities across the United States are using different scenarios to attract new residents and maintain current ones as they redevelop their neighborhoods and fight off urban sprawl. Research shows that people adjust their assessments to fit circumstances, but more work needs to focus on QOL perceptions among the most mobile, those who have many options. Furthermore, what patterns of communication are most likely to attract and attach residents to city neighborhoods? If neighborhoods are to be a viable option in people's search for meaning and community, more attention should be paid to how communication fits into the environment, because it is only through communication that people develop a "sense of community."

MAJOR CONCLUSIONS AND DIRECTIONS FOR FUTURE RESEARCH

In addition to the preceding summary, several conclusions can be drawn across the broader literature. These also point to directions for future research.

- **Urban neighborhoods need to be separated from the generic "community" concept in studies of pluralism and communication.**

The defining characteristic of size and the critical mass it represents is missing when the larger metro system of which a neighborhood is a subsystem provides this dimension. Rather than focus on size, other community characteristics are likely to be more important (e.g., ethnic and lifestyle diversity). Functions of grassroots media, specifically neighborhood newspapers, parallel those of the larger media in strengthening weak ties and fulfilling development, redevelopment and mobilization roles; however, the extent to which they "reflect" the "power structure" is questionable. They may reflect external influential interests or the community "group" interests (e.g., ethnic interests rather than status interests). Furthermore, the Internet provides ties that ignore geographic boundaries in point-to-point communication and in forms of both social and economic organization. Some people are locating in more distant, non-metropolitan areas because they seek a less harried life and can telecommute to their job; at the same time, cities are employing ideas of "new urbanism" (incorporating such old ideas as porches) in constructing neighborhoods that attract people who seek out the QOL represented by a denser urban lifestyle. We need to examine the consequences of older concepts of community context (size and diversity) when people are more mobile and communication allows them to be strongly integrated into jobs and communities outside their community.

- **The link between local media/communication channels and the power structure is increasingly tenuous, particularly in urban areas.**

There are two points to consider. First, the "local" nature of mass media and other communication channels is threatened by not only by the Internet but also by other changes. Ownership is increasingly concentrated (e.g., radio stations are being merged into groups that share resources and ignore local content), and the appearance of satellite radio may act as an even stronger threat to localism. In addition, newspapers increasingly are sharing resources with other media, particularly in Web ventures that reach out beyond the community. Second, media that see their economic survival depending on factors outside the community are less likely to "reflect" the concerns of local influentials. Of course, it's an empirical question whether media will increasingly reflect a homogeneous "national" constituency or whether their behavior will follow traditional paths, but we should question whether newspapers will reflect a "consensual" versus "conflict" model when their "local" audiences are increasingly integrated into national communication systems.

- **Decisions to settle in neighborhoods/communities are not mere reflections of kinship and economics. The motivational factors need to be viewed as not only tentative but also as complex reflections of people's searches for meaning in life.**

Neighborhoods still are a source of identification and meaning in people's lives, although proximity has been diminished as a basis for interaction and communication. The historical literature is a good foundation but probably not a terribly useful template for describing how people in a mobile society select neighborhoods and communities and how that selection is tied to searches for both privacy and "affiliation" with other people ("sense of community"), status and economics, safety and beauty, convenience and location. Furthermore, the decisions themselves often are tied to patterns of communication that have changed from the past; thus, people today are using the Internet to survey neighborhoods before moving to a new city. These factors need to be brought into models that help us understand complex relationships between social characteristics, the physical environment, and patterns of communication.

- **The network of interpersonal relationships is reflected in the network of communication relationships, but the two are not isomorphic.**

We need to examine communication networks in their own right and not assume they reflect the pattern of personal ties perfectly. In particular, we need to examine communication networks based on proximity, friendship, family relationships, group affiliations, and instrumental relationships (e.g., organizationally dependent relationships, those who communicate and work together because they're striving to reduce neighborhood crime through CB patrols, block clubs, etc.). The network and systems theories have the potential for integrating communication theories with those in the other social sciences—urban studies, sociology, political science, economics. To do so, we need to determine the extent to which a neighborhood communication system links people within the neighborhood geographic system and how it balances with the communication links pulling them out of the community. In other words, to what extent is the neighborhood a social system and a communication system?

- **We need to expand the expressive power of our concepts in describing neighborhoods as social and communication systems through the suggestions in chapter 8 and through inductive generalization from empirical examination of diverse sets of urban neighborhoods.**

More comparative research is needed in studies that focus explicitly on urban neighborhoods and contrast them with other types of communities; such research requires considerable resources but the stakes are high. Studies can show more recent patterns of "successful" and "unsuccessful" neighborhoods in terms of the various dimensions used to define diversity, communication, and sense of community. Success should be defined in terms of a neighborhood's ability to help its residents find meaning in and enhance the QOL, not merely in terms of the level of income or social status.

Endnotes

1. See Cronkhite (1986) for a discussion of communication as a discipline and an explication of the concept.

2. Logan and Spitze (1994) noted Wirth's (1938) vision of "urbanism as a way of life," where the

> neighborhood is regarded as having diminishing importance in people's social lives. The anonymity of the modern metropolis is thought to have freed people from ties previously imposed by the local community. Its heterogeneity allows them to choose social partners based on common interests wherever they may be found: through the workplace, or voluntary associations, or as friends of friends. Distance is becoming a weaker constraint on interaction in industrial society: people can cover a wider territory in their daily routines, they can maintain contact at greater distances through telecommunications, and they are more likely to change their place of residence. The resulting social networks are not bounded by geography and have been described as "community liberated" in Wellman's (1979) terms. (p. 453)

3. Logan and Spitze (1994) noted:

> there are many reasons to expect the residential neighborhood to continue to focus people's social interaction. Spatial proximity makes it convenient to spend time with others in the neighborhood and creates common interests. Neighbors have the same access to jobs and shopping, they have the same exposure to crime and receive the same protection from the police, their children typically attend the same schools, they suffer the same earthquakes.

Neighborhoods are often socially homogeneous, certainly more so than the metropolis as a whole. Thus neighbors typically share bonds of class, race and ethnicity, religion and even kinship. The resulting mixture of instrumental connections, social homogeneity, and sentiment can be a powerful basis for collective action. (pp. 453-454; also see Logan & Molotch, 1987)

4. Apparently, no one has attempted an operational definition of what level of relationships is sufficient for a geographic area to become a community and, subsequently, carried out a study characterizing areas as neighborhoods and residential areas along with accompanying characteristics.

5. Citing Weber (1978), Brow (1990) said that *community* "refers simply to 'a sense of belonging together.'" He adds that the sense of belonging together combines both affective and cognitive elements, a feeling of solidarity and an understanding of shared identity. Closely related is the notion of *communalization,* defined as any pattern of action that promotes a sense of belonging together. This is also captured in Weber's refashioning of the contrast between gemeinschaft and gesellschaft, between communal relationships in which people's social actions are based on a feeling that they belong together and relationships where actions are based on adjusted interests (Brow, 1990).

6. In addition to community and neighborhood, there also is a need to define city; Wirth (1938) provided a "minimum sociological definition of the city" as a "relatively large, dense and permanent settlement of socially heterogeneous individuals."

7. He described five types of environmental variables, including spatial organization (including how dwelling units are related to each other, functional distance of residents) expressed in terms of space, distance, and contact points that influence how people interact; functional focal points (location of common facilities not determined by chance but by pre-existing needs); casual contact centers (e.g., paths, corridors, porches); and visual perception of the neighborhood (characteristics that influence its image). See Nasar (1990) for a study of residents' evaluative image of the city.

8. These include casual neighboring, social participation, family solidarity, leisure, and privacy.

9. Dorren (1998) analyzed the notion of neighborhood in Haarlem, a Dutch town in Holland, during the 17th century, when that state was one of the most urbanized in Europe.

10. Also see Schwab's (1988, 1989) study, which found the life-cycle model had the greatest predictive value compared to two other models of neighborhood change. Taking a much longer perspective and looking at cities in other countries, Carey (1976) provided a different view of the significance of age as a variable.

11. In defining neighborhoods, the "city" or community of which they are a constituent part also should be defined. Wirth (1938) defined *city* as a "relatively large, dense and permanent settlement of socially heterogeneous individuals."

12. Hamm, Currie, and Forde (1988) factor analyzed data describing Winnipeg neighborhoods to develop a typology of changes.

13. "We need more in depth studies that explore the historical experience of the neighborhood as part of the city and that examine the changing nature of this relationship over time. By doing so, historians can establish a context in which the role of the neighborhood can further illuminate our understanding of American urbanism" (Melvin, 1987, p. 267).

14. Employing an ecological systems model integrates the physical with the human or social.

15. Lalli and Thomas (1989) looked at communities as open systems influenced by superordinate structures, which are located within an urban political system. Examining decision making about a development project in Germany, they found that the "dominant impression in the media that the project had wide-spread support was not correct, and that the diffuse public opinion in the town was not congruent with the subjective attitude of the population" (p. 445). They argue for more interdisciplinary approaches. See Claval (1987) for a discussion of the academic literature on the region as a geographical, economic, and cultural concept.

16. They noted that regional economy "essentially refers to the economic structure and process within a certain geographical area," with most of the labor force and economic activity occurring within the area. If *neighborhood economy* is defined similarly to include only the economic structure and process within geographic boundaries, most neighborhood economies would be quite small. However, the concept usually is defined so that it implies labor force participation, occupational distribution and earning power of neighborhood residents. Furthermore, local residents' earning power can be treated as exports in the regional economy and employment of nonresidents by neighborhood businesses as imports.

17. Teitz defined *neighborhood* as "a contiguous subarea within a city or region that is seen by its inhabitants and others as possessing internal coherence and social meaning. Such a perception is usually associated with some important characteristics that may include social composition, ethnicity, economic class and structure, or physical attributes" (p. 114). He added that such units may or may not be incorporated as formal local governments but the term generally is applied to units that are part of a larger urban governmental entity.

18. Namboodiri (1988) said the "systematic study of interdependence within and among social organizations" is the "core of sociology" (p. 622).

19. Operationally, these are the percentage of residents with relatives living in their neighborhood; percentage of residents with best social friend living in their neighborhood; and percentage of residents with the person they depend upon most to discuss their personal concerns living in their neighborhood.

20. Operationally, these included percentage of residents likely to borrow or exchange things with their neighbors and percentage of residents likely to help or be helped by their neighbors with small tasks such as repair work or grocery shopping.

21. Cassel (1999) analyzed data from General Social Surveys to test the effect of voluntary association and church involvement on presidential election turnout in the United States from 1972 to 1992, finding both religious and nonreligious group activities moderately important predictors of turnout in all elections. Increases in civic skills did not explain group effects, and she suggested that an increase in sense of community may explain how group involvement stimulates turnout, or group activity and turnout may be manifestations of some underlying social participation concept.

22. Although looking at social dimensions of urbanism, not neighborhoods, Abrahamson (1974) found that the demographic aspect of urbanism has been exaggerated and suggests that historical and cultural forces may be more influential (e.g., regional differences were noteworthy). The same thing might be expected to occur for neighborhoods.

23. Hill and Bier (1989) showed how neighborhoods and the regional economy are linked, using Cleveland as an example. "It stands to reason that if the impact of economic restructuring is felt disproportionately by specific groups of workers it will be transmitted to where they live. Some neighborhoods will benefit, others will lose" (p. 125). They used data on poverty and housing prices as indicators of neighborhood change. Data supported their expectations. "The effects of economic restructuring are widespread but uneven. The link between the regional economy and the structure of neighborhoods is direct but difficult to model" (p. 142).

> The true impact of economic restructuring is felt by more than just those who either lose or change jobs. Because restructuring does not affect a random group of workers spread evenly throughout a metropolis, it generates spillover effects that reach into neighborhoods. Economic restructuring affects classes of workers and their families based on the occupation of the worker. In the case of Cleveland the spatial effects of restructuring resulted in changes in the vitality and prospects of neighborhoods and their residents. (p. 143)

Also see Wiewel, Brown, and Morris (1989) on mechanisms linking economic development at the regional and the neighborhood level.

24. Simpson (1995) said that the term *pluralism* is first found in a book by Furnivall (1948), who coined the term to describe the force of economic and political circumstances in colonial situations and the level of equilibrium among different cultural groups.

25. D. Barker (1998) concluded that if an individual surrounds him or herself with social networks that do not challenge his or her political views, the individual may experience more personal confidence and believe that he or she has more opportunity to affect political decisions.

26. Demers (1998) conceptually defined *structural pluralism* as the number of groups in a community or social system.

27. For those using a macrosocial perspective, there is a distinction between two views that are often pitted against each other—social control versus social change (see Viswanath & Demers, 1999). The former refers to intentional or unintentional attempts by social institutions or the state to regulate or encourage conformity to norms via socialization or coercion. The ideological and philosophical basis for many following this approach is materialism or an emphasis on beginning one's search for truth in macro-level theories. In mass communication, this is often characterized as the "reflection hypothesis." The latter, social change, focuses on processes and relationships that generate changes rather than stability in society. In mass communication, this appears in the "effects tradition."

28. The research is based on qualitative interviews of residents in two Chicago suburbs.

29. Blau distinguished between nominal categories and status; the former refer to such ascriptive characteristics as race, gender, ethnicity, whereas the latter refer to one's position on graduated scales of income, education, and so on. In Blau's (1977) analysis of multiple parameters, *structural conditions* are defined as the correlation of parameters. He said that consolidated parameters reduce the rates of social association among people from different strata and weaken their integration. The relationship between structural complexity and communication is important for the maintenance of groups, such as ethnic groups.

30. One factor that may account for the difference is the stability of the neighborhood communication system while other neighborhood factors or systems are changing.

31. To measure *Neighboring,* respondents were asked to use the same 5-point scale to indicate how often they and their neighbors entertain one another in their homes or yards. A second item asked how many of the people they knew in the 10 houses or apartments closest to theirs. Responses to the two items were standardized and added (α = .39). Both items are modifications of those in Wallin's Scale for Measuring Women's Neighborliness (Wallin, 1953).

32. To measure *Neighborhood Activity,* respondents were asked to use a 5-point scale ranging from *almost never* to *all the time* to indicate how often they did various things in their neighborhood, including going to shops and banks, attending a church or religious institution, going to the public library, walking down a neighborhood street, going to a fraternal club or hall, going to a neighborhood park, eating at a neighborhood restaurant, going to a neighborhood pub or bar, visiting a recreation center, visiting a neighborhood school, and going to meetings of neighborhood groups such as block clubs or other organizations (α = .63). These items have been used by Jeffres, Dobos, and Lee (1991; Jeffres, Perloff, Atkin, & Neuendorf, 2000) to measure neighborhood activities across various contexts.

33. To measure *Neighborhood Attachment,* respondents used a 0-10 scale (where 0 = *completely disagree,* 5 = *neutral* and 10 = *completely agree*) to indicate the extent to which they agreed with the following three items: "I enjoy living in this neighborhood"; "I feel involved in my community"; and "If I had to move, I'd really miss my neighborhood" (α = .63).

34. To measure *Perceived Community Solidarity,* respondents were asked to use a 0-10 scale (where 0 = *completely disagree,* 5 = *neutral,* 10 = *completely agree*) to indicate the extent to which they agreed with the following four items tapping perceived community solidarity: "Real friends are hard to find in this community"; "I feel like I belong in this neighborhood"; "This neighborhood lacks real leaders"; "Almost everyone is polite and courteous to you in this neighborhood"; "People work together to get things done in this neighborhood" (α = .31). The items were taken from Fessler's (1952) scale. To measure *Perceived Neighborhood Quality of Life* a single item was used: "I'd like you to imagine a scale from 0 to 10, with 0 being the worst place to live and 10 being the best place to live. On this scale, how would you rank the neighborhood in which you live?" This item has been used in a variety of studies (Andrews, 1986; Campbell, Converse, & Rodgers, 1976; Jeffres & Dobos, 1993a, 1995; Jeffres, Dobos, & Sweeney, 1987). The solidarity and QOL measures were combined with community attachment for a scale of *Neighborhood Affect* using standardized scores from perceptions of neighborhood QOL, perceived community solidarity (Csolidar) and community attachment (Cattach).

35. In his own research on community involvement, Rothenbuhler (1991) examined the Guttman scale used by Stamm and others, finding that two communication variables—keeping caught up with the local news and getting together with other people—are necessary to the community involvement process. Referring back to Dewey's (1916/1966) point that communication and community have a necessary relation and one could not exist without the other, Rothenbuhler added, "Communication is the beginning of community involvement. But not just communication of any sort, rather both gathering information and interacting with others" (p. 75).

36. Psychological attachment to one's community was correlated with the strength of one's interpersonal network and with an emphasis on localism versus cosmopolitanism.

37. White (1997) is skeptical of claims that the new technologies will increase citizen participation and he suggests that they will have little impact on voter apathy.

38. In Blum's study testing Blau's theory, results showed that social structure constrained choice (e.g., religious and ethnic heterogeneity encourages social interactions among people from different ethnic or religious groups). Measures of intergroup relations were based on the number of people respondents reported socializing during the 3 months prior to the survey.

39. The measure of *Neighborhood Communication* used items with several different formats to tap the strength of one's involvement in the neighborhood communication network. Responses to each were standardized before they were summed up for the scale. First, respondents were asked to use a 5-point scale to indicate how often they talk over the fence or sit on the porch in their neighborhood. Second, they were asked how many of the 10 closest neighbors they knew well enough to say hello or good morning to when they met them on the street. Third, respondents were asked to use a 0-10 scale where 0 meant they *completely disagreed*, 5 was *neutral,* and 10 meant they *completely agreed* with the following statement: "I spend more time talking with my neighbors than most people do." Fourth, residents were asked if they had relatives living in the neighborhood and how many they talked with that day. Fifth, respondents were asked how many people in the neighborhood (other than relatives) they talked to that day, including neighbors or people at local stores, in public places, or on public transit (α = .55). These items come from a variety of sources.

40. To measure *Interest in Neighborhood News and News Sources*, residents were asked, "How interested are you in news about what's going on in the [name] neighborhood? On a 0-10 scale where 0 means you're not at all interested, 5 is neutral, and 10 means you're very interested, what number expresses how interested you are?" Then they were asked to use a 5-point scale ranging from *almost never* to *all the time* to indicate how often they get neighborhood news from (a) other people in the neighborhood, (b) local community organizations, (c) neighborhood newspapers such as [name], (d) from the [name of largely suburban weekly chain], (e) the [name of metro daily], and (f) from radio or television.

41. To measure *Total Interpersonal Communication Links*, respondents were asked to think about the number of people they talked with "today" in different contexts, including within their household, relatives in the neighborhood, others in the neighborhood (see item above), people at work (if they worked outside the home), people elsewhere in the city, and people they talked with by telephone, local and long distance.

42. To measure *Mass Media Use*, respondents were asked how many hours of TV they watched yesterday, how many hours they listened to the radio, how many days last week they read a newspaper, the number of different magazines read regularly, the number of books read in the past 6 months, the number of borrowed or rented videos watched in the past month, and the number of times they went out to see a movie in a theater in the past month. Responses to each were standardized and then added for an overall media-use scale (α =.26).

43. Because no sampling frame exists for neighborhood and community newspapers, a variety of sources and a set of procedures were used to compile a master list. Community papers often are so small that they are easily overlooked. They also make frequent

changes in staff, location, format, and function as they grow. The goal was to obtain a variety of representative community papers in major cities so representation from newspaper chains where multiple papers emanated from a single office was limited. Once the revised list was completed, a pre-mailing was sent to the papers announcing that a questionnaire would come and urging their participation. Then a six-page questionnaire was mailed, with a system of follow-ups that included a postcard reminder, a second questionnaire, and finally a personal phone call. Adjusting the sample to reflect information from the phone calls produced a list of 321 papers, with 141 usable questionnaires and 7 unusable questionnaires returned, for a response rate of 44%. Responses for cities included in the sample were as follows: Baltimore, 6; Boston, 8; Chicago, 12; Cleveland, 18; Columbus, 2; Dallas, 6; Washington, DC, 5; Detroit, 4; Denver, 1; El Paso, 1; Houston, 4; Indianapolis, 5; Los Angeles, 20; Memphis, 0; Miami, 3; Milwaukee, 1; Minneapolis, 9; New Orleans, 2; New York, 10; Philadelphia, 9; Phoenix, 1; Pittsburgh, 5; San Antonio, 0; San Diego, 2; San Francisco/San Jose, 2; Seattle, 5. See the authors for more information on the response rates by individual cities.

44. The questionnaire prepared for the editors solicited information on a wide variety of topics. In the section on newspaper goals, editors rated the importance of a long list of newspaper "goals often attributed to neighborhood and community newspapers," using a 4-point scale: *very important, somewhat important, not very important*, or *totally unimportant* (plus don't know). The list of goals was constructed using the traditional list of functions but expressing them in terms of familiar types of content in most cases. The list was pretested with some community editors of urban papers and items with a uniquely urban focus added. In addition, several items were designed to measure editor's perceptions of the importance of conflict reporting style as conceptualized by Tichenor, Donohue, and Olien (1980). These included bringing people in the neighborhood together is a goal; getting people involved in solving neighborhood problems; getting conflict out in the open so the neighborhood can deal with it; trying to develop consensus in the community; avoiding problems, focusing on positive things in the neighborhood. See Tichenor et al. (1980).

45. Three concepts often are intertwined in this research: size, structural pluralism, and diversity. In the mass communication literature, measures of the three often are combined to examine relationships with media organizations and performance. This section examines conceptual relationships among the three. Size of population is generally used as a measure of "system size," whereas structural pluralism focuses on the distribution of power within the system and diversity refers to heterogeneity in terms of ascriptive characteristics (e.g., ethnicity, race, gender). These are the traditional sociological descriptors that Talcott Parsons saw as central to sociological theory (Mann, 1984; Tomovic, 1979). Ascriptive refers to those that people generally "inherit" or are assigned, whereas achievement-oriented factors refer to those stemming from one's labor. As systems grow in size, there is greater social differentiation, and this is often expressed as "structural pluralism" (Tichenor, Donohue, & Olien, 1999) and as "diversity." For Blau (1977), social structure refers to role relations and all characteristics of people that influence such relations can be designated as group membership (e.g., ascriptive, nominal categories) or status (e.g., income). This distinction parallels that between "heterogeneity" (or diversity) and "inequality," the latter reflecting the distribution of status and differences in power. This does not mean that material wealth or income is the sole source of power, but it has been used as a key measure in many studies. Greater size leads to

greater structural pluralism and to greater diversity, but how are those two concepts linked? Focusing on the societal level, Simpson (1995) examined the evolution of the concept of pluralism and points out that "pluralism is not presumed in heterogeneity" (p. 462). Although heterogeneity describes the existence of multiple social components or groups sharing a set of social institutions, pluralism describes a situation in which multiple cultural enclaves have their own set of social institutions. Clearly, most societies exist somewhere between these two pictures. Simpson pointed out that the ambiguous applicability of heterogeneity and pluralism results from failure to examine the relationship between patterns of stratification and of social organizations within a society. Simpson summarized definitions and components of pluralism according to numerous scholars (e.g., M. Smith, 1971, made distinctions between cultural pluralism, social pluralism, and structural pluralism based on level of citizenship). After examining definitions of pluralism across the social sciences, Simpson argued that pluralism cannot be considered a function or property of a distinctive type of society because all societies are racially and ethnically diverse to some degree. The dispersion of power among different social groups is not equivalent to the level of ethnic and racial diversity in a society.

46. Blau's formula for variance across categories was used. The formula, which provides the equivalent to statistical variance when the categories are ordered or interval data, follows: Diversity = $1 - [(category1^2 + category2^2 + category3^2)/ (category1 + category2 + category3)^2]$. Following are two examples computing diversity in gender for two samples, one with 90 men and 10 women and another with 60 men and 40 women. The first example, for a sample of 90 men and 10 women, is: $1 - [(90x90)+(10x10)/(100x100)] = 1 - [(8100+100)/(10,000] = 1 - [.82] = .18$. The second example, for a sample of 60 men and 40 women, is: $1-[(60x60)+(40x40)/ (100x100)] = 1-[(3600+1600)/10,000] = 1-[5,200/10,000] = 1- [.52]=.48$. As the examples show, when the population is concentrated into a single category, the resulting figure is small (.18), but when gender is spread more equally between the two categories, the figure is larger (.48).

47. Although all three summary indices—ascriptive diversity, life-cycle diversity, and status differentiation—are correlated with population, that capturing ascriptive diversity (gender, race, and language) is strongest ($r = .42, p < .001$). Thus, the larger the community served, the greater the diversity in race, language, and gender. The size of the community covered (number of square miles) is correlated with the index of overall diversity ($r = .33, p < .01$), whereas the second geographic measure (number of blocks) is correlated with language diversity ($r = .31, p < .05$) and income differentiation ($r = .27, p < .10$). Population was correlated with only one dimension of newspaper goals/functions—emphasis on advertising and theater, whereas size is negatively related to the dimension representing importance of editorials and not emphasizing development news.

48. Population is negatively correlated with perceptions that power in the community is held by institutions ($r = -.19, p < .05$), but population is not correlated with attributions of power to others or to perceptions of social, political, or economic conflict in the community served.

49. In a factor analysis, measures of newspaper goals and functions yielded eight dimensions, including:

1. the watchdog function
2. civic journalism and activism
3. covering churches, organizations, and personals

4. covering ethnics and social services
5. advertising and theater coverage
6. covering festivals and clubs
7. people, features, and photos
8. providing editorials and not emphasizing development.

50. For example, Lacy and Fico (1990) looked at chain ownership in terms of news quality and Connery (1989) examined management issues and the independence given reporters.

51. Editors were asked to rate the perceived quality of life in the neighborhood or community the paper serves, using a 0–10 scale where 0 represents the worst place to live, 5 is neutral, and 10 is the best place to live. They also were asked to use the same scale to tell how they thought residents would rate their community, and why; the reasons were coded as dummy variables. Editors also were asked to describe the image of the neighborhood/community shared by its residents. Responses were coded and then grouped into those focusing on people (were leaders closely knit, good residents), nature–physical factors (size, environment), housing and culture (architecture, housing), negative factors (bad area, crime), positive factors (good, education), and attitudes/subjective factors (exciting, peaceful, glitz, history). The range for these variables was 0–2. Two open-ended questions asked editors for major assets and problems of the community/neighborhood. Responses about assets were grouped into those focusing on physical factors (e.g., nature, temperature, size), people (ethnicity, diversity, tolerance, values, etc.), leisure (entertainment, culture, parks), economics (money, stores, jobs, industry), services (police, airport, hospital, etc.), and subjective factors (energy, pride, feelings); the range was up to 0–4. Liabilities were grouped into the following categories: economic factors (taxes, jobs, business), people (apathy, homogeneity), poverty (income level, income, aging area), housing, crime, roads (traffic, parking), government (mayor, budget, zoning), schools, public services, urban ills (explicitly stated), race, and environment (noise, flooding, pollution); the range was 0–3.

52. Respondents were asked how strongly residents were attached to the neighborhood and asked to check which of the following describes residents' feelings about their community: Most people feel fiercely committed to their neighborhood and would avoid moving elsewhere if at all possible; a majority of residents are strongly committed to their neighborhood but the rest have weak attachments; a few residents are strongly committed to the neighborhood but most are weakly attached and some would move if they had the chance; although there are some residents strongly committed to the neighborhood, most are weakly attached and most would probably move if they had the chance; there is almost no sense of neighborhood, and most people would move if they had a choice. Editors also were asked two items to ascertain the level of interaction in the community. The first asked "How much do people talk and communicate with each other in the neighborhood/community served by your newspaper?" They were asked to check from the following: you often see people talking on street corners and you see a lot of street activity throughout the neighborhood; you see a lot of people talking in a few places in the neighborhood but most areas have little street life; most activity is private, with almost no street life and few people chatting on the street. The second item asked "to what extent do people in your neighborhood limit their interactions to other folks in the neighborhood/community?" They were asked to check one of the following: people keep mainly to themselves and interact very little, people interact only with peo-

ple in the immediate neighborhood, people interact only with people outside the neighborhood, people interact infrequently with people both inside the neighborhood and elsewhere in the city, people interact frequently with people both inside the neighborhood and elsewhere in the community; responses were recoded for two variables, one tapping internal–external focus and one tapping frequency of interaction. To ascertain perceptions of community activity, editors were asked about "how much activity goes on in formal organized groups like block watch, clubs, charities, scouts, etc." and they were asked to check one of the following responses: there are a lot formal groups and many activities, there are a few very active formal groups but not many, there are few formal groups and few people active, there are almost no formal groups in the neighborhood. A second item solicited "how much activity in the neighborhood/community served occurs in informal situations, for example, people visiting each other's homes, socializing while playing card games, parties, etc." They were asked to check one of the following responses: there is a lot of this activity in the neighborhood, there is a moderate amount of this activity in the neighborhood, there is only a little amount of this activity in the neighborhood, and there is almost none of this activity in the neighborhood. Respondents were told the following: "Based on your discussions with people in the neighborhood/community and what you've learned, how informed would you say people are about current events?" Then they were asked to check from among the following categories: almost all adults are well informed about current events, most people are well informed but a few aren't, a few people are well-informed but most are poorly informed, almost all adults are poorly informed.

53. Respondents were told that communities vary and a variety of things are found in different neighborhoods, then were asked to check from a list those located in the community served by their newspaper. The list included major factories, manufacturing areas, several churches, retail stores, a local library branch, a local hospital, a covered shopping mall, many small convenience stores, a local park, a local recreation center, private ethnic clubs, local schools attended by area youths. A summary score for the number of institutions checked also was computed. Editors also were asked to assess the diversity of their community by estimating the distribution of several social categories, including race (Black, White, Hispanic, Asian, other), religion (Catholic, Protestant, Jewish, other), education (less than high school graduate, high school graduate, some college, college graduate or more), SES (poor, unemployed residents, moderate incomes/working people, middle class, upper middle class, upper class), and life cycle (families with kids, retired people, single people, couples with no kids). Six measures of perceived diversity were constructed, using Blau's (1977) formula for variance across categories as described earlier. In addition to the individual measures of community diversity, summary variables were constructed to represent cumulative measures of heterogeneity across editors' perceptions of community diversity in education, income, life cycle, and so on. To obtain a measure of perceived sources of power in the community, respondents were told that "getting things done takes power" and asked "what individuals or groups would you say have the most clout for getting things done in the neighborhood/community?" Responses were grouped into those featuring community groups (civic, development, activist), money (merchants, banks, industry), institutions (schools, police, unions, etc.), media, and government. Editors were asked how people get along in the community and some examples of conflicts. Results were classified as social conflicts (ethnic, old vs. new residents, generational, etc.), political (zoning, with city government, etc.), or economic (landlords vs. renters, vs. developers, landowners vs. the poor).

54. The editor's individual characteristics also have little impact on his or her reports of residents' image of the community. A few statistically significant correlations appear for reports of community assets and liabilities (e.g., younger editors are more likely to stress schools as a liability, women are more likely to cite housing as a liability, whereas men are more likely to cite crime, and education is related to seeing economic problems). Also, older editors see less commitment to the area, whereas those with more education see residents as interacting more outside than inside the community. Older and more educated editors also are somewhat more likely to say residents are less informed about current events. Individual characteristics show few relationships with the institutional inventory and perceptions of who has power or types of neighborhood conflicts. Older editors see the media as having more power in the community. The third set of variables was perceptions of community characteristics. As Table 1 in the appendix shows, the level of education is positively related to perceptions of community diversity, including overall diversity, religious diversity, and SES diversity.

55. As the table shows, QOL ratings are lower when the source of revenue is greater from other sources, but none of the paper's characteristics affects QOL ratings. Also, residents' images of the area are not related to any newspaper characteristics, but several assessments of assets and liabilities are related. For example, papers that are sold and not freely distributed are less likely to cite people or leisure opportunities as area assets. When papers have larger editorial staffs, editors are more likely to cite physical features as area assets and in papers with a larger circulation, editors are more likely to cite leisure opportunities as major assets. Editors of free papers are more likely to cite crime as a liability, whereas editors of papers that are sold are more likely to cite environmental liabilities. Editors in papers with larger circulations and with larger editorial staffs also are more likely to cite environment as a liability. Editors of more frequently published papers are more likely to cite housing as a problem. When papers are members of a chain editors are less likely to cite positive factors when describing residents' image of the area and they are less likely to cite feelings or attitudes as area assets. Chain editors are more likely to cite people and housing as area liabilities, whereas non-chain editors are more likely to cite government, urban ills, and racial factors.

56. Looking at editors' descriptions of residents' behaviors shows that editors of papers that are sold are more likely to see interaction as occurring more outside the neighborhood and for interaction to be less frequent. Editors of less frequent papers see more local group activity in the neighborhood. In papers with larger editorial staffs, editors are more likely to report that interaction is more internal to the community than occurring outside the neighborhood; they also see more of such street or public interaction in the area. Chain editors see more formal group or organizational activity in the community. Editors of papers that get more of their revenue from sales see their residents as more informed about current events, and those with larger portions of their revenue from advertising see more internal versus external interaction.

57. In the third category, community characteristics, only sources of revenue are correlated with diversity perceptions. The higher the percentage of revenue from advertising, the lower the perception of religious diversity, and the higher the percentage of revenue from sales, the lower the perceived life-cycle diversity. However, numerous statistically significant correlations appear in the institutional inventory reported by editors. Editors of papers with larger circulations and larger editorial staffs are more likely to identify a larger number of institutions as present in the community served and to also cite a major

factory, manufacturing, a shopping mall, and a private ethnic club. Editors of papers with less frequent publication schedules cite fewer institutions and are less likely to identify manufacturing areas, shopping malls, retail stores, or private ethnic clubs as present in their communities. Editors of chain papers cite fewer community institutions and are less likely to say their community has a major factory, manufacturing area, or a recreation center. The higher the percentage of revenue from advertising, the more institutions cited in the community and the more likely editors noted the presence of parks, recreation centers, several churches, retail stores, and local schools attended by neighborhood youth. None of the newspaper characteristics were related to editors' perceptions of who has power in the community and only one correlation was found for editor's reports or neighborhood conflicts: The higher the percentage of revenue from advertising, the less likely editors reported political conflicts in the community.

58. The relationships between the age, publisher and origins of the paper and editors' perceptions are found in Table 3 in the appendix; none of the QOL ratings are related to these newspaper characteristics. Editors of papers published or founded by individuals are less likely to see the neighborhood image in terms of housing and culture; the reverse is found for papers founded by community groups and merchants, for whom housing and culture are image factors. For papers founded by activists, editors report neighborhood images in terms of attitudes. The older the paper, the more likely physical factors and services available are cited as assets and the less likely people factors are cited. When papers are founded by community groups, people are seen as the major asset, and merchant-founded papers are linked to economic factors as key assets. Looking at liabilities reported by editors shows that older papers are linked to racial factors. When papers are published by development organizations, editors report that residents' commitment to the area is higher, whereas the reverse is found when papers are founded by individuals. Chain editors report less street activity, whereas those founded by merchants report more of such activity. Looking at editors' community perceptions shows that editors of papers run by development organizations see less SES diversity and editors of those founded by merchants report less life-cycle diversity. Editors of papers founded by activists see more racial and religious diversity. The older the paper, the more institutions reported in the inventory and the more likely a library and ethnic club is noted. Editors of papers founded by development organizations and merchants report factories in their communities, whereas those editing papers founded by activists do not. When papers are published by chains the editor is more likely to see power in institutions, whereas papers founded by individuals are less likely to see power in money interests or in the media themselves. Editors of papers founded by development corporations are more likely to see power in neighborhood groups, whereas those founded by merchants and activists see power in money. Editors of papers published by development organizations are more likely to cite political conflicts in the community, whereas those published by individuals are less likely to see such conflicts. Social conflicts are noted by editors of papers founded by merchants but are less likely to be noted by editors of papers founded by individuals and community groups.

59. As Table 3.1 shows, larger population is associated with lower QOL assessments. Also, editors of suburban papers give lower QOL ratings, whereas those of city papers give higher QOL ratings, the reverse of what might be expected. Also, editors of papers serving city neighborhoods see residents with an image that stresses people factors. Only a few relationships are noted for major assets (e.g., community size is related to citing

leisure opportunities and larger population to citing feelings and attitudes as area assets). Several community characteristics are related to area liabilities. Editors in communities with smaller populations are more likely to cite housing as a problem. Editors of center-city papers are more likely to cite the government as a major liability. An examination of editors' perceptions of residents' behaviors shows that the size of the population is positively related to estimates of the amount of formal group activity in the area. Also editors of city papers see their residents as ill informed, whereas those of suburban papers see the reverse. The number of zip codes served is positively correlated with total perceived diversity and to perceptions of racial and religious diversity. The size of population and number of zip codes served are correlated with the number of institutions noted in the inventory and to the presence of recreation centers, shopping malls, private ethnic clubs, and a local hospital. Population is also related to the presence of factories and manufacturing areas. More institutions also are cited by editors of suburban papers, with corresponding citations that manufacturing, malls, ethnic clubs and local schools were present. Several community characteristics also were related to editors' perceptions of who has power in the community. Power is seen in institutions by editors of smaller communities, those covering fewer zips and those serving cities. City editors also say power is in the "money" interests.

60. Table 3.2 gives the relationship between variables based on the census data and editor's perceptions. QOL ratings are negatively associated with total diversity, as well as diversity in race, household, marital status, and occupation. However, income diversity is positively related to QOL ratings. When the reasons given for perceptions of residents' QOL assessments are examined, income diversity is negatively related to citing ethnic diversity. Also, in communities with language diversity, editors are more likely to say residents have strong values, have a strong sense of community, and spend their entire lives in the neighborhood. Several diversity measures are related to editors' reports of the area's assets. The greater the age diversity, the less likely leisure opportunities are cited as assets but the more likely availability of services is cited. The same pattern is found for household diversity, which also is negatively related to citing physical assets. An examination of area liabilities shows that total census diversity is positively associated with citations that poverty is a major liability and that schools are a problem. The higher the racial diversity, the more likely editors are to cite crime as a liability and the less likely they are to cite government. The greater the age diversity, the more likely racial factors are cited as liabilities and the less likely people factors are cited. The greater household diversity, the less likely urban ills are cited as problems. The greater diversity in marital status, the more likely editors are to cite crime and housing as problems and the less likely government is cited. Language diversity also is associated with poverty and less likelihood government is seen as a liability. The greater the occupational diversity, the less likely people and government are seen as problems but the more likely schools are cited as a liability. And the greater the income diversity, the more likely roads, government and urban ills are seen as liabilities and the less likely housing is seen as a problem. Community diversity variables also are related to reports of residents' behaviors. The greater the racial diversity, the higher the local interaction perceived but the lower street activity and group activity. The higher age diversity, the greater street activity and the greater formal group activity. Household diversity also is related to greater formal group activity. The higher the diversity of marital status, the lower the level of street activity reported. The greater educational diversity, the greater interaction

is more external than internal to the neighborhood. The greater the occupational diversity, the stronger the level of residents commitment to the neighborhood, according to editors, and the more informed residents are. And the higher the income diversity, the lower the level of commitment to the area, the lower formal group activity and the higher external interaction is versus internal neighborhood interaction. Looking at community perceptions of editors, one sees that diversity in the census data is strongly related to perceived racial diversity. The higher the overall census diversity, racial diversity, language diversity, educational diversity, and marital status diversity, the greater the perceived racial diversity in the neighborhood. However, income diversity is negatively related. Also, diversity in households in the census data is negatively associated with perceptions of religious, life-cycle and SES diversity. The reverse relationship is found for marital status, where diversity in the census data is positively associated with racial diversity and SES diversity. The greater the occupational diversity, the greater the perceived educational diversity and the lower the perceived life-cycle diversity. The greater the income diversity, the lower the perceived religious diversity. Community diversity measures are related to the institutional inventory. The greater the overall census diversity, the greater the number of institutions reported by editors in their communities, and the greater the likelihood editors report their neighborhoods/communities have a hospital, recreation center, shopping mall, and private ethnic club. Gender diversity is related to having a library and racial diversity to having a hospital and private ethnic club. The greater the occupational diversity, the more institutions reported in the community and the more likely the area has a factory, a hospital, a mall, retail stores, and a local school attended by area youth. The greater the income diversity, the less likely a factory is reported but the more likely a library is reported. Editors' perceptions of who has power in the community also are related to community census measures but reports of neighborhood conflicts are not related to any community variables. The greater the racial diversity, the more likely editors say power is in groups and not in "money interests." The greater the diversity in marital status, the more likely power is seen in neighborhood groups but not in institutions. Power in groups also is linked to language diversity. The greater the educational diversity, the less likely power is seen in media, and the greater the income diversity, the more likely power is seen in government but not in institutions.

61. Influence between communication and community runs in both directions. As Adams (2000) also noted, interpersonal communication may provide the building blocks for community but people generally are born into or join communities rather than build them one relationship at a time.

62. Parks and Roberts (1998) examined development of personal relationships on line, finding that 94% of users of MOOs (multi-user dimensions, object-oriented environment) formed ongoing personal relationships on MOOs, most of which were close friendships or romances with the opposite sex. Mitra (1996) noted how ethnic communities can be built around the world using the Internet. See Viswanath and Arora (2000); Y. Kim, Lujan, and Dixon (1998); and Jeffres (1983, 2000; Jeffres & Hur, 1981) for how communication patterns and ethnic media affect assimilation and integration as well as group maintenance.

63. LaRose and Mettler (1989) found that rural residents were just as likely to have access to information technology as urban residents. They also were just as likely to use technology regardless of income, age, or employment.

64. A study of 189 Ohio neighborhood-based organizations found that their small size and budgets limited Internet access, with only three having full access. See Urban University and Neighborhood Network (1997).

65. According to Doheny-Farina (1996):

> A community is bound by place, which always includes complex social and environmental necessities. It is not something you can easily join. You can't subscribe to a community as you subscribe to a discussion group on the net. It must be lived. It is entwined, contradictory, and involves all our senses. It involves the "continuing, unplanned interactions between the same people for a long period of time." Unfortunately, communities across the nation are being undermined and destroyed by a variety of forces. Global computer networks like the Internet, for example, represent a step in the continual virtualization of human relations. The hope that the incredible powers of global computer networks can create new virtual communities, more useful and healthier than the old geographic ones, is thus misplaced. (p. 37)

66. *Strengthening "weak ties": Using the Internet to improve neighborhood communication* (1999).

67. Of the organizations represented, more than one fourth (27%) were from social services, whereas slightly more than one fifth (22%) were businesses, one tenth (11%) churches, followed by various ethnic and civic groups. See Volumes 1 and 3 of the project report for more information on participants and the project: *Strengthening "weak ties": Using the Internet to improve neighborhood communication* (1999).

68. Hills described the differing views of cities held by three individuals: Frank Lloyd Wright (1958), who saw humanity divided between two psychological types, nomad individualists—who love adventure and wandering, and cave dwellers—who loved settled life and cities and who he saw as the "true" Americans; Mumford (1938, 1961), who conceptualized good city and regional form from an ecological perspective that is against the nation-state; and Jacobs (1961), whose city-based regionalism and urban views came just as central areas of U.S. cities were being sorted by urban renewal, cut by freeways and emptied of people by suburbia.

69. "Racism, ethnic chauvinism, and class devaluation, I suggest, grow partly from a desire for community; that is, from the desire to understand others as they understand themselves and from the desire to be understood as I understand myself. Practically speaking, such mutual understanding can be approximated only within a homogeneous group that defines itself by common attributes" (Young, 1986, pp. 12-13).

70. Young (1986) said that city life "embodies difference as the contrary of the face-to-face ideal expressed by most assertions of community. City life is the 'being-together' of strangers. Strangers encounter one another, either face to face or through media, often remaining strangers and yet acknowledging their contiguity in living and the contributions each makes to the others" (p. 21). "The unoppressive city is thus defined as openness to unassimilated otherness" (p. 22).

71. In summary, variables from each domain—macro status, individual demographics, interest, communication, neighboring/affect—have direct paths contributing to the level of neighborhood activity. The model identifies constraints but also suggests several entry points for programs to increase residents' involvement in their communities. First, neigh-

borhood status is an inhibitor, which is no surprise. With status comes lower density and less proximity, more resources to make outside links and more reasons for doing so. Within that constraint, age is a physical detriment to community involvement at some point and education acts as another negative constraint to be overcome. However, given the community, the positive link between education and media use suggests using those channels—particularly pint media—to stimulate community involvement; the positive direct path from education to neighborhood activity is either an indication of greater overall activity in life or of neighborhood involvement in general so the predisposition seems to exist. Both gender and age generate higher interest in neighborhood news, which shows positive relationships with the local communication measures, suggesting potential paths of influence targeted for people-to-people, organizations, and local community newspapers; in fact, older adults and women are more likely to be involved in these channels.

72. Moemeka (1998) discussed communication in a communal society, which may differ from communication in more individualistic or collectivist societies. This also should be reflected at the neighborhood level. Moemeka said that personalism is a growing norm in both individualistic and urban communalistic communities.

73. Noble (1987) compared 50 males and 50 females in their use of the telephone for intrinsic (psychological neighborhoods of family and friends) and instrumental (information and business) purposes. Women made and received more intrinsic calls than did men. Men received more instrumental calls than did women but there was no gender difference for instrumental calls made.

74. "Intimate network members are those whom respondents 'feel are closest to you outside your home.' Significant network members are those non-intimates whom respondents 'are in touch with in your daily life and who are significant in your life.' Intimate and significant network members jointly comprise the respondents' sets of active network members. Other studies' estimates of the total number of informal ties—not just active ties—range from 250 to 1,500 (Wellman & Tindall, 1993, p. 70; also see Bernard et al., 1990; Pool & Kochen, 1978).

75. Werner, Altman, and Brown (1992) concluded that "the physical environment provides opportunities for communication that can facilitate neighborhood cohesiveness" but the cues and messages vary with time and circumstances.

76. With the emerging "communication grid" (Dizzard, 1989) being built as the "information superhighway," all of these communication patterns—person-to-person, group, organizational, and mass communication—can occur in the same context. No doubt the changing technologies will affect existing patterns of communication. Thus, it seems imperative that scholars do a better job of understanding those patterns for subsequent points of comparison.

77. Often, communication scholars have shifted their focus from the symbolic activity that Cronkhite argued should be the fodder of our study and concentrated on, for example, the enduring relationships forming the dyad (interpersonal communication), group processes and tasks (group communication), organizational productivity (organizational communication), or media institutions (mass communication). The distinction is easier when researchers ask themselves to delineate the target to which they want to generalize based on their research. If the concern is on the context rather than the symbolic activity (in context), the focus is not on communication.

78. Mastin (2000) examined a concept of civic participation that included serving on a committee to improve civic life, writing letters or circulating literature or holding home meetings concerning public issues, belonging to organizations that take a stand on community issues and problems, contacting public officials and volunteering to work on a candidate's election campaign. Thus, the index mixes local community involvement with overall involvement in political campaigns and civic issues. However, in regression analysis, church involvement and national media (watching cable TV, reading general interest magazines, and reading news or political magazines) involvement were significant predictors of the civic participation scale, with local media's (local TV and the daily newspaper) contribution approaching significance. Interpersonal discussion of issues with others was not related and neither were any of the social categories—gender, age, education and income. The sample consisted of African Americans interviewed in person.

79. Items included: (CMU4) "I enjoy striking up conversations with people I don't know when I'm waiting in line, sitting next to someone in a waiting room or while having a cup of coffee somewhere"; (CMU5) "I feel more comfortable talking with people like myself than with people who are different"; (CMU7) "I enjoy reading about what's going on in the country and around the world more than news about the local area"; (CMU8) "I wish there were more news in the media about my neighborhood and less about Cleveland or the metro area in general; (CMU9) "I enjoy reading the entertainment, sports, and features in the daily newspaper more than the general news sections"; (CMU11) "If there was some way I could send a message to everyone in Cleveland using mail by telephone or some computer hookup, I'd do it regularly"; (CMU13) "Even if it cost more, I'd like to have a cable system that had 500 channels so there was always something that fit my personal tastes"; (CMU14) "Sometimes I wish I were a columnist for the Plain Dealer and could tell everybody what I thought about what's going on today"; (CMU17) "I often feel the need to express myself and wish I had a chance to be a writer or reporter"; (CMU18) "I wish I had a chance to spend more time talking with other people in my neighborhood"; (CMU19) "I hate being alone and sometimes just leave the house to go somewhere so I won't be lonely and can talk with people"; (CMU20) "I value my solitude and welcome the chance to be alone and not have to talk with other people."

80. Items include: (CMU2) "I seem to spend much of my time at work talking with customers, clients or coworkers"; (CMU3)"Many days I don't talk with anyone outside my family"; (CMU6) "The people I see most often live in the same part of town I do"; (CMU15) "I spend a lot of time talking with friends and associates about things I find interesting, like hobbies, personal interests, or current events"; (CMU16) "I think organizations and clubs are a good way to find people you can talk with about similar interests."

81. Measures included: *quality of life*: multiple measures of respondent's QOL, across such domains as the nation, the metro area, neighborhood, job, and family; *community knowledge:* knowledge of the metro area, including nine items tapping people, places, and things from the past to the present; *personal identification:* measures of identification, operationalized with a set of items that allowed people to indicate the importance of different aspects of their life—family, job, ethnicity, community (neighborhood and the metro area), hobbies-leisure activities, and religion.

82. Names of communication informants were solicited from editors of community newspapers asked for advice on individuals who lived in the neighborhood, interacted with others in the community and were knowledgeable about the area.

83. Ettema and Peer (1996) discussed the language used by journalists in writing about economically depressed areas.

84. These perceptions of newspaper goals and functions may be related to but are quite separate from role expectations and activities captured in the portraits of U.S. journalists; see, for example, Johnstone, Slawski, and Bowman (1976) and Weaver and Wilhoit (1986, 1996).

85. The items were providing news of local festivals, events; linking consumers with advertisers; telling residents about local clubs, organizations, and so on; alerting residents to social services available; announcing personal items like weddings, births, and so on; keeping an eye on local public officials; discussing political issues in the metro area; covering local schools; covering local churches; covering crime news; giving residents a chance to sell via classifieds; reporting news of ethnic communities in the neighborhood; providing news about local theaters and entertainment in the neighborhood; alerting residents to local problems, conflicts; investigative reporting; covering neighborhood sporting events; editorials giving the paper's point of view; reporting news about redevelopment projects; features on local people; letters to the editor; printing articles written by local residents; getting residents' pictures in the paper. In addition, several items were designed to measure editor's perceptions of the importance of conflict reporting style as conceptualized by Tichenor et al. (1980). These included bringing people in the neighborhood together is a goal; getting people involved in solving neighborhood problems; getting conflict out in the open so the neighborhood can deal with it; trying to develop consensus in the community; avoiding problems, focusing on positive things in the neighborhood.

86. Massey (1998) examined civic journalism's routine use of including more average citizens into the news, finding that the profile of elites was reduced more than the profile of nonelites was increased.

87. Six began from 1900 to 1909; 2, 1910 to 1919; 7, 1920 to 1929; 10, 1930 to 1939; 10, 1940 to 1949; 10, 1950 to 1959; 14, 1960 to 1969; 33, 1970 to 1979; 30, 1980 to 1989; 3, 1990s.

88. Civic journalism is defined as journalism that tries to get citizens more involved in civic life. It is based on the belief that there has been a deterioration of public life and civic engagement and that public participation are essential in a democracy. Definitions and interpretations often vary, with an emphasis on making a difference, getting involved in the community and helping people set the public agenda. See Charity (1995) and Gade et al. (1997).

89. The impact of an extensive network of communication and neighborhood involvement is illustrated by Novek (1995), who described the experiences of almost 100 adolescents who published a community paper and learned how communication is related to community building.

90. The 13 papers represented were 5 profit-making concerns operated as businesses by companies or small entrepreneurs; 5 papers operated by neighborhood associations and nonprofit neighborhood groups; and 3 papers operated by neighborhood development organizations. Two editors were interviewed from one of the papers (during different years). Ten of the editors lived in the middle of the neighborhoods served by their papers, but two lived slightly outside the boundaries and two lived further away. Two editors were high school graduates, whereas eight were college graduates, two had some

college, and one had a master's degree. They ranged in age from 25 to 71, with a mean of 40.3 years. Three were in their 20s, two in their 30s, three in their 40s, one in their 50s and two were 65 or older. Five were married, four single, and the others divorced or separated. There were eight men and six women.

91. See Lindlof (1988) for a discussion of the extent to which interpretation of media content is a function of community membership.

92. Scott (1988) also noted that the central question in the development of social network analysis has been how serious to take the metaphor of a social network, which, at its simplest, involves a set of points connected by lines.

93. Homans (1986) viewed the study of social networks as the application of mathematics to the analysis of social structures. "A social network is a pattern of positive or negative choices, on some criterion such as liking or disliking, made by individuals for or against other individuals in a small group or much larger assemblage of persons. The study of social networks grew out of such psychological researchers as 'balance theory' (Heider 1946) and the description of concrete networks in Homans (1950)" (p. xxvi). "Social networks arise out of the choices individuals make for interacting with other individuals, from the development of cliques, and the development of hierarchies within cliques and among them. Social network research, with the exception of a part of 'balance theory,' cannot deal with these matters. They will have to be explained by a more general theory of social behavior, derived from an individualistic behavioral psychology" (p. xxvi). A sociologist, Collins (1986), identified networks as an area for creative work. Milardo (1992) discussed four methods used to define social networks—global, significant other, exchange, and interactive.

94. Looking at public relations processes as a formalized bridge between organizations and their environment (including other organizations and the media), Danowski, Barnett, and Friedland (1987) looked at how interorganizational network structures are associated with media use by organizations and with the effects on images that audiences hold about these organizations. Analyzing the Fortune 100 industrial corporations, they found firms which were more central in interorganizational networks received more media coverage in business publications and had more favorable public images.

95. Burt and Schott (1985) argued that the meaning of a relation content can be derived in part from the pattern of coincidence relations linking the content to others. Two relationships are of different kinds to the extent that they contain different contents.

96. In their book on network analysis, Knoke and Kuklinski (1982) discussed attributes—intrinsic characteristics of people, objects, events, which themselves may be involved in relationships (actions or qualities that exist only if two or more entities are considered together).

> Where attributes persist across the various contexts in which an actor is involved (e.g., a person's age, sex, intelligence, income, and the like remain unchanged whether at home, at work, at church), relations are context specific and alter or disappear upon an actor's removal from interaction with the relevant other parties (e.g., a student/teacher relation does not exist outside a school setting; a marital relation vanishes upon death or divorce of a spouse). A wide variety of relational properties can be measured: the strengths of the relationships among pupils in a classroom, the kinship

obligations among family members, the economic exchanges between organizations. A systematic classification of relationships will be presented below. (Knoke & Kuklinski, 1982, pp. 10-11)

Many aspects of social behavior can be treated from both the attribute and the relational perspectives . . . for example, the value of goods that a nation imports in foreign trade each year is an attribute of the nation's economy, but the volume of goods exchanged between each pair of nations measures an exchange relationship. (p. 11)

97. "These elements possess some attribute(s) that identify them as members of the same equivalence class for purposes of determining the network of relations among them" (Knoke & Kuklinski, 1982, p. 12).

98. Burt and Schott (1985) noted the following:

With the notable exception of ethnographers, network analysts rarely capture the complexity of naturally occurring relations. Their concern is less the complexity of the typical relationship between a pair of individuals than it is the complexity of the structure of relations among many individuals as a system. The relations described are analytical constructs—a relation's form being its intensity or strength as a tendency to occur and its content being its substance as a reason for occurring. The form of a friendship relation, for example, would refer to the intensity or strength of the relation while its content, its substantive meaning, would be friendship. Network models of social structure typically describe the form of relations while taking the content of those relations as a given, an item exogenous to the model. The most general of these models purport to describe formal structure in multiple networks among individuals in a system where each network consists of relations having the same content. (p. 288)

99. "If network analysis were limited just to a conceptual framework for identifying how a set of actors is linked together, it would not have excited much interest and effort among social researchers. 'The structure of relations among actors and the location of individual actors in the network have important behavioral, perceptual, and attitudinal consequences both for the individual units and for the system as a whole'" (Knoke & Kuklinski, 1982, p. 13).

100. Acock and Hurlbert (1990) argued that network analysis is useful for studying families.

101. Some examples of relational concept are: transactional relations (control over physical or symbolic "media"); communication relations (links between actors are channels by which messages may be transmitted from one actor to another in the system); boundary penetration relations (ties consisting of constituent subcomponents held in common, such as overlapping membership in boards of directors); instrumental relations (actors contacting each other to secure goods, services, information, e.g., job, advice, abortion); sentiment relations (networks in which individuals express feelings of affection, admiration, deference, loathing); authority/power relations (networks indicating the rights and obligations of actors to issue and obey commands); kinship and descent relations (bonds indicate role relationships among family members; Knoke & Kuklinski, 1982).

102. Network analysis has two alternatives for identifying positions in a complete network and determining which actors jointly occupy each position: social cohesion (degree

to which actors in a position are connected directly to each other by cohesive bonds) and structural equivalence (actors are aggregated into a jointly occupied position or role to the extent that they have a common set of linkages to the other actors in the system", Knoke & Kuklinski, 1982, p. 20).

103. "Dense communication networks engender similarity of perceptions and opinions among their members" (Laumann & Marsden, 1979).

104. Rice (1993) looked at how network concepts can be used to understand social influence and information processing in organizations. "Social influence models in general, and the social information processing model in particular, include three essential components: the ambiguity or uncertainty of the situation, exposure to influence, and some 'source other' who is valued by the individual and who is the source of the social information" (p. 44). In general, people are more subject to influence from others during times of uncertainty and ambiguity, and in unfamiliar or new settings, new tasks, and so on. Social proximity is defined as "the extent to which one can be exposed to influence from others in a given social system" (p. 45).

105. Rice (1993) noted relational and positional views of organizational networks; for the relational view, an organization is a communication network in which actors or other units process resources and information (Dow, 1988). The key influence mechanism here is communication proximity, or the extent to which individuals are directly or indirectly linked (Rogers & Kincaid, 1981). In the positional network view, proximity refers to the extent to which individuals occupy the same (or similar) social roles or positions, rather than the extent to which two individuals communicate with each other. Others also have noted the distinction between relational and positional bases for interaction and influence (Ranson, Hinings, & Greenwood, 1980). A third potential mechanism for social information processing is spatial proximity. "Simply working close to one another increases the likelihood of interaction among individuals, who then may develop similar attitudes" (Rice, 1993, p. 52). Many studies show relationships between physical proximity and communication interaction (Johnson, 1988; Nahemov & Lawton, 1975). Davis (1984) proposed three elements of the physical environment: physical structure (the nature and placement of furnishings and location that influence occurrence and type of interaction), physical stimuli (in the environment that affect what people attend to and concentrate on), and symbolic artifacts (which guide interpretation of the social setting and indicate status differences; Rice, 1993). Also see Arquilla and Ronfeldt (1998), Bullis and Bach (1991), Larose, Bernier, Soucy, and Duchesne (1999).

106. Hill and Hughes (1997) examined electronic group formation, focusing on political content, finding that liberal political USENET groups were less organized than other USENET groups but that the political USENET groups behave similar to other socially cohesive groups.

107. Babe (1996) argued for a communication-centered worldview rather than an economic model for examining information exchange, or communication. Barnett and Choi (1995) looked at a nation's position in the international telecommunication network, finding that the world's communication network may be described as a star with a hub and three spokes, one for Latin America, one for Europe, and a third for Asia and the Middle East. Language accounted for nearly 28% of a network's structure, whereas physical location explained 17%.

108. Allen (1977) found that formal and informal communication are functionally inde-

pendent, although formal communication is slightly more important (Rice, 1993). Laying out the historical background of network research, particularly communication networks, Barnett, Danowski, and Richards (1993) noted the limiting view of researchers who have thought of "the relationship defining communication links only as one of overall message exchange. This has been called a cohesion approach. It requires direct exchange of information between nodes" (p. 10). Woelfel (1993) said that networks consist of sets of interrelated nodes and may be classified according to the characteristics of the nodes and characteristics of the relationships among them. He focused on communication networks defined as "sets of nodes whose state is at least partly a function of the states of other nodes in the set. A network is a communication network, then, if the state of any of its nodes changes as a function of the perturbation of the state of another node in the set" (p. 22). Thus, he included both neural networks (brain) as well as those composed of interpersonal and mediated networks. "On the individual level, neural networks provide the organic substrate on which individual human thought and feeling take place, while on the social level, interpersonal and media networks provide the mechanism which gives rise to collective cultural experience" (Woelfel, 1993, pp. 22-23). He defined communication as "flow of energy" (p. 26).

109. Bolton and Dewatripont (1994) looked at the internal organization of a firm as a communication network designed to minimize both the costs of processing new information and the costs of communicating this information among its agents. "In order to economize on overall communication costs, an efficient network must have a centralized design . . . efficient networks take a pyramidal form. There is a wide variety of pyramidal forms" (p. 811). Concepts here include total communication time, specialization in processing, minimizing delay in processing, efficiency, structure (layers, pyramidal network), number of communication links, collection of messages received by any agent in network.

110. MacDonald (1976) looked at two roles in communication networks of organizations: liaison and nonliaison persons, which are defined by their relationship with others in the communication network. *Role* here refers to perceptions of members of how they and others function, who communicates with whom, what they communicate about, at what frequencies they communicate and with what person-defining consequences. In the study, separate networks were constructed for each of three message functions and liaisons were identified within networks. A "liaison" is a member with frequent communication contacts in at least two communication groups, whether or not he or she is a group member. A communication group refers to a subsystem of a network. Results showed that liaisons made and received more communication choices than other members of the staff. Liaisons were perceived by their nonliaison frequent contacts to have more control over the flow of messages than themselves. Liaisons were more satisfied with their jobs than nonliaisons. Liaisons tended to have more formal supervisory positions. Liaisons also were in the organization longer.

111. Richards (1993) noted that network studies have been conducted on such organizational variables as vertical and horizontal communication (Dubin & Spray, 1964; Porter & Roberts, 1973, cited in Richards, 1993; Roberts, O'Reilly, Bretton, & Porter, 1974), network size (Meyer, 1972), work dependencies, and initiation patterns (Davis & Leinhardt, 1972). Other studies have focused on aspects of the relationships linking individuals (e.g., transitivity and structural balance, equivocality, and environmental variety or volatility).

112. In traditional network analysis, the roles, or positions that people occupy are defined functionally. These include isolates (those who communicate with no one else in a specified time slice), bridges (group members who link two or more groups together and provide one kind of communication channel between them), and liaisons (who do not belong to a single group but who link groups, thus having more control over the flow of information in a network). Liaisons often serve as opinion leaders as well as gatekeepers in a network (Wigand, 1977).

113. "Uniformity of belief or attitude and behavior is commonly associated with relatively closed (bounded) social systems in which communication among members is unrestricted" (Kincaid, 1993, p. 113; also see Kincaid, 1988, 1987).

114. Centrality of a network has been defined in graph theory (Harary, 1990). Also, Freeman (1979) developed three measures of centrality based on this notion. Kincaid (1993) explained that dividing the total number of nodes by the total possible number provides a measure of *density,* another indication of the network's internal cohesion. Centrality based on *closeness,* or distance, is defined as the average length of the "shortest path" (geodesic) connecting a node to all other nodes in a network. Another concept of centrality is based on *betweenness measures,* the extent to which a node lies along the geodesic paths linking other pairs of nodes in the network. A node that functions this way for many pairs in the network is in a position of influence. Betweenness is "the proportion of geodesics containing a node that connect a pair of nodes out of all of the geodesics connecting that pair of nodes, summed over all of the pairs of nodes in the network" (Kincaid, 1993, p. 115). These three measures of centrality apply to individual nodes in a network, and averaging these measures over all the members of a given network generates aggregate measures of centrality that apply to the network as a whole. If average closeness is low, then network members are relatively close to one another in terms of communication. Stephenson and Zelen (1989) proposed another concept of centrality, "information centrality," defined as the number of lines in all of the paths that connect a pair of nodes. This measure represents the maximum information for combining paths.

115. *Entropy*—the statistical measure of information, or uncertainty reduction—is a useful concept in network analysis. "Networks characterized by high entropy cohesion have an equally probable or evenly distributed distribution of participation across members of the network. Networks with low entropy cohesion have participation (communication) concentrated among, or dominated, by a few members of the network. In fact Mackenzie (1966) presents empirical evidence of an inverse relationship between entropy and structural centrality in a communication network" (Kincaid, 1993, p. 114). "The entropy measure is limited, however, in that it only takes into account the direct links among members, and ignores the structure generated by indirect links in the network" (p. 114).

116. Barnett (1993) described how correspondence analysis, a metric method of multidimensional scaling, can be used to describe communication networks. Applied to network data, it allows for the simultaneous presentation of nodes as both sources and receivers.

117. Looking at both social structure and communication at the community level, Wigand (1977) said that communities "need to be studied in terms of their communicative patterns or the lack thereof. To do this systematically, a discussion of communication network analysis becomes imperative" (p. 143). "The more interaction that exists between two members of a social system, the stronger is that communication link. The overall communication structure of the system is determined by the recognized patterns

of these communication links and their relative strengths" (Wigand, 1977, p. 145). He defined social structure as the "persisting pattern of social relationships among social positions and social relationship is any linkage between incumbents of different social positions that involves mutual orientations" (p. 145). The communication role that a given individual plays in a system is determined by his position in the communication network. Various specialized roles develop which are important to the flow of communication in communities.

118. This integration is reflected in the characteristics of the network. A resident's closest friends are themselves usually friends of each other, thus constituting an "interlocking network." In a contrasting "radial network," one's friends are not themselves friends and do not interact with one other. A radial network is open to its environment, whereas an interlocking network is closed. Thus, new information from the environment is less likely to penetrate the interlocking network (Wigand, 1977). Laumann (1969; cited in Wigand, 1977; also see Laumann, 1976) found dyadic relationships in interlocking networks more homogeneous on politics, education, SES, and religion than were radial networks.

119. The perspectives of Fischer (1982), D. Warren and Warren (1977), and others lead to the conclusion that the neighborhood is only one of the social networks in which urbanites live and can be characterized as "a proximity anchored helping network" (D. Warren, 1975). Using two factors, external linkage of the neighborhood system to outside social systems and the extent and nature of internal social organization, D. Warren identified six neighborhood types: integrated, parochial, stepping stone, transitory, and anomic.

120. Bass and Stein (1997) noted differences in measuring network ties, comparing the social support questionnaire and social network list.

121. Van Tilburg, Gierveld, Lecchini, and Marsiglia (1998) noted that loneliness is more prevalent in regions of Europe where community bonds are strongest and living alone rarest. This inverse macro-level association, they argue, could be explained by differences in individual social integration. Also see Barrera and Baca (1990) and Query and James (1989) on social support networks.

122. Jones (1992) found that parental divorce had little impact on functioning of the friendship network but family conflict did affect the size and quality of the friendship network and increase feelings of loneliness.

123. However, looking at Internet communication in Argentina, Boczkowski (1999) pointed to the mutual shaping of national identities, software, and hardware development and practices.

124. "Communication ties may vary in strength, which has been defined as the . . . 'combination of the amount of time, the emotional intensity, the intimacy (mutual confiding), and the reciprocal services" (Granovetter, 1973, cited in Weenig & Midden, 1991, p. 735).

125. Several theories in mass communication are based on the cumulative effect of people's exposure to media channels. Thus, cultivation theory suggests that people's perceptions of the real world begin to parallel that of the "TV world" through constant and repeated exposure to channels that are redundant in their representations of images of crime, and so on (Gerbner, 1972, 1990). Similarly, agenda-setting theory is built on the notion that the cumulative build-up of media reports of social problems and issues leads to increased salience among audiences (McCombs & Shaw, 1972, 1974). Generally,

interpersonal communication is seen as a mitigating factor or intervening variables in these and other theories of media effects. When people talk with others about media topics, media influence is reduced. Research in diffusion theory provides abundant examples, with media channels more important at creating awareness and interpersonal channels at persuasion (Rogers, 1962/1995). However, pitting interpersonal and mass communication against each other makes little sense in an environment where new technologics and the Internet are erasing contextual differences between forms of communication (see Jeffres & Atkin, 1996).

126. Items include Com. in public areas (CMU4): "I enjoy striking up conversations with people I don't know when I'm waiting in line, sitting next to someone in a waiting room or while having a cup of coffee somewhere"; Communication Homopholy (CMU5): "I feel more comfortable talking with people like myself than with people who are different"; Neighborhood Com. (CMU18): "I wish I had a chance to spend more time talking with other people in my neighborhood"; Need for Interpersonal Communication (CMU19): "I hate being alone and sometimes just leave the house to go somewhere so I won't be lonely and can talk with people"; Need for Solitude (CMU20): "I value my solitude and welcome the chance to be alone and not have to talk with other people"; Communication Sender Role Across Contexts (CMU11): "If there was some way I could send a message to everyone in [metro] using mail by telephone or some computer hookup, I'd do it regularly"; Mass Com. Sender Role (CMU14): "Sometimes I wish I were a columnist for the [metro daily] and could tell everybody what I thought about what's going on today"; Mass Com. Sender Role2 (CMU17): "I often feel the need to express myself and wish I had a chance to be a writer or reporter"; Mass Com. Receiver Role (CMU13): "Even if it cost more, I'd like to have a cable system that had 500 channels so there was always something that fit my personal tastes."

127. Measures were Interpersonal Communication (IPC) Pattern at Work (CMU2): "I seem to spend much of my time at work talking with customers, clients or coworkers"; Family vs. External Locus Pattern (CMU3): "Many days I don't talk with anyone outside my family"; Communication Homopholy Pattern (CMU6): "The people I see most often live in the same part of town I do"; Interpersonal Communication with Friends (CMU15): "I spend a lot of time talking with friends and associates about things I find interesting, like hobbies, personal interests, or current events"; Clubs/ Organizations as Context for Communication (CMU16): "I think organizations and clubs are a good way to find people you can talk with about similar interests."

128. Laszlo (1996) said that the science of Galileo and Newton developed because it could handle relatively simple relationships, which could be tested, and which presented a world picture of a universe reducible to such relationships. At the beginning of the 20th century, with the breakdown of mechanistic theory within physics, sets of interacting relationships came to occupy the center of attention with their "staggering complexity" (Laszlo, 1996). In biology, where the laws of physics were insufficient to explain the complex interactions in a living organism, new laws had to be postulated, "not laws of 'life forces,' but laws of integrated wholes, acting as such. . . . New laws were postulated, which did not contradict physical laws but 'complemented' them. They showed what highly complex sets of things, each subject to the basic laws of physics, do when they act together. In view of parallel developments in physics, chemistry, biology, sociology, and economics, many branches of the contemporary sciences become, in Warren Weaver's phrase, 'sciences of organized complexity'—that is 'systems' sciences" (Laszlo, 1996, p.

8). "Equipped with the concepts and theories provided by the contemporary systems sciences, we can discern strands of organized complexity wherever we look. We ourselves are a complex organized system, and so are our societies and our environment" (pp. 8-9).

129. Laszlo (1996) viewed a shift toward rigorous yet holistic theories, "thinking in terms of facts and events in the context of wholes, forming integrated sets with their own properties and relationships," which has replaced "uncoordinated specialization" (p. 16). He added, "Systems thinking gives us a holistic perspective for viewing the world around us, and seeing ourselves in the world. It is a way of organizing, or perhaps reorganizing, and our knowledge in terms of systems, systemic properties, and inter-system relationships" (p. 16).

130. "Contemporary science concentrates on organization: not what a thing is 'per se,' nor how one thing produces an effect on one other thing, but rather how sets of events are structured and how they function in relation to their 'environment'—other sets of things, likewise structured in space and time. These are invariances of process related to real-world systems. We shall call them 'invariances of organization'" (Laszlo, 1996, p. 17).

131. Laszlo (1996) offered the hypothetico-deductive method, setting up a working hypothesis as a working tool and seeing whether it works in experience, asking: "What are the characteristics any observed thing must have if it is to be considered a natural system?" (p. 24). This is more efficient than merely attempting to catalog anything that one comes across, and it's also in keeping with science as process across time.

132. According to the Second Law of Thermodynamics, natural systems/physical world run down, although the process may be postponed; a particular configuration of parts and relationships that is maintained in a self-maintaining system is called a *steady-state*, one in which energies are continually used to maintain the relationship of the parts and keep them from collapsing in decay. One might consider what is a steady state of a neighborhood or its communication system and what happens that might disrupt each and how they might return it to steady state (e.g., maintaining "sense of community").

133. Self-creativity is a response to changing conditions that cannot be offset by adjustments based on the existing structure, so self-creativity is a precondition of evolution. "If natural systems were merely to maintain the 'status quo' throughout the range of circumstances they encounter there would be no evolution, no patterns of development, and nothing we would call progress. . . . Natural systems evolve new structures and new functions; they create themselves in time" (p. 39). There are two forms of change, preprogrammed change such as evolution and growth of an embryo based on information coded into its genes, and, secondly, the creative advance into novelty, which in nature may be self-transformation of entire species; there are "change-buffering feedbacks within all open systems," where there is progressive modification of behaviors (Laszlo, 1996, p. 53).

134. According to Laszlo (1996):

> On the level of contemporary multiperson systems, macrodetermination is even more striking. We see corporations, universities, social organizations, and political regimes take on determinate structure, and we see that this structure does not impose mechanistic determinacy on their members. Sociocultural systems have openings for certain kinds of roles, from presidents to shoeshine boys. Persons with adequate qualifications can fill the jobs, regardless of their unique individuality. Roles are not made for given

individuals, but for "kinds" of individuals classes according to qualification. When the roles are filled, the particular personality of each new tenant is reflected in his interrelations with others, and it produces corresponding shifts within the organizational structure. There is flexibility within the system, as part adjusts to part. (p. 85)

It is due to such plasticity that complex systems remain viable under changing circumstances. Totally mechanistic systems have only two states: a functional one where all parts work in the rigorously determined manner, and a failing one where one or more parts have broken down. They lack the plasticity of natural systems, which act as dynamic, self repairing wholes in regard to any deficiency. (p. 86)

The inverse side of macrodetermination is "functional autonomy." The functional autonomy of parts within a natural system adds up to the macrodetermination of the whole. Functional autonomy does not mean independence. A fully autonomous (independent) set of units would not constitute a system, only a heap. Systemicity is imposed as a set of rules binding the parts among themselves. But these rules do not constrain the parts to act in one way and one way only; they merely prescribe that certain types of functions are carried out in certain sequences. The parts have options; as long as a sufficient number of sufficiently qualified units carries out the prescribed tasks, the requirements of systemic determination are met. (p. 86)

135. Cultures are "value-guided systems" that define man's need for such values as rationality, meaningfulness in emotional experience, richness of imagination, and depth of faith (Laszlo, 1996, pp. 76).

If we survey the conclusions that emerge from these findings, we find that our objective basic values are those which we share with all natural systems. Each of us "must" (in the sense that he or she cannot help but) commit himself to survival, creativity, and mutual adaptation within a society of his peers; the alternative to these is isolation and death. But there is no imperative attached to the cultural specification of these values. These we can choose according to our insights. Of course, we "must" (in the same sense as above) remain within the limits of general natural-systems values. Finding and respecting these limits is precisely the problem facing us today. (p. 80)

136. Laszlo (1996) said:

We know fairly clearly what constitutes organic health for our biological system; now we must likewise learn the norms of our manifold ecological, economic, political, and cultural systems. . . . The supreme challenge of our age is to specify, "and learn to respect," the objective norms of existence within the complex and delicately balanced holarchic order that is both in us and around us. There is no other way to make sure that we achieve a culture that is both viable and humanistic. (p. 92)

137. Hill (1988) added, "With respect to open participation in political processes, she is skeptical of the small neighborhood unit. She views political districts of 100,000 persons as necessary to have reasonable leverage on big city governments" (p. 306).

138. He defined community development as "planned intervention to stimulate social change for the explicit purpose of the 'betterment of the people'" (p. 360). Summers discussed different intervention strategies: authoritative (by an external agent), client-centered (with emphasis on equality and citizens' control over lives), radical reform (programs guided by radical reforms such as Marxism). Also see Christenson and Robinson (1980).

139. See Schuftan (1996) for an explication of the meaning of empowerment in community development.

140. Tulloss (1995) noted that the structure of residents' participation in development policy is constantly being challenged and shaped by developers, community residents, and public officials. She adds that the institutionalization of citizen participation in development policy in Boston, Massachusetts, is the result of current and historical economic conditions and political mobilization.

141. Ryan (1994) noted that the Community Development Society in its first 25 years viewed collective action as a product of the individual decisions of people who come together to pursue similar self interests. More recently, collective action is viewed as a product of both individuals and groups.

142. Senator Robert W. Kasten, Jr. of Wisconsin was quoted in an article by Neal R. Peirce, a contributing editor of the *National Journal*. "Election might shake the cities," *Plain Dealer*, Oct. 24, 1992, p. 7B.

143. See Bartsch (1989) for a review of government programs promoting community development.

144. Oropesa (1992b) noted that the patterns of membership are consistent with the Chicago School and community of limited liability perspectives, both of which suggest that length of residence in an area is positively correlated with membership.

145. Also, organizations claiming larger areas were more representative of their residents than those of less populous neighborhoods, but this may be due to geographic location of the larger neighborhoods in suburbs, which have fewer problems.

146. Concern with people's pursuit of happiness did not originate in the modern era. Happiness was a significant preoccupation of the eighteenth century when Thomas Jefferson included the pursuit of happiness as an endowed right in his draft of the Declaration of Independence (Campbell, 1981).

147. In psychological approaches, origins of QOL are found in the satisfaction of personal needs, which are viewed from a variety of perspectives (e.g., Maslow's, 1954, hierarchy of needs and notion of self-actualization; also see Sirgy, 1986), and other internal states (Abbey & Andrews, 1986; Bryant & Veroff, 1986) such as perceived control over one's life (positively related to positive QOL perceptions; Campbell, 1981, pp. 214-215). Abbey and Andrews (1986) used structural modeling to analyze a data set of outpatient pharmacy clients, finding that internal control, social support and performance increased QOL while stress and depression decreased QOL, and control by others was unrelated. Juster and Courant (1986) look at the relationship between QOL and "process benefits," or enjoyment of the activities themselves rather than outcomes (e.g., one may dislike

housecleaning but feel good about having a clean house); they found the two measures almost unrelated across a variety of activities. Economic approaches view QOL maximization in terms of resource distribution. Looking at people with material and postmaterial values in their cross-national data, Inglehart and Rabier (1986) found relatively little difference on overall QOL satisfaction measures but differences on the value of different domains and activities (e.g., materialists valued leisure time, doing interesting things, getting along with friends, and the views of others that one was useful and well thought of). Lightsey (1996) noted that personality traits and psychological resources are important for human well-being.

148. Younger adults are less satisfied with where they live (Brennan, 1986); levels of satisfaction for all aspects of life except health rise with age (Campbell, Converse, & Rodgers, 1976; Herzog & Rodgers, 1986). See Raphael, Renwick, Brown, and Rootman (1996) for approaches that consider QOL in relation to health. See Powell (1998) for the QOL and "myths of aging" and Abeles, Gift, and Ory (1994) for research on factors affecting the QOL over the life span.

149. Income is positively related to both subjective and objective QOL measures (Ackerman & Paolucci, 1983; Campbell, 1981), but income explained only a small part of the variance of subjective QOL in cross-national data (Inglehart & Rabier, 1986). Also see Sirgy (1998).

150. Occupation makes minor contributions overall; executives and professionals are highest in perceived QOL and the unemployed are lowest. Job satisfaction was related to overall QOL perceptions (Michalos, 1986). Also see Warburton and Suiter (1996) for the impact of job dissatisfaction on QOL.

151. Bryant and Veroff (1986) found both men and women use the same six dimensions in making personal QOL assessments. Also see Camporese, Freguja and Sabbadini (1998) for a recent survey looking at women's lifestyles and QOL.

152. Education is unrelated or only modestly related to quality of life, Campbell et al. (1976) noted, but modest relationships were found in cross-national data. Ross and Van Willigen (1997) propose that education improves well-being because it increases access to nonalienated paid work and economic resources that increase sense of control over life and access to stable social relationships, including marriage. Two national surveys in 1990 and 1995 found well-educated people have lower levels of emotional distress and physical distress but not of dissatisfaction.

153. Marriage contributes to overall happiness in cross-national and U.S. data (Campbell et al., 1976). Keith and Schafer (1998) looked at three marital types (e.g., equal partners) and the QOL. Others have examined the QOL during widowhood (Shea & Schewe, 1995) and of single-parent homeless families (Cline, 1995). See Keith and Schafer (1998) for research on QOL and marital types. A study in Slovenia found life satisfaction associated with good family relationships, as well as good health, living in a nonpolluted environment and opportunities to learn and apply knowledge at work (Svetlik, 1996).

154. Urbanites are less satisfied (Fernandez & Kulik, 1981). Also see Parfect and Power (1997) for planning as a factor affecting urban QOL. McCormick (1997) found that the QOL in three small rural communities was linked to remote locations and size. Baldassare and Wilson (1995) noted the decline of suburban QOL ratings. Also see M. Jensen and Leven (1997).

155. Ethnic differences on QOL have been found but there is an interaction between race and income (Campbell et al., 1976). See Kar et al. (1995-1996) for research on an exploration of Indo-American quality of life; Kar, Jimenez, Campbell, and Sze (1998) for research on QOL and acculturation; and Hughes and Thomas (1998) for the continuing significance of race on QOL assessments.

156. Health is important for older people and a priority when problems exist (Campbell et al., 1976). Bowling (1997) looked at measurement of health as a factor in one's QOL.

157. People judged as more attractive say they are more positive but not "more satisfied" with their lives (Campbell et al., 1976).

158. International comparisons show many similarities in perceived QOL (Inglehart & Rabier, 1986; Szalai & Andrews, 1980). Veenhoven (1996) used a "happy life expectancy" index to measure QOL in terms of output, length of life, and level of happiness within a country. Empirical data from 48 countries collected in the early 1990s shows happy life expectancy highest in northwest Europe and lowest in Africa. Happy life expectancy is higher in nations that are more affluent, educated, free, and tolerant, variables that explain 70% of the statistical variation in happy life expectancy.

159. These are viewed from different perspectives (e.g., Maslow's, 1954, hierarchy of needs and notion of self-actualization).

160. Abbey and Andrews (1986) found that social support, internal control, and performance increased QOL while stress and depression decreased QOL; control by others was unrelated.

161. Cross-national data found few differences on overall QOL measures but differences on value of different domains and activities (Inglehart & Rabier, 1986).

162. Religious commitment is positively related to QOL (Hadaway & Roof, 1978; also see Campbell, 1981; Francis & Evans, 1996; Inglehart & Rabier, 1986, p. 17).

163. See Research Associates of Washington (1994).

164. Also see Ervin (1984) for a study relating residential structure with measures of the QOL.

165. The surveys were conducted in the winter of 1992-1993 (Survey 1), the spring of 1993 (Survey 2), the fall of 1993 (Survey 3), the spring of 1995 (Survey 4), and the spring of 1996 (Survey 5), and spring of 1999 (Survey 6). Sample sizes were Survey 1, 331; Survey 2, 320; Survey 3, 302; Survey 4, 313; Survey 5, 377; Survey 6, 321. The response rate for each survey was either slightly above or below 50%. See the authors for more details about the individual studies.

166. In four surveys, respondents were asked to use 0-10 scales to indicate how "satisfied" they were with "how things are going in your job or at work" (Perceived Job QOL), "how things are going in your family" (Perceived Family QOL), and "how things are going in the nation today" (Perceived National QOL). The quality of the local media was assessed three times (Perceived Media Quality): in the first survey respondents used the 0-10 scale to rate their "confidence in the greater [metropolitan] area media"; in the second survey respondents used the same scale to tell how "satisfied" they were with the "local media—newspapers, radio and TV"; in the fourth survey they used the same scale to tell how "satisfied" they were with "the quality of the local media—newspapers, radio and TV." In one survey respondents assessed their "confidence" in three metro domains using 0-10 scales; they evaluated their local schools, local police department and public

transportation in the metro area. In the second and sixth surveys respondents were asked to indicate on a 0-10 scale how satisfied they were with "your personal life" and also asked how happy/unhappy they were. All QOL measures were standardized and a Quality of Life Index was formed by summing across the standard scores, creating a summary QOL measure. Following are the alpha's for the quality of life indices: Survey 1, α =.61; Survey 2, α = .42; Survey 3, α = .60; Survey 4, α = .56; Survey 5, α = .44; Survey 6, α = .68.

167. To keep the length of the interviews to 10 to 15 minutes and to accommodate special interests in specific surveys, all media use measures could not be included in each survey.

168. Respondents indicated the extent to which they agreed or disagreed with three statements: (a) The Internet will change the world for the better, (b) The Internet violates people's rights to privacy, and (c) the Internet will provide lots of information. The scale for the second was reversed in the coding, responses to all three were standardized, and the responses were summed up for an index.

169. For results involving other QOL indicators, see Jeffres, Neuendorf, and Atkin (2000).

170. Checkoway (1995) identified six strategies of community change: mass mobilization, social action, citizen participation, public advocacy, popular education, and local services development.

171. Breakdown theory is the "classic sociological explanation of contentious forms of collective action such as riots, rebellion and civil violence. The crux of the theory is that these sorts of events occur when the mechanisms of social control lose their restraining power" (Useem, 1998, p. 215) and their origins are in nonrational, emotional impulses (Pichardo, 1988). In the 1970s, researchers concluded the theory could not account for the social movements and collective violence of the 1960s and 1970s, or for newly collected historical data.

172. Useem (1998) concludes that resource mobilization theory is less successful than breakdown theory in explaining the urban riots of the 1960s as well as ethnic violence, arguing that defiant or nonroutine forms of collective action occur when mechanisms of social control falter or every-day routines are disrupted. Looking for foundations on which to build future work identifying breakdown processes, Useem (1998) suggested examining social capital theory, which says that strong networks of cooperation and high levels of interpersonal trust associated with such networks are required for economic prosperity. Second, he suggested looking at Huntington's (1996) argument that with the end of the Cold War, the world is becoming divided along lines of culture and religion rather than economics or ideology; thus, the basis of the most hostile conflicts will come from the clash between the world's seven or eight major civilizations.

173. Urban theorists agree that protest movements arise more frequently in cities than rural areas or small towns (Hirsch, 1993). However, there is disagreement on explanations for involvement and motivation in such movements. The Chicago school argued that such movements are driven by socially disorganized urbanites seeking social direction. Marxists argue that protest movements are based on the consciousness of objective economic class interests. Resource mobilization theorists see urbanization as a source of political tools with which previously powerless groups can challenge government, big business, and other major institutions. Hirsch's (1993) analysis of a squatters movement

in the 1980s led him to argue for a fourth, that protest movements occur when relatively isolated social groups are denied routine political access.

174. Pichardo (1992) noted that both the professional organizer and political process models of resource mobilization theory place the contributions and actions of influentials above those of the indigenous community. He argued that the indigeneous perspective treats the level of indigenous involvement as an empirical matter and does not a priori restrict the level of such community involvement of subordinates to that of elites.

175. See Strang and Soule (1998) for a review of the literature on diffusion and social movements.

176. "Diffusion of innovations and network analysis have complemented one another for over 30 years. Diffusion of innovations research has been greatly enhanced by network analysis because it permits more exact specification of who influences whom during the diffusion process. Network analysis has benefited from diffusion research by providing a real-world application to compare and clarify network models" (Valente, 1995, p. 2).

177. The history of network models can be traced from Coleman, Katz, and Menzel's (1966; Menzel & Katz, 1955) and Rogers' (1962/1995; Rogers, Ascroft, & Roling, 1970, cited in Valente, 1995) opinion leadership to Granovetter's (1973, 1982) strength-of-weak-ties, to Rogers and Kincaid's (1981) communication networks and to Burt's (1987) structural equivalence model.

178. According to Valente (1995):

> The first and most powerful network model was the use of nominations to determine who in the social system is considered an opinion leader. "Opinion leaders" were defined as those individuals with the highest number of nominations and were theorized to be a significant influence on the rate of adoption. Once identified, opinion leaders were discovered to be earlier adopters of innovations, and it was postulated that opinion leaders then passed on information to opinion followers. This pattern of opinion leaders being early adopters and then passing on information about the innovation to opinion followers is called the two-step flow hypothesis. (pp. 33-34)

179. This model says that people in the same group can be expected to have similar adoption times. Group membership increases social pressure on an individual to adopt an innovation so that the entire group can share the benefits (Valente, 1995). There are several ways to define group membership in network analysis (e.g., Scott, 1991). One approach is to treat an individual as a member of a group if at least half of his or her communication is with others in that group. In another practice, any set of three or more individuals is considered a group if their communication density is greater than the communication density for the network (Richards, 1989). These group definitions suffer in that an individual may be a member of numerous groups in the network. Valente (1995) chose to examine the components of the network; a component is a set of points linked to one another, and two individuals are members of the same component if they can reach one another through any series of intermediaries. Using three data sets, Valente found that component membership was not associated with innovation adoption (i.e., individuals in the same component were not more likely to adopt innovations at about the same time than those in other components).

180. The personal network density model focuses on the extent to which an individual's personal network is interconnected (i.e., in a dense personal network, the people one communicates with communicate frequently with each other). A neighborhood resident with a dense network in the community is not likely to receive much information from outside his or her own network (Danowski, 1986), so they are likely to hear of an innovation being diffused into the neighborhood later than those whose networks are less dense and neighborhood centered. Valente (1995) found support in his secondary analyses that personal network density/radiality was associated with early adoption. He also found that network density (more frequent communication among individuals in the network) facilitated faster diffusion of innovations. However, network density was not related to more extensive diffusion (adoption by a greater proportion of the network).

181. Personal network exposure refers to the extent that an individual is exposed to an innovation through one's personal network. Individual influence is the amount of exposure that an individual receives through patterns of interaction in the network. One's connectedness in a social system influences adoption behavior. Connectedness refers to the number of others in a social system with whom an individual is linked. If one is connected to many others who have adopted an innovation, exposure is higher. Analyzing a medical doctor data set, Valente (1995) found a relationship between personal network exposure and adoption.

182. Valente (1995) noted that, "A 'network' is the pattern of friendship, advice, communication, or support that exists among members of a social system" and "networks may be constructed by asking respondents to name others with whom they communicate. Once these nominations are made, a graph of the communication structure can be drawn that indicates who communicates with whom. This graph is called a 'sociogram'" (p. 31). All network studies of communities or some other designated system are conceptually limited, since a network/system can be broken down into overlapping structures differentiated by function, content (Knoke & Kukulinski, 1982).

183. "In a sense, this is a false dichotomy because relation and structure are inevitably entwined. The crucial difference is that for structural models, the overall pattern of network nominations determines the position or role the individual has during the diffusion process. Thus, any individual's adoption behavior is seen through the behavior of the whole network" (Valente, 1995, p. 47). Structural models focus on how the structure of the social system influences diffusion of innovations.

184. By the late 1960s and early 1970s, several schools of network analysis had developed (Scott, 1991).

185. If neighborhood had been left out of the trio, the focus would have shifted drastically as the turf covered expands to include virtually all of society (see, e.g., Shepherd & Rothenbuhler, 2000, and, more specifically, Depew & Peters, 2000, for a such a treatment of community and communication). Despite concerns with urban problems and America's cities today, researchers interested in communication and related phenomena often seem hesitant to examine geographically based communities as a primary focus rather than a convenient context. This book sought to remedy that somewhat by surveying the existing literature, adding unpublished pertinent data, and integrating the strands representing communication, urban studies, and sociology.

References

Abbey, A., & Andrews, F. (1986). Modeling the psychological determinants of life quality. In M. Andrews (Ed.), *Research on the quality of life*. Ann Arbor: Institute for Social Research, University of Michigan.

Abbott, C. (1974). The neighborhoods of New York, 1760-1775. *New York History, 55*, 35-54.

Abbott, E.A. (1988). *The volunteer newspaper: A communication solution for small rural communities? A case study*. Paper presented to the Newspaper Division at the annual conference of the Association for Education in Journalism and Mass Communication, Portland, OR.

Abeles, R., Gift, H., & Ory, M. (Eds.). (1994). *Aging and quality of life*. New York: Springer.

Abrahamson, M. (1974). The social dimensions of urbanism. *Social Forces, 52*, 376-383.

Abrahamson, M., & Carter, V.J. (1986). Tolerance, urbanism and region. *American Sociological Review, 51*, 287-294.

Ackerman, N., & Paolucci, B. (1983). Objective and subjective income adequacy: Their relationship to perceived life quality measures. *Social Indicators Research, 12*, 25-48.

Acock, A.C., & Hurlbert, J.S. (1990). Social network analysis: A structural perspective for family studies. *Journal of Social and Personal Relationships, 7*, 245-264.

Adams, C.H. (2000). Prosocial bias in theories of interpersonal communication competence: Must good communication be nice? In G.J. Shepherd & E.W. Rothenbuhler (Eds.), *Communication and community* (pp. 37-52) Mahwah, NJ: Erlbaum.

Ahlbrandt, R. S., Jr. (1986). Using research to build stronger neighborhoods: A study of Pittsburgh's neighborhoods. In R. B. Taylor (Ed.), *Urban neighborhoods, research and policy* (pp. 285-309). New York: Praeger.

Alba, R.D. (1978). Ethnic networks and tolerant attitudes. *Public Opinion Quarterly, 42,* 1-16.

Albrecht, T.L., & Hall, B. (1991). Relational and content differences between elites and outsiders in innovation networks. *Human Communication Research, 17,* 535-561.

Allen, L.R. (1990). Benefits of leisure attributes to community satisfaction. *Journal of Leisure Research, 22*(2), 183-196.

Allen, T. (1977). *Managing the flow of technology.* Cambridge, MA: MIT Press.

Altschull, J.H. (1996). A crisis of conscience: Is community journalism the answer? *Journal of Mass Media Ethics, 11,* 166-172.

Andrews, F. M. (Ed.). (1986). *Research on the quality of life.* Ann Arbor: Institute for Social Research, University of Michigan.

Andrews, F., & Withey, S. (1976). *Social indicators of well being: American's perceptions of life quality.* New York: Plenum Press.

Arquilla, J., & Ronfeldt, D. (1998). Preparing for information-age conflict: Part 1 conceptual and organizational definitions. *Information Communication & Society, 1,* 1-22.

Atkinson, T. (1982). The stability and validity of quality of life measures. *Social Indicators Research, 10,* 113-132.

Babe, R.E. (1996). Economics and information: Toward a new (and more sustainable) worldview. *Canadian Journal of Communication, 21,* 161-178.

Badran, M.H. (1992). *Integrated neighborhood shopping centers: One means of meeting community needs.* Unpublished master's thesis, University of Waterloo, Canada.

Badura, B. (1986). Social networks and the quality of life. In D. Frick (Ed.), *The quality of urban life* (pp. 55-60). New York: Walter de Gruyter.

Baldassare, M., & Wilson, G. (1995). More trouble in paradise: Urbanization and the decline in suburban quality-of-life ratings. *Urban Affairs Review, 30,* 690.

Bandura, A. (1986). *Social foundations of thought and action.* Englewood Cliffs, NJ: Prentice-Hall.

Banks, S.P., Altendorf, D.M., Greene, J.O., & Cody, M.J. (1987). An examination of relationship disengagement: Perceptions, breakup strategies and outcomes. *Western Journal of Speech Communication, 51,* 19-41.

Barbee, A.P., & Cunningham, M.R. (1995). An experimental approach to social support communications: Interactive coping in close relationships. *Communication Yearbook, 18,* 381-413.

Barker, D.C. (1998). The talk radio community: Nontraditional social networks and political participation. *Social Science Quarterly, 79,* 261-272.

Barker, J.R., & Tompkins, P.K. (1994). Identification in the self-managing organization: Characteristics of target and tenure. *Human Communication Research, 21,* 223-240.

Barnett, G.A. (1993). Correspondence analysis: A method for the description of communication networks. In B. Dervin & M. Voigt (Eds.), *Progress in communication sciences* (Vol. 6, pp. 135-163). Norwood, NJ: Ablex.

Barnett, G.A., & Choi, Y. (1995). Physical distance and language as determinants of the international telecommunications network. *International Political Science Review, 16*(3), 249-265.

Barnett, G.A., & Danowski, J.A. (1992). The structure of communication: A network analysis of the International Communication Association. *Human Communication Research, 19*, 264-285.

Barnett, G.A., Danowski, J.A., & Richards, W.D., Jr. (1993). Communication networks and network analysis: A current assessment. In W.D. Richards, Jr., & G.A. Barnett (Eds.), *Progress in communication sciences* (Vol. 12, pp. 1-20). Norwood, NJ: Ablex.

Barrera, M., Jr., & Baca, L.M. (1990). Recipient reactions to social support: Contributions of enacted support, conflicted support and network orientation. *Journal of Social and Personal Relationships, 7*, 541-551.

Bartsch, C. (1989). Government and neighborhoods: Programs promoting community development. *Economic Development Quarterly, 3*(2), 157-168.

Bass, L.A., & Stein, C. (1997). Comparing the structure and stability of network ties using the social support questionnaire and the social network list. *Journal of Social and Personal Relationships, 14*, 123-132.

Belanger, F., Lafrance, A.A., & Taylor, J.R. (1990). Computerization in a polycentric enterprise: A case study. *Canadian Journal of Communication, 15*, 31-58.

Bell, W., & Force, M.T. (1956). Urban neighborhood types and participation in formal association. *American Sociological Review, 21*, 25-34.

Bellah, R.N., Madsen, R., Sullivan, W.M., Swidler, A., & Tipson, S.M. (1985). *Habits of the heart: Individualism and commitment in American life*. New York: Harper & Row.

Bennett, L. (1993). Rethinking neighborhoods, neighborhood research, and neighborhood policy: Lessons from uptown. *Journal of Urban Affairs, 15*, 245-257.

Berg, J.H., & McQuinn, R.D. (1989). Loneliness and aspects of social support networks. *Journal of Social and Personal Relationships, 6*, 359-372.

Berkowitz, D., & TerKeurst, J.V. (1999). Community as interpretive community: Rethinking the journalist-source relationship. *Journal of Communication, 49*, 125-136.

Bernard, H.R., Killworth, P., Johnsen, E., Shelley, G.A., McCarty, C., & Robinson, S, (1990). Comparing four different methods for measuring personal networks. *Social Networks, 12*, 179-216.

Birru, M. (1991). *Communication as a tool for participatory development by community development organizations*. Unpublished doctoral thesis, University of Pittsburgh, PA.

Blau, P.H. (1977). *Inequality and heterogeneity: A primitive theory of social structure*. New York: The Free Press.

Bleiker, A.H. (1972). The proximity model and urban social relation. *Urban Anthropology, 1*(2), 151-175.

Blum, T.C. (1985). Structural constraints on interpersonal relations: A test of Blau's macrosociological theory. *American Journal of Sociology, 91*(3), 511-521.

Boczkowski, P.J. (1999). Mutual shaping of users and technologies in a national virtual community. *Journal of Communication, 49*, 86-108.

Bogart, L., & Orenstein, F.E. (1965). Mass media and community identity in an interurban setting. *Journalism Quarterly, 42*, 179-188.

Bolan, M. (1997). The mobility experience and neighborhood attachment. *Demography, 34*(2), 225-237.

Bolton, P., & Dewatripont, M. (1994). The firm as a communication network. *The Quarterly Journal of Economics, 109*(4), 809-839.

Bowling, A. (1997). *Measuring health: A review of quality of life measurement scales.* Philadelphia, PA: Open University Press.

Braithwaite, D.O., Waldron, V.C., & Finn, J. (1999). Communication of social support in computer-mediated groups for people with disabilities. *Health Communication, 11*, 123-151.

Brennan, J. (1986). *Majority of Americans like where they live* [A report on an ABC News/*Washington Post* poll conducted in February 1986]. New York: ABC News.

Bridger, J.C. (1996). Community imagery and the built environment. *Sociological Quarterly, 37*(3), 353-374.

Brow, J. (1990). Notes on community, hegemony, and the uses of the past, *Anthropological Quarterly, 63*(1), 1-6.

Bryant, F., & Veroff, J. (1986). Dimensions of subjective mental health in American men and women. In F. Andrews (Ed.), *Research on the quality of life* (pp. 117-146). Ann Arbor: Institute for Social Research.

Bryant, R. (1978). "The View": A community newspaper. *Community Development Journal, 13*(1), 43-46.

Buckley, W. (Ed.). (1968). *Modern systems research for the behavioral scientist. A sourcebook.* Chicago: Aldine.

Buckley, W. (1967). *Sociology and modern systems theory.* Englewood Cliffs, NJ: Prentice-Hall.

Bullis, C., & Bach, B.W. (1991). An explication and test of communication network content and multiplexity as predictors of organizational identification. *Western Journal of Speech Communication, 55*, 180-197.

Bulmer, M. (1985). The rejuvenation of community studies? Neighbours, networks and policy. *Sociological Review, 33*, 430-448.

Bursik, R.J., & Grasmick, H. (1993). *Neighborhoods and crime: The dimensions of effective neighborhood control.* New York: Lexington Books.

Bursik, R.J., & Webb, J. (1982). Community change and patterns of delinquency. *American Journal of Sociology, 88*, 24-42.

Burt, R.S. (1987). Social contagion and innovation: Cohesion versus structural equivalence. *American Journal of Sociology, 92*, 1287-1335.

Burt, R.S., & Schott, T. (1985). Relation contents in multiple networks. *Social Science Research, 14*, 287-308.

Calhoun, C. (1998). Community without propinquity revisited: Communications technology and the transformation of the urban public sphere. *Sociological Inquiry, 68*, 373-397.

Campbell, A. (1981). *The sense of well-being in America: Recent patterns and trends.* New York: McGraw-Hill.

Campbell, A., Converse, P., & Rodgers, W. (1976). *The quality of American life.* New York: Russell Sage.

Camporese, R., Freguja, C., & Sabbadini, L. (1998, May). Time use by gender and quality of life. *Social Indicators Research, 44*, 119-144.

Carey, G.W. (1976). Land tenure, speculation, and the state of the aging metropolis. *The Geographical Review, 66*(3), 253-265.

Carey, J.W. (1998). The Internet and the end of the national communication system: Uncertain predictions of an uncertain future. *Journalism and Mass Communication Quarterly, 75*, 28-34.

Carley, K.M., & Kaufer, D.S. (1993). Semantic connectivity: An approach for analyzing symbols in semantic networks. *Communication Theory, 3*, 183-213.

Cartwright, D. (1968). The nature of group cohesiveness. In D. Cartwright & A. Zander (Eds.), *Group dynamics: Research and theory* (3rd ed., pp. 91-109). New York: Harper & Row.

Cassel, C.A. (1999). Voluntary associations, churches and social participation theories of turnout. *Social Science Quarterly, 80*, 504-517.

Chaffee, S.H., & Berger, C.R. (1987). Levels of analysis: An introduction. In C.R. Berger & S.H. Chaffee (Eds.), *Handbook of communication science* (pp. 143-145). Newbury Park, CA: Sage.

Charity, A. (1995). *Doing public journalism.* New York: Guilford Press.

Checkoway, B. (1985). Neighborhood planning organizations: Perspectives and choices. *Journal of Applied Behavioral Science, 21*(4), 471-486.

Checkoway, B. (1995). Six strategies of community change. *Community Development Journal, 30*, 2-20.

Christenson, J.A., & Robinson, J.W., Jr. (Eds.). (1980). *Community development in America.* Ames: Iowa State University Press.

Claval, P. (1987). The region as a geographical, economic and cultural concept. *International Social Science Journal, 39*(112), 159-172.

Clevenger, T., Jr. (1977). Communication and the survival of democracy. In W.E. Arnold & J.L. Buley (Eds.), *Urban communication: Survival in the city* (pp. 119-127). Cambridge, MA: Winthrop.

Cline, M. (1995). Supporting the quality of life of single parent homeless families: A case study. In J. Sirgy & A. Samli (Eds.), *New dimensions in marketing/quality-of-life research* (pp. 137-150). Westport, CT: Quorum Books.

Coleman, J.S., Katz, E., & Menzel, H. (1966). *Medical innovation: A diffusion study.* New York: Bobbs Merrill.

Collins, R. (1986). Is 1980s sociology in the doldrums? *American Journal of Sociology, 91*(6), 1336-1355.

Collin-Jarvis, L. (1992). *A causal model of the reciprocal relationship between community attachment and community newspaper use.* Paper presented to the Communication Theory & Methodology Division at the annual conference of the Association for Education in Journalism and Mass Communication, Montreal.

Conason, J. (1975). Community newspapers: A press for the people. *The Nation, 221*, 467-468.

Connery, T. (1989). Management commitment and the small daily. *Newspaper Research Journal, 10*, 59-76.

Contractor, N.S., & Seibold, D.R. (1993). Theoretical frameworks for the study of structuring processes in group decision support systems: Adaptive structuration theory and self-organizing systems theory. *Human Communication Research, 19*, 528-563.

Cook, C.C. (1988). Components of neighborhood satisfaction: Responses from urban and suburban single-parent women. *Environment and Behavior, 20*(2), 115-149.

Corbett, J.B. (1992). Rural and urban newspaper coverage of wildlife: Conflict, community and bureaucracy. *Journalism Quarterly, 69*, 929-937.

Corman, S.R., & Scott, C.R. (1994). Perceived networks, activity foci, and observable communication in social collectives. *Communication Theory, 4*, 171-190.

Creedon, P.J. (1993). Acknowledging the infrasystem: A critical feminist analysis of systems theory. *Public Relations Review, 19*, 157-166.

Crenshaw, E., & St. John, C. (1989). The organizationally dependent community. A comparative study of neighborhood attachment. *Urban Affairs Quarterly, 24*(3), 412-434.

Cronkhite, G. (1986). On the focus, scope and coherence of the study of human symbolic activity. *The Quarterly Journal of Speech, 72*, 231-245.

Csikszentmihalyi, M., & Rochberg-Halton, E. (1987). *The meaning of things: Domestic symbols and the self.* Cambridge: Cambridge University Press.

Cuba, L., & Hummon, D. (1993). A place to call home: Identification with dwelling, community and region. *The Sociological Quarterly, 34*, 111-131.

Dahl, R. (1961). *Who governs?* New Haven, CT: Yale University Press.

Danowski, J.A. (1986). Interpersonal network structure and media use: A focus on radiality and non-mass media use. In G. Gumpert & R. Cathcart (Eds.), *Intermedia* (3rd ed., pp. 168-175). New York: Oxford University Press.

Danowski, J.A., Barnett, G.A., & Friedland, M.H. (1987). Interorganizational networks via shared public relations firms' centrality, diversification, media coverage and publics' images. *Communication Yearbook, 10*, 808-830.

Davis, J.A., & Leinhardt, S. (1972). The structure of positive interpersonal relations in small groups, In J. Berger, M.J. Zelditch, & B. Anderson (Eds.), *Sociological theories in progress* (Vol. 2). New York: Houghton-Mifflin.

Davis, M. (1997). Fragmented by technologies: A community in cyberspace. *Interpersonal Computing and Technology, 5*, 7-18.

Davis, T. (1984). The influence of the physical environment in offices. *Academy of Management Review, 9*(2), 271-283.

Davison, W.P. (1972). Public opinion research as communication. *Public Opinion Quarterly, 36*, 311-322.

Davison, W.P. (1988). *Mass media, civic organizations and street gossip: How communication affects the quality of life in an urban neighborhood.* New York: Gannett Center for Media Studies.

Demerath, N.J., & Peterson, R.A. (Eds.). (1967). *System, change and conflict.* New York: The Free Press.

Demers, D. (1994). Relative constancy hypothesis, structural pluralism and national advertising expenditures. *Journal of Media Economics, 7*, 31-48.

Demers, D. (1996a). Does personal experience in a community increase or decrease newspaper reading? *Journalism and Mass Communication Quarterly, 73*, 304-318.

Demers, D. (1996b). *The menace of the corporate newspaper. Fact or fiction?* Ames: Iowa State University Press.

Demers, D. (1998). Structural pluralism, corporate newspaper structure and news source perceptions: Another test of the editorial vigor hypothesis. *Journalism & Mass Communication Quarterly, 75*, 572-592.

Demers, D., & Merskin, D. (1998). *Effect of structural pluralism and corporate news structure on news source perceptions of critical content.* Paper presented to the Newspaper Division at the annual conference of the Association for Education in Journalism and Mass Communication, Baltimore, MD.

Demers, D., & Viswanath, K. (Eds.). (1999). *Mass media, social control and social change: A macrosocial perspective.* Ames: Iowa State University Press.

Depew, D., & Peters, J.D. (2000). Community and communication: The conceptual background. In G.J. Shepherd & E.W. Rothenbuhler (Eds.), *Communication and community* (pp. 3-21) Mahwah, NJ: Erlbaum.

Dervin, B. (1975). *Strategies for dealing with the information needs of urban residents: Information or communication?* Paper presented to the Information Systems Division at the annual conference of the International Communication Association, Chicago.

Dervin, B. (1977). A conceptual perspective on the information needs of urban residents. In W.E. Arnold & J.L. Buley (Eds.), *Urban communication. Survival in the city* (pp. 206-231). Cambridge, MA: Winthrop.

Deseran, F.A. (1978). Community satisfaction as definition of the situation: Some conceptual issues. *Rural Sociology, 43*, 235-249.

Dewey, J. (1966). *Democracy and education.* New York: The Free Press (Original work published 1916)

Diener, E., & Suh, E. (1997). Measuring quality of life: Economic, social and subjective indicators. *Social Indicators Research, 40*, 189-216.

Dizzard, W.P., Jr. (1989). *The coming information age* (3rd ed.). New York: Longman.

Doheny-Farina, S. (1996). *The wired neighborhood.* New Haven, CT: Yale University Press.

Donnelly, P.G., & Majka, T.J. (1996). Change, cohesion, and commitment in a diverse urban neighborhood. *Journal of Urban Affairs, 18*(3), 269-284.

Dorren, G. (1998). Communities within the community: Aspects of neighbourhood in seventeenth-century Haarlem. *Urban History, 25*, 173-188.

Dow, G. (1988). Configurational and coactivational views of organizational structure. *Academy of Management Review, 12*(1), 53-64.

Downs, A. (1981). *Neighborhoods and urban development.* Washington, DC: Brookings Institution.

Doyle, D.P., & Luckenbill, D.F. (1993). Socioeconomic status, perceived need and the mobilization of officials. *The Social Science Journal, 30*, 151-162.

Dubin, R., & Spray, S. (1964). Executive behavior and interaction. *Industrial Relations, 3*, 99-108.

Duncan, J.S. (1976). Landscape and the communication of social identity. In A. Rapoport (Ed.), *The mutual interaction of people and their built environments* (pp. 391-402). Paris: Mouton.

Dunwoody, S., & Griffin, R.J. (1999). Structural pluralism and media accounts of risk. In D.K. Demers & K. Viswanath (Eds.), *Mass media, social control, and social change: A macrosocial perspective* (pp. 139-158). Ames: Iowa State University Press.

Edelstein, A.S., & Larsen, O.N. (1960). The weekly press' contribution to a sense of urban community. *Journalism Quarterly, 37*, 489-498.

Eggert, L.L., & Parks, M.R. (1987). Communication network involvement in adolescents' friendships and romantic relationships. *Communication Yearbook, 10,* 283-322.

Eisenstadt, S.N. (1985). Macro-societal analysis—Background, development and indications. In S.N. Eisenstadt & H.J. Helle (Eds.), *Macro-sociological theory: Perspectives on sociological theory* (pp. 7-24). Newbury Park, CA: Sage.

Emig, A.G. (1995). Community ties and dependence on media for public affairs. *Journalism and Mass Communication Quarterly, 72,* 402-411.

Ervin, D.J. (1984). Correlates of urban residential structure. *Sociological Focus, 17,* 59-75.

Ettema, J.S., & Peer, L. (1996). Good news from a bad neighborhood: Toward an alternative to the discourse of urban pathology. *Journalism and Mass Communication Quarterly, 73,* 835-856.

Eulau, H., & Rothenberg, L. (1986). Life space and social networks as political contexts. *Political Behavior, 8*(2), 130-157.

Feeley, T.H., & Barnett, G.A. (1997). Predicting employee turnover from communication networks. *Human Communication Research, 23,* 370-387.

Feld, S.L. (1981). The focused organization of social ties. *American Journal of Sociology, 86,* 1015-1036.

Fernandez, R.M., & Kulik, J.C. (1981). A multilevel model of life satisfaction: Effects of individual characteristics and neighborhood composition. *American Sociological Review, 46,* 840-850.

Fessler, D.R. (1952). The development of a scale for measuring community solidarity. *Rural Sociology, 17,* 144-152.

Fischer, C.S. (1975a). The effects of urban life on traditional values. *Social Forces, 53,* 420-432.

Fischer, C.S. (1975b). Toward a subcultural theory of urbanism. *American Journal of Sociology, 80,* 1319-1341.

Fischer, C. (1975c). *The urban experience.* New York: Harcourt Brace Jovanovich.

Fischer, C.S. (1982). *To dwell among friends: Personal networks in town and city.* Chicago: University of Chicago Press.

Fischer, C.S. (1984). *The urban experience* (2nd ed.). New York: Harcourt Brace Jovanovich.

Fischer, C. with Jackson, R., Stueve, C., Gerson, K., Jones, L., & Baldassare, M. (1977). *Networks and places: Social relations in the urban setting.* New York: The Free Press.

Fishbein, M., & Ajzen, I. (1975). *Belief, attitude, intention and behavior: An introduction to theory and research.* Reading, MA: Addison-Wesley.

Fisher, B.A. (1978). *Perspectives on human communication.* New York: Macmillan.

Fitzsimmons, S.J., & Ferb, T.E. (1977). Developing a community attitude assessment scale. *Public Opinion Quarterly, 41,* 356-378.

Folwell, A., Chung, L., Nussbaum, J., Bethea, L., & Grant, J. (1997). Differential accounts of closeness in older adult sibling relationships. *Journal of Social and Personal Relationships, 14,* 843-849.

Francis, L., & Evans, T. (1996, Winter). The relationship between personal prayer and purpose in life among churchgoing and non-churchgoing twelve-to-fifteen-year-olds in the UK. *Religious Education, 9,* 9-21.

Frandsen, K.D., & Millis, M.A. (1993). On conceptual, theoretical and empirical treatments of feedback in human communication: Fifteen years later. *Communication Reports, 6*, 79-91.

Franz, P., & Warren, D.I. (1987). Neighborhood action as a social movement. Perspectives on trends in the United States and West Germany. *Comparative Political Studies, 20*(2), 229-246.

Freeman, L.C. (1979). Centrality in social networks. *Social Networks, 1*, 215-239.

Freudenberg, W. (1986). The density of acquaintanceship: An overlooked variable in community research? *American Journal of Sociology, 92*, 27-63.

Fried, M. (1986). The neighborhood in metropolitan life: Its psychosocial significance. In R.B. Taylor (Ed.), *Urban neighborhoods, research and policy* (pp. 331-363). New York: Praeger.

Friedkin, N. (1980). A test of structural features of Granovetter's strength of weak ties theory. *Social Networks, 2*, 411-422.

Friedkin, N. (1982). Information flow through strong and weak ties in intraorganizational social networks. *Social Networks, 3*, 273-285.

Furlong, M.S. (1989). An electronic community for older adults: The SeniorNet network. *Journal of Communication, 39*, 145-153.

Furnivall, J.S. (1948). *Colonial policy and practice: A comparative study of Burma and Netherlands India.* New York: New York University Press.

Gade, P., Abel, S., Antecol, M., & others (1997). *Civic journalism: The practitioner's perspective.* Paper presented at the annual conference of the Association for Education in Journalism and Mass Communication, Chicago.

Galaskiewicz, J. (1985). Professional networks and the institutionalization of a single mind set. *American Sociological Review, 50*, 639-658.

Galaskiewicz, J., & Krohn, K.R. (1984). Positions, roles, and dependencies in a community interorganizational system. *Sociological Quarterly, 25*, 527-550.

Gans, H.J. (1964). Social and physical planning for the elimination of urban poverty. In B. Rosenberg, I. Gerver, & F.W. Horton (Eds.), *Mass society in crisis: Social problems and social pathology* (pp. 629-644). New York: Macmillan.

Gardner, J. (1996). Building community. *Community Education Journal, 23*, 6-9.

Garoogian, D. (Ed.). (1999). *America's top-rated cities: A statistical handbook.* Lakeville, CT: Grey House.

Gaunt, T.P. (1998). Communication, social networks, and influence in citizen participation. *Journal of the Community Development Society, 29*, 276-297.

Gaziano, C. (1974). Readership study of paper subsidized by government. *Journalism Quarterly, 51*, 323-326.

Gaziano, C. (1985). Neighborhood newspapers and neighborhood leaders: Influences on agenda setting and definitions of issues. *Communication Research, 12*, 568-594.

Gaziano, C. (1989). Mass communication and class communication. *Mass Communication Review, 16*, 29-38.

Gaziano, C., & McGrath, K. (1987). Newspaper credibility and relationships of newspaper journalists to communities. *Journalism Quarterly, 64*, 317-318.

Gaziano, E., & Gaziano, C. (1999). Social control, social change and the knowledge gap hypothesis. In D.K. Demers & K. Viswanath (Eds.), *Mass media, social control and social change: A macrosocial perspective* (pp. 117-136). Ames: Iowa State University Press.

Gerbner, G. (1972). Violence and television drama: Trends and symbolic functions. In G. Comstock & E. Rubinstein (Eds.), *Television and social behavior, Vol. 1: Media content and control* (pp. 28-187). Washington, DC: U.S. Government Printing Office.

Gerbner, G. (1990). Epilogue: Advancing on the path of righteousness (maybe). In N. Signorielli & M. Morgan (Eds.), *Cultivation analysis: New directions in media effects research* (pp. 249-262). Newbury Park, CA: Sage.

Gerbner, G., & Gross, L. (1976). Living with television: The violence profile. *Journal of Communication, 26*(2), 173-199.

Gerson, K., Stueve, C.A., & Fischer, C.S. (1977). Attachment to place. In C.S. Fischer, R.M. Jackson, C.A. Stueve, K. Gerson, L.M. Jones, & M. Baldassare (Eds.), *Networks and places* (pp. 139-161) New York: The Free Press.

Ginsberg, Y. (1975). Joint leisure activities and social networks in two neighborhoods in Tel Aviv. *Journal of Marriage and the Family, 37*(3), 668-676.

Giugni, M.G. (1998). Was it worth the effort? The outcomes and consequences of social movements. *Annual Review of Sociology, 98*, 371-393.

Gladney, G.A. (1990). Newspaper excellence: How editors of small and large papers judge quality. *Newspaper Research Journal, 11*, 58-72.

Goheen, P.G. (1974). Interpreting the American city. *The Geographical Review, 64*, 362-384.

Goodwin, R.N. (1974, January 28). The American condition. *The New Yorker*, p. 38.

Gotham, K.F. (1999). Political opportunity, community identity and the emergence of a local anti-expressway movement. *Social Problems, 46*, 332-354.

Gottlieb, B.H. (1985). Social support and the study of personal relationships. *Journal of Social and Personal Relationships, 2*, 351-375.

Gould, J.M. (1986). *Quality of life in American neighborhoods: Levels of affluence, toxic waste, and cancer mortality in residential zip code areas*. Boulder, CO: Westview Press.

Granovetter, M. (1973). The strength of weak ties. *American Journal of Sociology, 78*, 1360-1380.

Granovetter, M. (1978). Threshold models of collective behavior. *American Journal of Sociology, 83*, 1420-1443.

Granovetter, M. (1982). The strength of weak ties: A network theory revisited. In P.V. Marsden & N. Lin (Eds.), *Social structure and network analysis* (pp. 105-130). Newbury Park: Sage.

Greer, S. (1962). *The emerging city: Myth and reality*. New York: The Free Press.

Greer, S. (1989). Urbanism and urbanity. Cities in an urban-dominated society. *Urban Affairs Quarterly, 24*(3), 341-352.

Greider, T., & Krannich, R.S. (1985). Neighboring patterns, social support and rapid growth. A comparison analysis from three western communities. *Sociological Perspectives, 28*(1), 51-70.

Griffin, R.J. (1990). Energy in the eighties: Education, communication and the knowledge gap. *Journalism Quarterly, 67*, 554-566.

Guest, A.M. (1974). Neighborhood life cycles and social status. *Economic Geography, 50*, 228-243.

Guest, A.M., & Lee, B.A. (1983). The social organization of local areas. *Urban Affairs Quarterly, 19*, 217-240.

Guest, A.M., & Wierzbicki, S.K. (1999). Social ties at the neighborhood level: Two decades of GSS evidence. *Urban Affairs Review, 35*, 92-111.

Gunnell, J.G. (1996). The genealogy of American pluralism: From Madison to behavioralism. *International Political Science Review, 17*, 253-265.

Hadaway, C.K., & Roof, W.C. (1978). Religious commitment and the quality of life in American society. *Review of Religious Research, 19*, 295-307.

Haeberle, S.H. (1987). Neighborhood identity and citizen participation. *Administration & Society, 19*(2), 178-196.

Haeberle, S.H. (1988). People or place. Variations in community leaders' subjective definitions of neighborhood. *Urban Affairs Quarterly, 23*(4), 616-634.

Hamm, B., Currie, R.F., & Forde, D.R. (1988). Research notes/A dynamic typology of urban neighborhoods: The case of Winnipeg. *Canadian Review of Sociology and Anthropology, 25*(3), 439-455.

Hansson, R.O., Jones, W.H., & Fletcher, W.L. (1990). Troubled relationships in later life: Implication for support. *Journal of Social and Personal Relationships, 7*, 451-463.

Harary, F. (1990). *Distance in graphs*. New York: Addison & Wesley.

Harris, J.C. (1996). Enhancing quality of life in low-income neighborhoods: Developing equity-oriented professionals. *Quest, 48*, 366-377.

Heider, F. (1946). Attitudes and cognitive organization. *Journal of Psychology, 21*, 107-112.

Herzog, A., & Rodgers, W. (1986). Satisfaction among older adults. In F. Andrews (Ed.), *Research on the quality of life* (pp. 235-251). Ann Arbor: Institute for Social Research.

Hill, D.R. (1988). Jane Jacobs' ideas on big, diverse cities: A review and commentary. *Journal of the American Planning Association, 54*(3), 302-314.

Hill, E.W., & Bier, T. (1989). Economic restructuring: Earnings, occupations, and housing values in Cleveland. *Economic Development Quarterly, 3*(2), 123-144.

Hill, K.A., & Hughes, J.E. (1997). Computer-mediated political communication: The USENET and political communities. *Political Communication, 14*, 3-27.

Hillery, G.A. (1955). Definitions of community: Areas of agreement. *Rural Sociology, 20*, 111-123.

Hindman, D. (1996). Community newspapers, community structural pluralism and local conflict with nonlocal groups. *Journalism & Mass Communication Quarterly, 73*, 708-721.

Hindman, D., & Homstad, C. (2000). *Community structural pluralism and newspaper adoption and use of information technologies*. Paper presented at the annual conference of the Midwest Association for Public Opinion Research, Chicago, IL.

Hindman, D., & Richardson, M. (1998). *Community newspaper editor definitions of community problems*. Paper presented at the annual conference of the Midwest Association for Public Opinion Research, Chicago, IL.

Hindman, E., Littlefield, R., Preston, A., & Neumann, D. (1999). Structural pluralism, ethnic pluralism and community newspapers. *Journalism & Mass Communication Quarterly, 76*, 250-263.

Hindman, E.B. (1998a). Community, democracy and neighborhood news. *Journal of Communication, 48*, 27-39.

Hindman, E.B. (1998b). "Spectacles of the poor": Conventions of alternative news. *Journalism and Mass Communication Quarterly, 75*, 177-193.

Hirsch, E.L. (1993). Protest movements and urban theory. *Research in Urban Sociology, 3,* 159-180.

Homans, G.C. (1950). *The human group.* New York: Harcourt, Brace.

Homans, G.C. (1986). Fifty years of sociology. *Annual Review of Sociology, 12,* 13-30.

Homel, R., Burns, A., & Goodnow, J. (1987). Parental social networks and child development. *Journal of Social and Personal Relationships, 4,* 159-177.

Hoover, E.M., & Vernon, R. (1962). *Anatomy of a metropolis.* Garden City, New York: Anchor Books; Cambridge, MA: Harvard University Press. (Original work published 1959)

Huckfeldt, R., & Sprague, J. (1987). Networks in context—The social flow of political information. *American Political Science Review, 81,* 1197-1216.

Hughes, M., & Thomas, M. (1998). The continuing significance of race revisited: A study of race, class, and quality of life in America, 1972 to 1996. *American Sociological Review, 63,* 785.

Hunter, A. (1971). The ecology of Chicago: Persistence and change, 1930-1960. *American Journal of Sociology, 77,* 425-444.

Hunter, A. (1974a). Community change. *American Journal of Sociology, 79,* 923-947.

Hunter, A. (1974b). *Symbolic communities.* Chicago: University of Chicago Press.

Hunter, A. (1979). The urban neighborhood: Its analytical and social contexts. *Urban Affairs Quarterly, 14,* 267-288.

Huntington, S.P. (1996). *The clash of civilizations and the remaking of the world order.* New York: Simon & Schuster.

Ikkink, K., & van Tilburg, T. (1998). Do older adults' network members continue to provide instrumental support in unbalanced relationships? *Journal of Social and Personal Relationships, 15,* 59-75.

Inglehart, R., & Rabier, J. (1986). Aspirations adapt to situations—but why are the Belgians so much happier than the French? In F. Andrews (Ed.), *Research on the quality of life* (pp. 1-56). Ann Arbor: Institute for Social Research.

Jacob, H. (1971). Black and white perceptions of justice in the city. *Law & Society Review, 5,* 69-89.

Jacobs, J. (1961). *The death and life of great American cities.* New York: Vintage Books.

Jang, H. (1997). Cultural differences in an interorganizational network: Shared public relations firms among Japanese and American companies. *Public Relations Review, 23,* 327-341.

Janowitz, M. (1967). *The community press in an urban setting: The social elements of urbanism* (2nd ed.). Chicago: University of Chicago Press. (Original work published 1952)

Janowitz, M., & Suttles, G. (1978). The social ecology of citizenship, In R. Sarri & Y. Hasenfeld (Eds.), *The management of human services* (pp. 80-104) New York: Columbia University Press.

Jeffres, L.W. (1983). Communication, social class and culture. *Communication Research, 10,* 219-246.

Jeffres, L. (1994). *Mass media processes.* Prospect Heights, IL: Waveland Press.

Jeffres, L. (1997). *Mass media effects.* Prospect Heights, IL: Waveland Press.

Jeffres, L. (2000). Ethnicity and ethnic media use. *Communication Research, 27,* 496-535.

Jeffres, L.W., & Atkin, D. (1996). Predicting use of technologies for communication and consumer needs. *Journal of Broadcasting & Electronic Media, 40*, 318-330.

Jeffres, L.W., Cutietta, C., Lee, J., & Sekerka, L. (1999). Differences of community newspaper goals and functions in large urban areas. *Newspaper Research Journal, 20*, 86-98.

Jeffres, L.W., Cutietta, C., Sekerka, L., & Lee, J. (2000). Newspapers, pluralism and diversity in an urban context. *Mass Communication & Society, 3*, 157-184.

Jeffres, L.W., & Dobos, J. (1983). Neighborhood newspaper audiences. *Newspaper Research Journal, 4*, 31-42.

Jeffres, L.W., & Dobos, J. (1984). Communication and neighborhood mobilization. *Urban Affairs Quarterly, 20*, 97-112.

Jeffres, L.W., & Dobos, J. (1993a). Communication and public perceptions of the quality of life. In M.J. Sirgy & A.C. Samli (Eds.), *New dimensions in marketing/quality-of-life research*. Westport, CT: Quorum Books.

Jeffres, L.W., & Dobos, J. (1993b). Perceptions of leisure opportunities and the quality of life in a metropolitan area. *Journal of Leisure Research, 25*, 203-217.

Jeffres, L.W., & Dobos, J. (1995). Separating people's satisfaction with life and public perceptions of the quality of life in the environment. *Social Indicators Research, 34*, 181-211.

Jeffres, L.W., Dobos, J., & Lee, J. (1988). Media use and community ties. *Journalism Quarterly, 65*, 575-581, 677.

Jeffres, L.W., Dobos, J., & Lee, J. (1991). *An exploration of communication patterns and perceptions of the neighborhood: Community newspaper editors and their audiences*. Paper presented at the annual conference of the Midwest Association for Public Opinion Research, Chicago.

Jeffres, L.W., Dobos, J., & Sweeney, M.M. (1987). Communication and commitment to community. *Communication Research, 14*, 619-643.

Jeffres, L.W., & Hur, K.K (1981). Communication channels within ethnic groups. *International Journal of Intercultural Communication, 5*, 115-132.

Jeffres, L.W., Latkovich, M., & Ceasar, J. (1983). Grassroots journalism in the city: Cleveland's neighborhood newspapers. *CRC Monographs, 6*.

Jeffres, L.W., & Lee, J. (1999). *Journalists as expert observers: Assessing audiences and communities*. Paper presented at the annual conference of the Midwest Association for Public Opinion Research, Chicago.

Jeffres, L.W., Neuendorf, K., & Atkin, D. (2000). Media use patterns and public perceptions of the quality of life. *Proceedings of The Second International Conference on Quality of Life in Cities* (Vol. 2, pp. 369-385). Singapore: National University of Singapore.

Jeffres, L.W., Perloff, R., Atkin, D., & Neuendorf, K. (2000). *Neighborhoods, communication and political beliefs*. Paper presented to the Communication Theory and Methodology Division at the annual conference of the Association for Education in Journalism and Mass Communication, Phoenix.

Jensen, M., & Leven, C. (1997). Quality of life in central cities and suburbs. *Annals of Regional Science, 31*, 431.

Jensen, R.J., & Hammerback, J.C. (1998). Your tools are really the people: The rhetoric of Robert Parris Moses. *Communication Monographs, 65*, 126-140.

Jensen, R.J., & Hammerback, J.C. (2000). Working in "quite places": The community organizing rhetoric of Robert Parris Moses. *Howard Journal of Communication, 11*, 1-18.

Johnson, J.D. (1988). On the use of communication gradients. In G. Goldhaber & G. Barnett (Eds.), *Handbook of organizational communication* (pp. 361-384). Norwood, NJ: Ablex.

Johnson, J.D., Meyer, M.E., Berkowitz, J.M., Ethington, C.T., & Miller, V.D. (1997). Testing two contrasting structural models of innovativeness in a contractual network. *Human Communication Research, 24*, 320-348.

Johnstone, B. (1990). *Stories, community, and place: Narratives from middle America.* Bloomington: Indiana University Press.

Johnstone, J.W.C., Slawski, E.J., & Bowman, W.W. (1976). *The news people: A sociological portrait of American journalists and their work.* Urbana: University of Illinois Press

Jones, D.C. (1992). Parental divorce, family conflict and friendship networks. *Journal of Social and Personal Relationships, 9*, 219-235.

Juster, F., & Courant, P. (1986). Integrating stocks and flows in quality of life research. In F. Andrews (Ed.), *Research on the quality of life* (pp. 147-170). Ann Arbor: Institute for Social Research, University of Michigan.

Kadushin, C. (1966). The friends and supporters of psychotherapy. *American Sociological Review, 31*, 786-802.

Kang, N., & Choi, J.H. (1999). Structural implications of the crossposting network of international news in cyberspace. *Communication Research, 26*, 454-481.

Kar, S.B., Jimenez, A., Campbell, K., & Sze, F. (1998, Spring). Acculturation and quality of life: A comparative study of Japanese-Americans and Indo-Americans. *Amerasia Journal, 24*, 129-142.

Kasarda, J., & Janowitz, M. (1974). Community attachment in mass society. *American Sociological Review, 39*, 328-339.

Kaufman, A. (1985, January 23). Define needs, city told. Urban expert says leaders must use media. *Plain Dealer*, p. 14A.

Kaufman, H.F. (1959). Toward an interactional conception of community. *Social Forces, 38*, 8-17.

Keith, P., & Schafer, R. (1998). Marital types and quality of life. *Marriage & Family Review, 27*, 19-35.

Keizer, G. (1997). Questioning community. *Pathways* [a publication of the Ohio Humanities Council], *21*(2), 3-4

Keller, S. (1968). *The urban neighborhood.* New York: Random House.

Keller, S. (1977). The telephone in new and old communities. In I. de Sola Pool (Ed.), *The social impact of the telephone* (pp. 281-298). Cambridge, MA: MIT Press.

Kemmis, D. (1990). *Community and the politics of place.* Norman: University of Oklahoma Press.

Kim, H.J., & Stiff, J.B. (1991). Social networks and the development of close relationships. *Human Communication Research, 18*, 70-91.

Kim, K., & Barnett, G.A. (1996). The determinants of international news flow: A network analysis. *Communication Research, 23*, 323-352.

Kim, Y.Y. (1977). Communication patterns of foreign immigrants in the process of acculturation. *Human Communication Research, 4*, 66-77.

Kim, Y.Y. (1978). A communication approach to the acculturation process: A study of Korean immigrants in Chicago. *International Journal of Intercultural Relations, 2*, 197-224.

Kim, Y.Y. (1979). Toward an interactive theory of communication-acculturation. In D. Nimmo (Ed.), *Communication yearbook 3* (pp. 435-453). New Brunswick, NJ: Transaction Books.

Kim, Y.Y. (1982). Communication and acculturation. In L.A. Samovar & R.E. Porter (Eds.). *Intercultural communication: A reader* (3rd ed., pp. 359-372). Belmont, CA: Wadsworth.

Kim, Y.Y. (1988). *Communication and cross-cultural adaptation: An integrative theory.* Philadelphia: Multilingual Matters.

Kim, Y.Y. (1994). Interethnic communication: The context and the behavior. In S.A. Deetz (Ed.), *Communication yearbook 17* (pp. 511-538). Thousand Oaks, CA: Sage.

Kim, Y.Y. (1995a). Cross-cultural adaptation: An integrative theory. In R. Wiseman (Ed.), *Intercultural communication theory* (pp. 170-193). Thousand Oaks, CA: Sage.

Kim, Y.Y. (1995b). Identity development: From cultural to intercultural. In H. Mokros (Ed.), *Information and behavior: Vol. 5. Interaction & identity* (pp. 347-369). New Brunswick, NJ: Transaction.

Kim, Y.Y., Lujan, P., & Dixon, L.D. (1998). Patterns of communication and interethnic integration: A study of American Indians in Oklahoma. *Canadian Journal of Native Education, 22*, 120-137.

Kincaid, D.L. (1987). The convergence theory of communication, self-organization, and cultural evolution. In D.L. Kincaid (Ed.), *Communication theory: Eastern and western perspectives* (pp. 209-221). New York: Academic Press.

Kincaid, D.L. (1988). The convergence theory of communication: Its implications for intercultural communication In Y.Y. Kim (Ed.), *International and Intercultural Annual: Vol. 12. Theoretical perspectives on international communication* (pp. 280-298). Beverly Hills: Sage.

Kincaid, D. L. (1993). Communication network dynamics: Cohesion, centrality and cultural evolution. In W.D. Richards Jr., & G.A. Barnett (Eds). *Progress in communication sciences* (Vol. 12, pp. 111-133). Norwood, NJ: Ablex.

Klein, J., Fontan, J., & Tremblay, D. (1998). *Territory and innovation in the urban environment: The case of Montreal.* Paper presented to the International Sociological Association, San Francisco, CA.

Knoke, D., & Kuklinski, J.H. (1982). *Network analysis.* Newbury Park, CA: Sage.

Korte, C. (1988). Increasing help exchange in an urban neighborhood: The effects of a neighborhood directory. *Journal of Applied Social Psychology, 18*(3), 228-251.

Kramer, M.W. (1996). A longitudinal study of peer communication during job transfers: The impact of frequency, quality and network multiplexity on adjustment. *Human Communication Research, 23*, 59-86.

Kurian, G.T. (1997). *The illustrated book of world rankings.* Armonk, NY: Sharpe Reference.

Lacy, S., & Fico, F. (1990). Newspaper quality and ownership: Rating the groups. *Newspaper Research Journal, 11*, 42-56.

Lalli, M., & Thomas, C. (1989). Public opinion and decision making in the community. Evaluation of residents' attitudes towards town planning measures. *Urban Studies, 26*, 435-447.

LaRose, R., & Mettler, J. (1989). Who uses information technologies in rural America? *Journal of Communication, 39*, 48-60.

Larose, S., Bernier, A., Soucy, N., & Duchesne, S. (1999). Attachment style dimensions, network orientation and the process of seeking help from college teachers. *Journal of Social and Personal Relationships, 16*, 225-247.

Lasswell, H. (1948). The structure and function of communication in society. In L. Bryson (Ed.), *The communication of ideas* (pp. 37-51). New York: Harper.

Laudeman, G. (1995). *Networks, people, and place: A model for networking communities.* Unpublished master's thesis, Michigan State University, Ann Arbor.

Laumann, E.O. (1973). *Bonds of pluralism: The form and substance of urban social networks.* New York: Wiley.

Laumann, E.O. (1976). *Networks of collective action: A perspective on community influence systems.* New York: Academic Press.

Laumann, E., & Marsden, P. (1979). The analysis of oppositional structures in political elites: Identifying collective actors. *American Sociological Review, 44*, 713-732.

Laszlo, E. (1996). *The systems view of the world: A holistic vision for our time.* Cresskill, NJ: Hampton Press.

Lee, B.A., Oropesa, R.S., Metch, B.J., & Guest, A.M. (1984). Testing the decline-of-community thesis: Neighborhood organizations in Seattle, 1929 and 1979. *American Journal of Sociology, 89*, 1161-1188.

Lehman, D.R., & Hemphill, K.J. (1990). Recipients' perceptions of support attempts and attributions for support attempts that fail. *Journal of Social and Personal Relationships, 7*, 563-574.

Lemert, J.B. (1984). News content and the elimination of mobilizing information: An experiment. *Journalism Quarterly, 61*, 243-249.

Lemert, J.B., & Ashman, M.G. (1983). Extent of mobilizing information in opinion and news magazines. *Journalism Quarterly, 60*, 657-662.

Lenz-Romeiss, F. (1973). *The city—new town or home town?* (E. Kustner & J.A. Underood, Trans.). New York: Praeger. (Original work published 1970)

Lerner, M. (1957). *America as a civilization.* New York: Simon & Schuster.

Leslie, L.A. (1989). Stress in the dual-income couple: Do social relationships help or hinder? *Journal of Social and Personal Relationships, 6*, 451-461.

Librero, F. (1993). Towards a methodology for problematique analysis: A Philippine experience. *Asian Journal of Communication, 3*, 84-102.

Lichtman, A.J. (1986). Competing models of the debate process. *Journal of the American Forensic Association, 22*, 147-151.

Lieske, J. (1990). The correlates of life quality in U.S. metropolitan areas. *Publius, 20*, 43-54.

Lightsey, O. (1996). What leads to wellness? The role of psychological resources in well-being. *Counseling Psychologist, 24*, 589-735.

Lindlof, T.R. (1988). Media audiences as interpretive communities. *Communication Yearbook, 11*, 81-107.

Lindstrom, B. (1997). A sense of place: Housing selection on Chicago's North Shore. *The Sociological Quarterly, 38*(1), 19-39.

Liu, B. (1978). Variations in social quality of life indicators in medium metropolitan areas. *American Journal of Economics and Sociology, 37*, 241-260.

Liu, B. (1979). Variations in social quality of life indicators in medium metropolitan areas. *Ekistics* (Athens), *46*, 152-161.

Logan, J.R., & Molotch, H. (1987). *Urban fortunes: The political economy of place.* Berkeley & Los Angeles: University of California Press.

Logan, J.R., & Spitze, G.D. (1994). Family neighbors. *American Journal of Sociology, 100*(2), 453-476.

Long, N.E. (1975). Ethos and the city: The problem of local legitimacy. *Ethnicity, 2*, 43-51.

Longo, B. (1995). Choice or chance: Questioning dimensions within the idea of community. *Journal of Technical Writing and Communication, 25*, 393-400.

MacDonald, D. (1976). Communication roles and communication networks in a formal organization. *Human Communication Research, 2*(4), 365-375.

Mackensen, R. (1986). Social networks. In D. Frick (Ed.), *The quality of urban life* (pp. 49-53). New York: Walter de Gruyter.

Madsen, A. (1989). General systems theory and counterplan competition. *Argumentation and Advocacy, 26*, 71-82.

Maitland, C. (1998). Global diffusion of interactive networks: The impact of culture. *Electronic Journal of Communication, 8* (3/4).

Mandelbaum, S.J. (1985). Thinking about cities as systems. Reflections on the history of an idea. *Journal of Urban History, 11*(2), 139-150.

Mandell, L. (1974). *Industrial location decisions in the Detroit area.* Ann Arbor, MI: Survey Research Center.

Mann, M. (Ed.). (1984). *The international encyclopedia of sociology.* New York: Continuum.

Marans, R.W., & Rodgers, W. (1975). Toward an understanding of community satisfaction. In A. Hawley & V. Rock (Eds.), *Metropolitan America in contemporary perspective* (pp. 299-352). New York: Wiley.

Markowitz, F. (1992). Community without organizations. *City and Society, 6*, 141-155.

Marlin, J.T., Ness, I., & Collins, S.T. (1986). *Book of world city rankings.* New York: The Free Press.

Marsden, P.V. (1987). Core discussion networks of Americans. *American Sociological Review, 52*, 122-131.

Marshall, A.A., & Stohl, C. (1993). Participating as participation: A network approach. *Communication Monographs, 60*, 137-157.

Martindale, D. (1988). *The nature and types of sociological theory.* Prospect Heights, IL: Waveland Press.

Maslow, A. (1954). *Motivation and personality.* New York: Harper & Row.

Massey, B.L. (1998). Civic journalism and nonelite sourcing: Making routine newswork of community connectedness. *Journalism and Mass Communication Quarterly, 75*, 394-407.

Mastin, T. (2000). Media use and civic participation in the African-American population: Exploring participation among professionals and nonprofessionals. *Journalism and Mass Communication Quarterly, 77*, 115-127.

McAdam, D. (1982). *Political process and the development of black insurgency, 1930-1970.* Chicago: University of Chicago Press.

McAlister, A., Johnson, W., Guenther-Grey, C., Fishbein, M., Higgins, D., O'Reilly, K., and the AIDS Community Demonstration Projects (2000). Behavioral journalism for HIV prevention: Community newsletters influence risk-related attitudes and behavior. *Journalism and Mass Communication Quarterly, 77,* 143-159.

McCarthy, J.D., & Zald, M.N. (1973). *The trend of social movements in America: Professionalism and resource mobilization.* Morristown, NJ: General Learning.

McCombs, M. (1997). Building consensus: The news media's agenda-setting roles. *Political Communication, 14,* 433-443.

McCombs, M., & Shaw, D. (1972). The agenda setting function of mass media. *Public Opinion Quarterly, 36,* 176-187.

McCombs, M., & Shaw, D. (1974). *The emergence of American political issues: The agenda-setting function of the press.* St. Paul, MN: West.

McCormick, P. (1997). Ethnography and a sense of place: Alternative measures for quality of life in eastern Arizona small towns. *Small Town, 27,* 12-19.

McLeod, J.M., Daily, K., Guo, Z., Eveland, Jr., W.P., Bayer, J., Yang, S., & Wang, H. (1996). Community integration, local media use and democratic processes. *Communication Research, 23,* 179-209.

McMillan, J.J., & Northern, N.A. (1995). Organizational codependency: The creation and maintenance of closed systems. *Management Communication Quarterly, 9,* 6-45.

McQuail, D. (1994). *Mass communication theory* (3rd ed.). Thousand Oaks, CA: Sage.

McQuail, D., & the Euromedia Research Group. (1990). Caging the beast: Constructing a framework for the analysis of media change in western Europe. *European Journal of Communication, 5,* 313-331.

Meltzer, E. (1998). *The new book of American rankings.* New York: Facts on File.

Melvin, P.M. (1987). *The organic city: Urban definition and community organization, 1880-1920.* Lexington: University Press of Kentucky.

Menzel, H., & Katz, E. (1955). Social relations and innovation in the medical profession: The epidemiology of a new drug. *Public Opinion Quarterly, 19,* 337-352.

Meyer, M.W. (1972). Size and the structure of organizations: A causal analysis. *American Sociological Review, 37,* 434-441.

Michalos, A. (1986). Job satisfaction, marital satisfaction and the quality of life: A review and a preview. In F. Andrews (Ed.), *Research on the quality of life* (pp. 57-83). Ann Arbor: Survey Center.

Mier, R. (1989). Neighborhood and region: An experiential basis for understanding. *Economic Development Quarterly, 3*(2), 169-174.

Milardo, R.M. (1992). Comparative methods for delineating social networks. *Journal of Social and Personal Relationships, 9,* 447-461.

Mitchell, J.C. (1969). The concept and use of social networks. In J.C. Mitchell (Ed.), *Social networks in urban situations* (pp. 1-50). Manchester, England: Manchester University Press.

Mitra, A. (1996). Nations and the Internet: The case of a national newsgroup, 'soc.cult.Indian.' *Convergence, 2,* 44-75.

Moemeka, A.A. (1998). Communalism as a fundamental dimension of culture. *Journal of Communication, 48,* 118-141.

Morgan, D.L. (1986). Personal relationships as an interface between social networks and social cognitions. *Journal of Social and Personal Relationships, 3,* 403-422.

Morgan, D.L., & March, S.J. (1992). The impact of life events on networks of personal relationships: A comparison of widowhood and caring for a spouse with Alzheimer's disease. *Journal of Social and Personal Relationships, 9,* 563-584.

Mumford, L. (1938). *The culture of cities.* New York: Harcourt, Brace.

Mumford, L. (1961). *The city in history.* New York: Harcourt, Brace.

Nachmias, C., & Palen, J. (1986). Neighborhood satisfaction, expectations, and urban revitalization. *Journal of Urban Affairs, 8,* 51-61.

Nahemov, L., & Lawton, M. (1975). Similarity and propinquity in friendship formation. *Journal of Personality and Social Psychology, 32,* 205-213.

Namboodiri, K. (1988). Ecological demography: Its place in sociology. *American Sociological Review, 53,* 619-633.

Nasar, J.L. (1990). The evaluative image of the city. *Journal of the American Planning Association, 56*(1), 41-53.

Neuendorf, K., Jeffres, L.W., & Atkin, D. (1998). *Public opinion and communication mapping.* Paper presented at the annual conference of the American Association for Public Opinion Research, St. Louis, MO.

Newby, G.B., & Bishop, A.P. (1996). Community system users and uses. *Proceedings of the ASIS Annual Meeting, 33,* 118-126.

Newcomb, M.D. (1986). Cohabitation, marriage and divorce among adolescents and young adults. *Journal of Social and Personal Relationships, 3,* 473-494.

Noble, G. (1987). Discriminating between the intrinsic and instrumental domestic telephone user. *Australian Journal of Communication, 11,* 63-85.

Northington, K.B. (1992). Split allegiance: Small-town newspaper community involvement. *Journal of Mass Media Ethics, 7,* 220-232.

Novek, E.M. (1995). Buried treasure: The community newspaper as an empowerment strategy for African American high school students. *Howard Journal of Communication, 6,* 69-88.

Nussbaum, J.F. (1983). Relational closeness of elderly interaction: Implications for life satisfaction. *Western Journal of Speech Communication, 47,* 229-243.

O'Connell, L. (1984). An exploration of exchange in three social relationships: Kinship, friendship and the marketplace. *Journal of Social and Personal Relationships, 1,* 333-345.

O'Connor, T., Hetherington, E., & Clingempeel, W. (1997). Systems and bi-directional influences in families. *Journal of Social and Personal Relationships, 14,* 491-504.

Oldenburg, R. (1989). *The great good place.* New York: Paragon House.

Olien, C.N., Tichenor, P.J., Donohue, G.A., Sandstrom, K.L., & McLeod, D.M. (1990). Community structure and editor opinions about planning. *Journalism and Mass Communication Quarterly, 67,* 119-127.

Olsen, M., Perlstadt, H., Fonseca, V., & Hogan, J. (1989). Participation in neighborhood associations. *Sociological Focus, 22*(1), 1-17.

Oropesa, R.S. (1989). The social and political foundations of effective neighborhood improvement associations. *Social Science Quarterly, 70,* 723-743.

Oropesa, R.S. (1992a). *The ironies of human resource mobilization by neighborhood associations.* Paper presented to the American Sociological Association, Pittsburgh, PA.

Oropesa, R.S. (1992b). Social structure, social solidarity and involvement in neighborhood improvement associations. *Sociological Inquiry, 62,* 107-117.

O'Sullivan, P.B. (1995). Computer networks and political participation: Santa Monica's teledemocracy project. *Journal of Applied Communication, 23*, 93-107.

Palisi, B.J. (1985). Formal and informal participation in urban areas. *Journal of Social Psychology, 125*(4), 429-447.

Palisi, B.J., & Palisi, R.J. (1984). Status and voluntary associations: A cross-cultural study of males in three metropolitan areas. *Journal of Voluntary Action Research, 13*, 32-43.

Palisi, B.J., & Ransford, H.E. (1987). Friendship as a voluntary relationship: Evidence from national surveys. *Journal of Social and Personal Relationships, 4*, 243-259.

Papa, M.J. (1990). Communication network patterns and employee performance with new technology. *Communication Research, 17*, 344-368.

Parfect, M., & Power, G. (1997). *Planning for urban quality: Urban design in towns and cities.* New York: Routledge.

Park, R.A. (1952). *Human communities.* Glencoe, IL: The Free Press.

Park, R. E. (1916). The city: Suggestions for the investigation of human behavior in the urban environment. *American Journal of Sociology, 20*, 577-613.

Park, R.E. (1925). The urban community as a spatial pattern and as a moral order. In E. Burgess (Ed.), *The urban community* (pp. 3-11). Chicago: University of Chicago Press.

Park, R.E. (1967). The city: Suggestions for the investigation of human behavior in the human environment. In R.E. Park, E.W. Burgess & R.D. McKenzie (Eds.), *The city* (pp. 1-46). Chicago: University of Chicago Press. (Original work published 1925)

Park, R.E., Burgess, E., & McKenzie, R.D. (1925). *The city.* Chicago: University of Chicago Press.

Parks, M.R. (1977). Anomia and close friendship communication networks. *Human Communication Research, 4*(1), 48-57.

Parks, M.R., & Roberts, L.D. (1998). "Making MOOsic": The development of personal relationships on line and a comparison to their off-line counterparts. *Journal of Social and Personal Relationships, 15*, 517-537.

Patterson, B.R. (1995). Communication network activity: Network attributes of the young and elderly. *Communication Quarterly, 43*, 155-166.

Peirce, N.R. (1992, October 24). Election might shake the cities. *Plain Dealer*, p. 7B.

Perkins, D.V. (1988). Neighborhoods as contexts for human behavior. *Contemporary Psychology, 33*(11), 946-947.

Peyrot, M., & Fenzel, M. (1994). *Neighborhood surveys as community organizing.* Paper presented to the American Sociological Association, Los Angeles.

Phillips, W.C. (1940). *Adventuring for democracy.* New York: Social Unit Press.

Pichardo, N.A. (1988). Resource mobilization: An analysis of conflicting theoretical variations. *Sociological Quarterly, 29*, 97-110.

Pichardo, N.A. (1992). *The role of community infrastructure grievances in the rise of social movements.* Paper presented to the American Sociological Association, Pittsburgh, PA.

Pilotta, J.J., Widman, T., & Jasko, S.A. (1988). Meaning and action in the organizational setting: An interpretive approach. *Communication Yearbook, 11*, 310-334.

Pool, I. de Sola & Kochen, M. (1978). Contacts and influence. *Social Networks, 1*, 5-51.

Powell, D. (1998). *The nine myths of aging: Maximizing the quality of later life.* New York: Freeman.

Query, J., & James, A. (1989). The relationship between interpersonal communication competence and social support among elderly support groups in retirement communities. *Health Communication, 1,* 165-184.

Rabrenovic, G. (1995). Deindustrialization and urban poverty: Struggle for survival in a low income neighborhood. *Research in Community Sociology, 5,* 183-200.

Ramsay, M. (1996). The local community: Maker of culture and wealth. *Journal of Urban Affairs, 18,* 95-118.

Ranson, S., Hinings, B., & Greenwood, R. (1980). The structuring of organizational structures. *Administrative Science Quarterly, 25,* 1-17.

Raphael, D., Renwick, R., Brown, I., & Rootman, I. (1996). Quality of life indicators and health: Current status and emerging conceptions. *Social Indicators Research, 39,* 65-88.

Ray, E.B. (1991). The relationship among communication network roles, job stress and burnout in educational organizations. *Communication Quarterly, 39,* 91-102.

Research Associates of Washington. (1994). *Across America.* Washington, DC: Author.

Revenson, T.A., & Majerovitz, S.D. (1990). Spouses' support provision to chronically ill parents. *Journal of Social and Personal Relationships, 7,* 575-586.

Rice, R.E. (1993). Using network concepts to clarify sources and mechanisms of social influence. In W.D. Richards, Jr. & G.A. Barnett (Eds.), *Progress in communication sciences* (Vol. 12, pp. 43-62). Norwood, NJ: Ablex.

Richards, W.D. (1989). *The NEGOPY network analysis program.* Vancouver, Canada: Department of Communication, Simon Fraser University.

Richards, W.D., Jr. (1993). Communication/information networks, strange complexity, and parallel topological dynamics. In W.D. Richards, Jr., & G.A. Barnett (Eds.), *Progress in communication sciences* (Vol. 12, pp. 165-195). Norwood, NJ: Ablex.

Roberts, K.H., O'Reilly, C.A., Bretton, G., & Porter, L.W. (1974). Organizational theory and organizational communication: A communication failure? *Human Relations, 27,* 501-524.

Robinson, J.P. (1973, March). *Measures of the quality of urban life.* Paper prepared for the City in History: Idea and Reality Conference, Center for Coordination of Ancient and Modern Studies, University of Michigan, Ann Arbor.

Robinson, J.P. (1976). Interpersonal influence in election campaigns: Two step-flow hypotheses. *Public Opinion Quarterly, 40,* 304-319.

Robinson, T. (1996). Inner-city innovator: The non-profit community development corporation. *Urban Studies, 33,* 1647-1670.

Rogers, E.M. (1976a). Communication and national development: The passing of dominant paradigm. *Communication Research, 3,* 213-240.

Rogers, E.M. (1976b). New perspectives on communication and development. *Communication Research, 3,* 99-106.

Rogers, E.M. (1987). Progress, problems and prospects for network research: Investigating relationships in the age of electronic communication technologies. *Social Networks, 9,* 285-310.

Rogers, E.M. (1995). *Diffusion of innovations.* New York: The Free Press. (Original work published 1962)

Rogers, E.M., & Kincaid, L. (1981). *Communication networks: Toward a new paradigm for research*. New York: The Free Press.

Rohrle, B., & Hellmann, I. (1989). Characteristics of social networks and social support among long-term and short-term unemployed teachers. *Journal of Social and Personal Relationships, 6,* 463-473.

Rosel, N. (1983). The hub of a wheel: A neighborhood support network. *International Journal of Aging and Human Development, 16*(3), 192-200.

Ross, C., & Van Willigen, M. (1997). Education and the subjective quality of life. *Journal of Health and Social Behavior, 38,* 275-297.

Rothenbuhler, E.W. (1991). The process of community involvement. *Communication Monographs, 58,* 63-78.

Rothenbuhler, E.W. (2000). Revising communication research for working on community. In G.J. Shepherd & E.W. Rothenbuhler (Eds.), *Communication and community* (pp. 159-179) Mahwah, NJ: Erlbaum.

Rothenbuhler, E.W., Mullen, L.J., DeLaurell, R., & Ryu, C.R. (1996). Communication, community attachment and involvement. *Journalism & Mass Communication Quarterly, 73,* 445-466.

Rubin, A.M. (1994). Media uses and effects: A uses-and-gratifications perspective. In J. Bryant & D. Zillmann (Eds.), *Media effects: Advances in theory and research* (pp. 417-436). Hillsdale, NJ: Erlbaum

Rubinyi, R.M. (1989). Computers and community: The organizational impact. *Journal of Communication, 39,* 110-123.

Ryan, V.D. (1994). Community development and the ever elusive "collectivity." *Journal of the Community Development Society, 25,* 5-19.

St. John, C., & Cosby, V. (1995). Life cycle differences in neighborhood satisfaction. *Sociological Spectrum, 15,* 147-160.

Sampson, R.J. (1988). Local friendship ties and community attachment in mass society: A multilevel systemic model. *American Sociological Review, 53,* 766-779.

Sanoff, H. (1971). The social implications of residential environments. *International Journal of Environmental Studies, 2,* 13-19.

Sartori, G. (1997). Understanding pluralism. *Journal of Democracy, 8,* 58-69.

Savageau, D., with D'Agostino, R. (2000). *Places rated almanac.* Foster City, CA: IDG.

Schooler, C., Flora, J.A., & Farquhar, J.W. (1993). Moving toward synergy: Media supplementation in the Stanford five-city project. *Communication Research, 20,* 587-610.

Schramm, W., & Lerner, D. (Eds.). (1976). *Communication and change: The last ten years—and the next.* Honolulu: University Press of Hawaii, East-West Center.

Scheufele, D.A., Shanahan, J., & Kim, S. (2000). *Who cares about local politics? Media influences on local political awareness, issue awareness and attitude strength in a local community.* Paper presented at the annual conference of the Midwest Association for Public Opinion Research, Chicago, IL.

Schuessler, K., & Fisher, G. (1985). Quality of life research and sociology. *Annual Review of Sociology, 11,* 129-149.

Schuftan, C. (1996). The community development dilemma: What is really empowering? *Community Development Journal, 31,* 260-264.

Schulman, M. (1985). *Neighborhood radio as community communication.* Harlem, NY: City College of New York, Local Media, Communication Theory.

Schumaker, P. (1991). *Critical pluralism, democratic performance, and community power.* Lawrence: University of Kansas Press.

Schwab, W.A. (1988). Alternative explanations of neighborhood change: An evaluation of neighborhood life-cycle, composition, and arbitrage models. *Sociological Focus, 20*(1), 81-93.

Schwab, W.A. (1989). Divergent perspectives on the future of Cleveland's neighborhoods: Economic, planning, and sociological approaches to the study of neighborhood change. *Journal of Urban Affairs, 11*(2), 141-154.

Schwartz, D.F. (1969). *Liaison roles in the communication structure of a formal organization: A pilot study.* Paper presented at the annual meeting of the National Society for the Study of Communication, Cleveland.

Schwirian, K.P. (1983). Models of neighborhood change. *Annual Review of Sociology, 9,* 83-102.

Scott, J. (1988). Trend report. Social network analysis. *Sociology, 22*(2), 109-127.

Scott, J. (1991). *Network analysis: A handbook.* Newbury Park, CA. Sage.

Shade, L.R. (1999). Roughing it in the electronic bush: Community networking in Canada. *Canadian Journal of Communication, 24,* 179-198.

Shah, D., Schmierbach, M., Hawkins, J., Espino, R., Ericson, M., Donavan, J., & Chung, S. (2000). *Untangling the ties that bind: The relationship between Internet use and engagement in public life.* Paper presented at the annual conference of the Midwest Association for Public Opinion Research, Chicago, IL.

Shea, L., & Schewe, C. (1995). Enhancing the quality of life during widowhood: A marketing challenge. In J. Sirgy & A. Samli (Ed.), *New dimensions in marketing/quality-of-life research* (pp. 137-150). Westport, CT: Quorum Books.

Shen, S., & Lai, Y. (1998). Optimally scaled quality-of-life indicators. *Social Indicators Research, 44,* 225-254.

Shepherd, G.J., & Rothenbuhler, E.W. (Eds.). (2000). *Communication and community.* Mahwah, NJ: Erlbaum.

Shoemaker, P.J., & Reese, S.D. (1991). *Mediating the message: Theories of influences on mass media content.* New York: Longman.

Signorielli, N., & Morgan, M. (1990). *Cultivation analysis: New directions in media effects research.* Newbury Park, CA: Sage.

Silver, C. (1985). Neighborhood planning in historical perspective. *American Planning Association Journal, 51*(2), 161-174.

Silverman, C. J. (1986). Neighboring and urbanism. Commonality versus friendship. *Urban Affairs Quarterly, 22*(2), 312-328.

Silverman, C.J. (1992). Neighbourhood life, communication and the metropolis. *Asian Journal of Communication, 2,* 92-105.

Simpson, J.C. (1995). Pluralism: The evolution of a nebulous concept. *American Behavioral Scientist, 38,* 459-477.

Sirgy, M.J. (1998). Materialism and quality of life. *Social Indicators Research, 43,* 227-260.

Slovak, J.S. (1986). Attachments in the nested community. Evidence from a case study. *Urban Affairs Quarterly, 21*(4), 575-597.

Smith, K.A. (1987). *Effects of newspaper coverage on neighborhood and community issue concerns.* Paper presented at the annual conference of the Association for Education in Journalism and Mass Communication, San Antonio, TX.

Smith, M.G. (1971). Institutional and political conditions of pluralism. In L. Kuper & M.G. Smith (Eds.), *Pluralism in Africa* (pp. 27-67). Berkeley: University of California Press.

Smith, R.L. (1982). *Neighborhoods inside and out: Comparative perspectives on the meaning of "neighborhood."* Unpublished doctoral dissertation, University of Minnesota, Minneapolis.

Sodeur, W. (1986). Social networks in urban neighborhoods. In D. Frick (Ed.), *The quality of urban life* (pp. 61-72) New York: Walter de Gruyter.

Stamm, K.R. (1985). *Newspaper use and community ties: Toward a dynamic theory.* Norwood, NJ: Ablex.

Stamm, K.R. (2000). Of what use civic journalism: Do newspapers really make a difference in community participation? In G.J. Shepherd & E.W. Rothenbuhler (Eds.), *Communication and community* (pp. 217-234) Mahwah, NJ: Erlbaum.

Stamm, K.R., Emig, A.G., & Hesse, M.B. (1997). The contribution of local media to commmunity involvement. *Journalism and Mass Communication Quarterly, 74,* 97-107.

Stamm, K.R., & Guest, A.M. (1991). Communication and community integration: An analysis of the communication behavior of newcomers. *Journalism and Mass Communication Quarterly, 68,* 644-656.

Steiner, J.F. (1929, April 15). Whither the community movement? *Survey,* pp. 130-131.

Stephenson, K., & Zelen, M. (1989). Rethinking centrality: Methods and examples. *Social Networks, 11,* 1-7.

Stinner, W.F., Van Loon, M., Chung, S., & Byun, Y. (1990). Community size, individual social position, and community attachment. *Rural Sociology, 55,* 494-521.

Stoecker, R. (1995). Community, movement, organization: The problem of identity convergence in collective action. *The Sociological Quarterly, 36,* 111-130.

Stolle, D. (1998). Bowling together, bowling alone: The development of generalized trust in voluntary associations. *Political Psychology, 19,* 497-525.

Stolle, D., & Rochon, T.R. (1998). Are all associations alike? *The American Behavioral Scientist, 41,* 47-65.

Stone, G.C., & Morrison, J. (1976). Content as a key to the purpose of community newspapers. *Journalism Quarterly, 53,* 494-498.

Stone, G.C., O'Donnell, M.K., & Banning, S. (1997). Public perceptions of newspaper's watchdog role. *Newspaper Research Journal, 18,* 86-102.

Straits, B.C. (1991). Bringing strong ties back in: Interpersonal gateways to political information and influence. *Public Opinion Quarterly, 55,* 431.

Strang, D., & Soule, S.A. (1998). Diffusion in organizations and social movements: From hybrid corn to poison pills. *Annual Review of Sociology, 24,* 265-290.

Strengthening "weak ties": Using the Internet to improve neighborhood communication (Vol. 1-3). (1999). Cleveland, OH: Collaborative Research Project, Department of Communication, Cleveland State University.

Summers, G.F. (1986). Rural community development. *Annual Review of Sociology, 12,* 347-371.

Surra, C.A. (1987). Reasons for change in commitment: Variations by courtship type. *Journal of Social and Personal Relationships, 4,* 17-33.

Suttles, G. (1972). *The social construction of communities.* Chicago: University of Chicago Press.

Svetlik, I. (1996). Satisfaction with life and work. *Druzboslovne Razprave, 12,* 22-23.

Swindell, D. (2000). Issue representation in neighborhood organizations: Questing for democracy at the grassroots. *Journal of Urban Affairs, 22,* 123-137.

Szalai, A., & Andrews, F.M. (1980). *The quality of life: Comparative studies.* Beverly Hills, CA: Sage.

Tardy, R.W., & Hale, C.L. (1998). Getting "plugged in": A network analysis of health-information seeking among "stay-at-home" moms. *Communication Monographs, 65,* 336-357.

Teitz, M.B. (1989). Neighborhood economics: Local communities and regional markets. *Economic Development Quarterly, 3*(2), 111-122.

Thompson, B., Corbett, K., Bracht, N., & Pechacek, T. (1993). Community mobilization for smoking cessation: Lessons learned from COMMIT. *Health Promotion International, 8,* 69-83.

Tichenor, P.J., Donohue, G.A., & Olien, C.N. (1980). *Community, conflict and the press.* Beverly Hills, CA: Sage.

Tichenor, P.J., Donohue, G.A., & Olien, C.N. (1999). Preface. In D. Demers & K. Viswanath (Eds.), *Mass media, social control, and social change: A macrosocial perspective.* Ames: Iowa State University Press.

Tilly, C. (1978). *From mobilization to revolution.* Reading, MA: Addison-Wesley.

Toennies, F. (1957). *Community and society* (C.P. Loomis, Trans.). New York: Harper Torchbook. (Original work published 1887)

Togeby, L. (1993). Grass roots participation in the Nordic countries. *European Journal of Political Research, 24,* 159-175.

Tomeh, A.K. (1967). Informal participation in a metropolitan community. *Sociological Quarterly, 8,* 85-102.

Tomovic, V.A. (Ed.). (1979). *Definitions in sociology: Convergence, conflict and alternative vocabularies.* St. Catharines, Ontario, Canada: Diliton Publications.

Trachtman, L.E. (1991). *Response to a community-based information and communication system.* Paper presented at the annual Conference of the Speech Communication Association, Atlanta, GA.

Treno, A.J., & Holder, H.D. (1997). Community mobilization: Evaluation of an environmental approach to local action. *Addiction, 92,* S173-S187.

Trinke, S., & Bartholomew, K. (1997). Hierarchies of attachment relationships in young adulthood. *Journal of Social and Personal Relationships, 14,* 603-625.

Tulloss, J.K. (1995). Citizen participation in Boston's development policy: The political economy of participation. *Urban Affairs Review, 30,* 514-537.

Turner, N.E. (1999). *Voluntary associations in low-income neighborhoods: Untapped community resources.* Paper presented to the American Sociological Association, Chicago, IL.

Turow, J. (1992). The organizational underpinnings of contemporary media conglomerates. *Communication Research, 19,* 682-704.

Tutzauer, F. (1993). Statistical comparison of communication networks. In W.D. Richards, Jr. & G.A. Barnett (Eds.), *Progress in communication sciences* (Vol. 12, pp. 95-110). Norwood, NJ: Ablex.

Urban University and Neighborhood Network. (1997, November). *Limited access: The information superhighway and Ohio's neighborhood based organizations.* ERIC No. ED414384.

Useem, B. (1998). Breakdown theories of collective action. *Annual Review of Sociology, 24*, 215-238.

Valente, T.W. (1995). *Network models of the diffusion of innovations.* Cresskill, NJ: Hampton Press.

Valenty, L. (1976). *The impact of the neighborhood newspaper on the urban community.* Unpublished master's thesis, University of Minnesota School of Journalism and Mass Communication.

van Every, E.J., & Taylor, J.R. (1998). Modeling the organization as a system of communication activity: A dialogue about the language/action perspective. *Management Communication Quarterly, 12*, 128-147.

van Tilburg, T. (1992). Support networks before and after retirement. *Journal of Social and Personal Relationships, 9*, 433-445.

van Tilburg, T., Gierveld, J., Lecchini, L., & Marsiglia, D. (1998). Social integration and loneliness: A comparative study among older adults in the Netherlands and Tuscany, Italy. *Journal of Social and Personal Relationships, 15*, 740-754.

Veenhoven, R. (1996). Happy life-expectancy: A comprehensive measure of quality-of-life in nations. *Social Indicators Research, 39*, 1-58.

Veiel, H.O.F., Crisand, M., Stroszeck-Somschor, H., & Herrle, J. (1991). Social support networks of chronically strained couples: Similarity and overlap. *Journal of Social and Personal Relationships, 8*, 279-292.

Viall, E.K. (1992). Measuring journalistic values: A cosmopolitan/community continuum. *Journal of Mass Media Ethics, 7*, 41-53.

Viswanath, K., & Arora, P. (2000). Ethnic media in the United States: An essay on their role in integration, assimilation and social control. *Mass Communication & Society, 3*, 39-56.

Viswanath, K., & Demers, D.K. (1999). Mass media from a macrosocial perspective. In D.K. Demers & K. Viswanath (Eds.), *Mass media, social control and social change: A macrosocial perspective* (pp. 3-28). Ames: Iowa State University Press.

Viswanath, K., & Finnegan, J.R., Jr. (1991, May). *The knowledge gap hypothesis: Twenty years later.* Paper presented at the annual conference of the International Communication Association, Chicago.

Viswanath, K., Finnegan, J.R., Jr., Rooney, B., & Potter, J. (1990). Community ties in a Midwest community and use of newspapers and cable TV. *Journalism Quarterly, 67*, 899-911.

Voakes, P.S. (1999). Civic duties: Newspaper journalists' views on public journalism. *Journalism and Mass Communication Quarterly, 76*, 756-774.

von Bertalanfry, L. (1968). *General system theory.* New York: George Braziller.

Wacquint, J.D., & Wilson, W.J. (1989). The cost of racial and class exclusion in the inner city. *Annals of the American Academy of Political and Social Science, 501*, 8-25.

Wallin, P. (1953). A Guttman scale for measuring women's neighborliness. *American Journal of Sociology, 59*, 243-246.

Wandersman, A., & Giamartino, G.A. (1980). Community and individual difference characteristics as influences in initial participation. *American Journal of Community Psychology, 8*, 217-228.

Wang, T.T. (1995). *Agenda-setting and -promoting as power in urban communities: The relationship between neighborhood organizations and the mass media.* Unpublished doctoral thesis, Northwestern University, Chicago, IL.

Warburton, D., & Suiter, J. (1996). The costs of job dissatisfaction. In D. Warburton & N. Sherwood (Eds.), *Pleasure and quality of life* (pp. 13-28). New York: Wiley.

Ward, J. (1980). *The Little Red Hen effect: Sources of media diversity in the central city.* Paper presented at the midwinter meeting. Association for Education in Journalism. University of Minnesota, School of Journalism and Mass Communication, Minneapolis.

Ward, J., & Gaziano, C. (1976). A new variety of urban press: Neighborhood public affairs publications. *Journalism Quarterly, 53*(1), 61-67, 116.

Warren, D. (1975). *Black neighborhoods: An assessment of community power.* Ann Arbor: University of Michigan Press.

Warren, D., & Warren, R.B. (1977). *The neighborhood organizer's handbook.* Notre Dame, IN: University of Notre Dame Press.

Warren, D.I. (1986). The helping roles of neighbors: Some empirical patterns. In R.B. Taylor (Ed.), *Urban neighborhoods, research and policy* (pp. 310-330). New York: Praeger.

Warren, R. (1978). *Community in America.* Chicago: Rand McNally College.

Waste, R.J. (1987). *Power and pluralism in American cities.* New York: Greenwood.

Weaver, D., & Wilhoit, G.C. (1996). *The American journalist in the 1990s: U.S. news people at the end of an era.* Mahwah, NJ: Erlbaum.

Weaver, D.H., & Wilhoit, G.C. (1986) *The American journalist: A portrait of U.S. news people and their work.* Bloomington: Indiana University Press.

Webb, E.T., Campbell, D.T., Schwartz, R.D., Sechrest, L., & Grove, J. (1981). *Nonreactive measures in the social sciences* (2nd ed.). Boston: Houghton Mifflin.

Weber, M. (1978). *Economy and society* (Vol. 1, 2). Berkeley: University of California Press.

Weenig, M.W.H. (1993). The strength of weak and strong communication ties in a community information program. *Journal of Applied Social Psychology, 23,* 1712-1731.

Weenig, M.W.H., & Midden, C.J.H. (1991). Communication network influences on information diffusion and persuasion. *Journal of Personality & Social Psychology, 61,* 734-742.

Weenig, M.W.H., & Midden, C.J.H. (1997). Mass-media information campaigns and knowledge-gap effects. *Journal of Applied Social Psychology, 27,* 945-958.

Weimann, G. (1983). The strength of weak conversational ties in the flow of information and influence. *Social Networks, 5,* 245-267.

Weissman, H.H. (1970). *Community councils and community control.* Pittsburgh: University of Pittsburgh Press.

Wellman, B. (1979). The community question: The intimate network of East Yorkers. *American Journal of Sociology, 84,* 1201-1231.

Wellman, B. (1983). Network analysis: Some basic principles. In R. Collins (Ed.), *Sociological theory* (pp. 155-200). San Francisco: Jossey-Bass.

Wellman, B. (1992). Men in networks: Private communities, domestic friendships. In P. Nardi (Ed.), *Men's friendships* (pp. 74-114). Newbury Park, CA: Sage.

Wellman, B., & Leighton, B. (1979). Networks, neighborhoods and communities: Approaches to the study of the community question. *Urban Affairs Quarterly, 14,* 363-390.

Wellman, B., Salaff, J., Dimitrova, D., Garton, L., Gulia, M., & Haythornthwaite, C. (1996). Computer networks as social networks: Collaborative work, telework and virtual community. *Annual Review of Sociology, 22*, 213-238.

Wellman, B., & Tindall, D.B. (1993). How telephone networks connect social networks. In W.D. Richards, Jr. & G.A. Barnett (Eds.), *Progress in communication sciences* (Vol. 12, pp. 63-93). Norwood, NJ: Ablex.

Werner, C.M., Altman, I., & Brown, B.B. (1992). A transactional approach to interpersonal relations: Physical environment, social context and temporal qualities. *Journal of Social and Personal Relationships, 9*, 297-323.

White, C.S. (1997). Citizen participation and the Internet: Prospects for civic deliberation in the information age. *Social Studies, 88*, 23-28.

White, W.J. (1999). Academic topographies: A network analysis of disciplinarity among communication faculty. *Human Communication Research, 4*, 604-617.

Whyte, W.F. (1943). *Street corner society*. Chicago: University of Chicago Press.

Wiewel, W., Brown, B., & Morris, M. (1989). The linkage between regional and neighborhood development. *Economic Development Quarterly, 3*(2), 94-110.

Wigand, R.T. (1977). Communication network analysis in urban development. In W.E. Arnold & J.L. Buley (Eds.), *Urban communication: Survival in the city* (pp. 137-170). Cambridge, MA: Winthrop.

Wilkinson, K.P. (1986). In search of the community in the changing countryside. *Rural Society, 51*, 1-17.

Willis, A. (1993). *American suburbs rating guide and fact book*. Milpitas, CA: Toucan Valley Publications.

Wilson, T.C. (1986). Community population size and social heterogeneity: An empirical test. *American Journal of Sociology, 91*(5), 1154-1169.

Winters, C. (1979). The social identity of evolving neighborhoods. *Landscape, 23*(1), 8-14.

Wirth, L. (1938). Urbanism as a way of life. *American Journal of Sociology, 44*, 3-24.

Woelfel, J. (1993). Cognitive processes and communication networks: A general theory. In W.D. Richards Jr. & G.A. Barnett (Eds.), *Progress in communication sciences* (Vol. 12, pp. 21-42). Norwood, NJ: Ablex.

Woolever, C. (1992). A contextual approach to neighborhood attachment. *Urban Studies, 29*, 99-116.

Wright, C.R. (1960). Functional analysis and mass communication. *Public Opinion Quarterly, 24*, 605-620.

Wright, F.L. (1958). *The living city*. New York: New Horizon Press.

Wyatt, R.O., Katz, E., & Kim, J. (2000). Bridging the spheres: Political and personal conversation in public and private spaces. *Journal of Communication, 50*, 71-92.

Wyatt, R.O., Kim, J., & Katz, E. (2000). How feeling free to talk affects ordinary political conversation, purposeful argumentation and civic participation. *Journalism & Mass Communication Quarterly, 77*, 99-114.

Yerby, J. (1995). Family systems theory reconsidered: Integrating social construction theory and dialectical process. *Communication Theory, 5*, 339-365.

Young, I.M. (1986). The ideal of community and the politics of difference. *Social Theory and Practice, 12*(1), 1-26.

Appendix:
Additional Tables

TABLE 1
Relationships Between Editor's Characteristics and Editor's Community Perceptions

	Age	Gender (hi = female)	Education (1 = yes; 2 = no)	Lives in Community
			Editor's Characteristics	
Editor's Perceptions of Community				
Quality of Life Variables				
Quality of Life Ratings				
Editor's community QOL rating	.14	.10	.11	-.06
How think residents rate QOL	.10	.07	.13	-.00
Residents' Image of Area				
People focus (Imagpeop)	-.10	.13	.00	.05
Nature-Physical emphasis	-.15#	.14	-.09	-.11
Housing-Culture	-.03	-.05	-.04	-.02
Negative	-.02	-.02	.04	.03
Positive	.01	-.03	.03	.15#
Attitude	-.01	.03	-.00	.06
Major Assets of Area				
Physical (Assphyen)	-.06	-.03	-.03	-.18*
People	.01	-.18*	.02	-.09
Leisure opp.	-.05	.02	.15#	.14
Economic factors	.05	-.07	-.06	-.01
Services avlb.	-.08	.12	-.15#	.02
Feelings, attitudes	-.03	.00	.06	-.09
Area's Major Liabilities				
Economic (Liabecon)	-.01	-.08	.19*	-.08
People	-.06	.02	.03	-.06
Poverty	.05	-.01	-.23**	-.06
Housing	-.15#	.18*	-.06	.09
Crime	-.11	-.19*	.13	.15#
Roads	.02	-.08	.07	.01
Government	-.02	.01	-.07	-.03
Schools	-.20*	.04	.06	-.03
Public services	-.11	-.13	-.04	.20*
Urban ills	-.07	-.05	-.03	.15#
Racial factors	.15#	.08	.08	-.12
Environment	.13	.08	-.03	.08
Perceptions of Residents Behaviors				
Level of commitment to area	-.21*	-.14	-.05	.06
Talkfreq (frequency talk)	.07	-.05	-.05	-.13
Inout (internal-external links)	.06	.03	.23**	-.13
Wheretlk (street/public activity)	.11	.02	-.06	.08
GR1 (amount of formal group activity)	.02	-.10	-.10	-.01

TABLE 1 (cont.)

	Editor's Characteristics			
	Age	Gender (hi = female)	Education (1 = yes; 2 = no)	Lives in Community
GR2 (how much group activity exists)	-.08	.10	-.00	-.07
Informd (informed about current events)	-.17#	-.05	-.17#	.08
Demrep (who won last pres. race in community vote)	-.15	.14	-.01	-.03
Community Perceptions				
Diversity Perceptions				
Total Perceived Diversity	-.16#	-.02	.23**	-.13
Racial Diversity	-.08	-.01	.06	-.11
Religious Diversity	-.18#	-.06#	.26**	-.03
Educational Diversity	-.22*	.09	.02	-.03
Life-cycle Diversity	-.07	-.04	.17#	-.01
SES Diversity	-.13	-.09	.25**	-.10
Institutions Reported in Community by Editors				
No. institutions cited (Instcom)	-.10	-.07	.13	.05
Major factory (Factry)	-.04	-.18*	.15#	.04
Library (Libry)	-.03	.08	-.02	-.01
Park (Park)	-.05	.05	-.04	.01
Manufacturing arcas (mfg)	-.07	-.11	.12	.02
Local hospital (hosptl)	-.09	-.12	.13	.07
Recreation center (recon)	-.09	.00	.04	-.00
Several churches (church2)	-.07	.04	.09	.14
Shopping mall (mall)	.04	-.02	.08	-.03
Private ethnic club (club)	-.04	-.14	.05	.10
Retail stores (retail)	.00	.04	.09	.06
Small convenience stores (constor)	-.17*	.13	.09	-.06
Local schools attended by area youth (locsch)	-.09	-.01	.01	.04
Editor's Perceptions of Who Has Power in Community				
Neighborhood groups (Powngrps)	-.10	-.00	-.04	.19*
Money (Powmoney)	-.01	.07	.11	-.07
Institutions (Powinst)	-.05	.08	.04	-.04
Media (Powmedia)	.23**	-.01	.07	-.08
Government (Powgov)	-.02	.06	-.00	-.05
Editor's Reports of Neighborhod Conflicts				
Social, group conflicts (consocl)	.07	-.06	.10	-.02
Political conflicts (Conpol)	-.05	-.03	-.03	.14#
Economic conflicts (Conecon)	-.00	.02	-.11	-.05

Note. Sample sizes for variables in the survey are 141, with occasional missing data. The sample size for correlations involving one of the variables based on census area are 81, with occasional missing data.

TABLE 2
Relationships Between Newspaper Characteristics and Editor's Community Perceptions

| | Newspaper Characteristics | | | | | % Revenue from | | |
	Free-Paid (hi=paid)	Circ.	Freq. (low= more often)	Size Editorial Staff	Chain (low=chain)	Adv.	Sales	Other
Quality of Life Perceptions								
Quality of Life Ratings								
How editor rates community QOL	.06	-.04	.01	-.07	-.01	.04	.02	-.24**
How think residents rate QOL	.06	.10	-.04	.03	.02	.14#	.07	-.30***
Residents' Image of Area								
People focus	-.13	-.03	-.07	-.07	.09	.07	.04	-.01
Nature-Physical emphasis	.03	-.06	.01	-.10	-.05	-.00	-.14#	-.04
Housing-Culture	.14	-.06	.03	.03	.02	-.02	-.06	-.05
Negative	-.09	-.05	.01	-.05	-.13	.07	-.04	-.07
Positive	-.05	-.03	.00	-.06	.16#	.12	.05	-.03
Attitude	.00	-.01	-.03	-.06	-.03	.14	-.01	.02
Major Assets of Area								
Physical	.03	.12	-.00	.17*	-.05	.01	.00	-.04
People	-.27***	-.09	.13	-.08	.06	-.08	.04	.14#
Leisure opportunities	-.21*	.21*	-.12	.12	.06	-.00	.05	.02
Economic factors	.07	.06	.01	.14	-.09	.11	.12	-.08
Services available	.03	-.03	-.06	.01	.02	.12	.02	.08
Feelings, attitudes	.04	.00	-.12	-.06	.15#	.01	-.07	.07

Area's Major Liabilities

Economic	-.14	.17#	-.10	.22**	-.08	.05	.03	-.12
People	-.12	-.01	-.02	.00	-.15#	.06	.02.	.03
Poverty	-.01	-.06	-.15#	-.05	.01	.02	.04	.36***
Housing	-.10	-.12	.25**	-.11	-.15#	-.05	.01	.12
Crime	-.17*	.13	.11	-.03	.09	-.03	.02	-.09
Roads	-.10	-.02	-.07	.10	.11	.07	.14#	-.09
Government	.09	-.07	-.06	-.10	.24**	-.04	-.15#	.03
Schools	-.08	-.05	.07	-.09	.06	-.03	.03	.08
Public services	-.07	.01	-.09	-.06	.03	.11	.00	.06
Urban ills	-.11	.02	-.10	.05	.15#	.09	.06	-.03
Racial factors	.06	.02	-.03	.06	.16#	.14#	-.03	-.07
Environment	.18*	.25**	-.15#	.48***	.05	.04	.09	-.04
Perceptions of Residents Behaviors								
Commitment to area	-.10	.10	.08	-.00	-.08	-.13	-.06	-.05
Talkfreq (freq. talk)	-.09	.08	-.11	.10	-.07	.09	.12	.09
Inout (internal-external)	.16#	-.11	.07	-.20*	-.06	-.17*	.05	.01
Wheretlk (street/public activity)	.16#	.13	-.10	.19*	.08	.01	-.05	-.04
GR1 (amount of formal group activity)	-.11	-.05	.06	.05	-.24**	.05	.01	.10
GR2 (how much group activity exists)	-.00	.02	.15#	.08	.08	-.06	-.14	-.09
Informd (informed about current events)	-.06	.08	.13	-.00	.11	.04	.24**	.07
Demrep (who won last pres. race in community	-.15	-.17#	.20*	-.18#	-.17#	-.08	-.02	.21*

(continues)

TABLE 2 (cont.)

			Newspaper Characteristics			% Revenue from		
	Free-Paid (hi=paid)	Circ.	Freq. (low= more often)	Size Editorial Staff	Chain (low=chain)	Adv.	Sales	Other
Community Perceptions								
Diversity Perceptions								
Total Perceived Diversity	-.01	.12	-.02	.06	.09	-.06	.02	-.05
Racial Diversity	-.08	.00	.09	-.06	-.09	-.14	.04	.06
Religious Diversity	.01	.06	-.08	.05	.06	-.15#	-.06	-.05
Educational Diversity	-.08	.06	.01	-.03	.10	-.03	.07	-.02
Life-cycle Diversity	.05	.09	-.02	.06	.00	-.01	-.15#	-.07
SES Diversity	-.03	.12	-.10	.10	.10	.05	.09	-.04
Institutions Reported in Community by Editors								
No. institutions cited (Instcom)	-.09	.19*	-.20*	.15#	.21*	.21*	.13	.03
Major factory (Factry)	-.04	.20*	-.04	.19*	.25**	.12	.19*	-.11
Library (Libry)	.02	.07	-.06	.04	.14#	.11	.03	.10
Park (Park)	-.06	.03	-.11	.03	.05	.32***	.05	.10
Manufacturing areas (mfg)	-.03	.20*	-.19*	.14#	.25**	.11	.10	.08
Local hospital (hosptl)	-.10	.14	-.10	.09	.07	.03	.03	.03
Recreation center (recon)	-.12	.11	-.10	.06	.21*	.19*	.12	.03
Several churches (church2)	.00	.01	-.06	.00	-.03	.16*	.01	.05
Shopping mall (mall)	-.13	.20*	-.21*	.16#	.11	.03	.02	-.00
Private ethnic club (club)	-.01	.14#	-.22*	.16#	.13	.04	-.02	.04
Retail stores (retail)	.01	.07	-.16*	.05	.05	.27***	.10	.05
Small convenience stores (constor)	-.03	.05	-.05	.03	.11	.13	.00	-.09

254

Local schools attended by area youth (locsch)	-.12	.06	-.07	.01	.05	.19*	.17*	.01
Editor's Perceptions of Who Has Power in Community								
Neighborhood groups (Powngrps)	-.01	-.07	.05	-.08	.09	-.03	.01	.09
Money (Powmoney)	.08	.02	.02	.06	.07	.11	-.11	-.00
Institutions (Powinst)	-.03	-.08	.11	.07	-.04	.12	-.08	-.05
Media (Powmedia)	-.11	-.06	-.07	.12	-.13	-.06	.10	-.09
Government (Powgov)	.01	-.08	-.07	-.01	.01	.01	.01	.02
Editor's Reports of Neighborhood Conflicts								
Social, group conflicts (consocl)	.02	-.07	-.01	-.07	-.05	.12	.05	-.12
Political conflicts (Conpol)	-.03	-.05	.06	-.07	.05	-.16*	-.03	.10
Economic conflicts (Conecon)	-.01	.04	-.01	.02	-.02	.06	-.05	.04

Note. Sample sizes for variables in the survey are 141, with occasional missing data. The sample size for correlations involving one of the variables based on census area are 81, with occasional missing data.

TABLE 3
Relationship Between Age/Origins of Paper, and Editor's Perceptions of the Quality of Life in the Community

	Age of Paper	Who Publishes Paper					Who Founded Paper			
		Individual	Chain	Dev. Org.	Individual	Community Group	Dev. Org.	Merchants	Activists	Other
Quality of Life Perceptions										
Quality of Life Ratings										
Editor's QOL rating	-.15	.09	-.15#	.04	.08	-.05	-.03	.08	-.14	.00
How think residents rate QOL	-.01	.09	-.06	.07	.09	-.11	-.05	.12	-.13	-.01
Residents' Image of Area as Reported by Editors										
People focus	-.01	-.08	-.09	.16#	-.05	-.04	.05	.15#	-.08	.11
Nature-Physical	-.04	-.08	.01	.07	-.06	-.02	.00	-.06	.01	.05
Housing-Culture	.10	-.17*	.07	.08	-.16#	.17*	.07	.21*	-.09	-.04
Negative	.03	-.01	.05	.05	-.02	-.07	.07	.01	.06	-.05
Positive	-.04	.08	-.06	.02	.05	-.08	.04	-.01	-.13	.09
Attitude	.12	-.01	.05	-.10	-.07	-.10	-.00	.01	.22**	-.07
Major Assets of Area										
Physical	.21*	.00	.09	.08	-.16#	.05	-.05	.09	.02	.04
People	-.26**	-.11	-.01	-.06	.00	.26**	.03	-.11	-.10	.01
Leisure opp.	.01	.06	-.08	-.04	.02	-.12	-.02	.05	.03	.03
Economic factors	-.04	.05	-.15#	.02	-.11	-.12	.05	.21*	.00	.11
Services avlb.	.18*	.05	-.04	-.11	.02	-.11	.07	.01	-.01	.10
Feelings, attitudes	.09	-.06	.09	-.06	.04	.01	-.04	-.05	.07	-.08
Area's Major Liabilities										
Economic	.11	.06	.01	-.02	-.05	-.02	.07	.08	-.03	.09
People	.10	.07	.00	-.09	.04	-.02	-.09	-.06	.00	-.07
Poverty	.06	-.04	.18*	-.10	-.11	.11	-.09	.05	.09	.03
Housing	-.13	-.12	.00	.19*	-.12	.11	.06	-.02	.13	-.08

Crime	-.06	-.07	-.03	.12	-.08	.01	.06	-.02	.07	.01
Roads	.09	.02	.01	.00	.06	.14#	-.05	-.11	-.08	.10
Government	-.01	-.05	.16#	-.14#	.20*	.05	-.13	-.12	-.09	-.01
Schools	-.07	-.04	.08	.03	.00	-.04	.06	-.02	.02	.02
Public services	-.02	-.06	.00	.06	.08	-.06	-.06	-.08	-.01	-.04
Urban ills	-.05	.13	-.15#	.07	.00	-.01	.01	-.04	-.03	.05
Racial factors	.20*	-.04	.03	-.07	.06	-.07	.06	.00	-.04	-.05
Environment	.15	.08	-.06	.02	-.05	-.03	.04	.07	.09	-.06
Editors Reports of Residents' Activity										
Commitment to area	-.02	.03	-.01	.18*	-.24**	-.01	.11	.03	-.02	.23**
Talkfreq (freq. talk)	.05	.01	-.02	.02	.02	-.09	.11	-.01	.07	-.19#
Inout (internal-external)	-.11	-.01	-.06	.12	.00	-.05	.01	-.02	.06	.03
Wheretlk (street/public activity)	.12	-.13	.18*	-.06	.14	.03	-.04	-.17*	-.07	-.01
GR1 (amount of formal group activity)	-.02	.02	-.03	-.02	-.06	.03	.07	.08	-.03	-.05
GR2 (how much group activity exists)	.07	-.08	.12	-.11	.06	.07	-.04	-.08	-.03	.02
Informed about events	.02	-.08	.14	-.00	.01	.08	-.04	-.05	-.10	.08
Who won last pres. race	-.14	.06	-.17*	.19*	-.23**	.26**	.11	-.07	.19*	-.12
Community Perceptions										
Diversity Perceptions										
Total Perceived Diversity	.12	.01	.10	-.02	-.10	.06	-.04	-.02	.08	.03
Racial Diversity	.06	-.06	.13	.03	-.03	-.12	-.06	-.08	.18*	.12
Religious Diversity	-.08	.07	.01	.13	-.13	.03	-.07	-.05	.18*	.04
Educational Diversity	.04	-.03	.02	.04	-.05	.02	-.06	.05	.06	-.08
Life-cycle Diversity	.07	-.08	.13	.06	-.05	.12	-.04	-.19*	.10	.04
SES Diversity	.06	.06	.10	-.17*	-.12	.06	-.01	.04	.09	-.02
Institutions Reported in Community by Editors										
No. institutions cited										
(Instcom)	.15#	-.14#	.14	-.09	-.06	-.01	.02	.11	-.02	.07

(continues)

TABLE 3 (cont.)

	Age of Paper	Who Publishes Paper			Who Founded Paper					
		Individual	Chain	Dev. Org.	Individual	Community Group	Dev. Org.	Merchants	Activists	Other
Major factory (Factry)	.03	-.13	.08	-.04	-.06	.01	.19*	.16#	-.14#	-.07
Library (Libry)	.19*	-.12	.19*	-.06	-.05	.02	.00	.06	-.00	.07
Park (Park)	.11	-.12	.17*	.01	-.06	.01	-.01	.05	.04	.07
Manufacturing areas (mfg)	.12	-.10	.09	-.11	-.06	.00	.00	.12	.02	-.04
Local hospital (hosptl)	.15#	-.13	.13	-.06	-.03	.00	.09	-.03	-.00	.12
Recreation center (recon)	.05	-.02	-.01	-.05	.10	-.05	-.09	.02	-.09	.10
Several churches (church2)	.08	-.19*	.20*	-.01	-.04	-.01	.08	-.05	.07	.06
Shopping mall (mall)	-.02	.08	.01	-.07	-.03	-.02	-.08	.14#	-.05	.10
Private ethnic club (club)	.17*	-.07	.04	-.07	.00	-.07	.11	-.05	-.01	.03
Retail stores (retail)	.09	-.10	.13	-.12	-.02	.04	-.07	.14#	-.08	.08
Small convenience stores (constor)	.10	-.16#	.09	.02	-.18*	.02	.00	.13	.11	.07
Local schools attended by area youth (locsch)	.07	-.12	.05	-.06	-.05	.02	-.18*	.13	.11	-.04
Editor's Perceptions of Who Has Power in Community										
Neighborhood groups (Powngrps)	.10	-.11	.08	.02	-.09	-.03	.18*	-.04	.11	-.15#
Money (Powmoney)	.02	.01	.01	-.02	-.19*	-.10	.00	.15#	.19*	-.07
Institutions (Powinst)	.02	-.07	.20*	-.04	-.11	-.04	.06	-.02	.12	.12

258

Media (Powmedia)	-.04	.01	-.10	.05	-.14#	.05	-.01	.06	.11	.04
Government (Powgov)	-.03	-.03	.05	.08	-.01	.02	-.06	.12	-.02	.01

Editor's Reports of Neighborhood Conflicts

Social, group conflicts

(consocl)	.02	-.07	.02	.02	-.14#	-.15#	-.03	.18*	.12	.10

Political conflicts

(Conpol)	.03	-.16#	.01	.26**	-.03	.00	.11	-.04	-.08	.06

Economic conflicts

(Conecon)	.11	.02	.03	-.06	-.05	-.06	.06	.09	-.03	.10

Note. Sample sizes for variables in the survey are 141, with occasional missing data. The sample size for correlations involving one of the variables based on census area are 81, with occasional missing data.

TABLE 4
Strength of Mass Communication Linkages

Number of hours watched television yesterday

0 hours	56	17.1%	6 hours	12	3.7%	Total =	327
up to 1 hour	46	14.1%	7 hours	2	.6%	Mean =	2.8 hours
2 hours	66	20.2%	8 hours	5	1.5%	Median =	2.0 hours
3 hours	54	16.5%	9 hours	0	0	Std.Dev. =	2.5 hours
4 hours	44	13.5%	10 hours	5	1.5%		
5 hours	30	9.2%	over 10 hours	7	2.1%		

Number of hours listened to the radio yesterday

0 hours	126	38.8%	6 hours	6	1.8%	Total =	325
up to 1 hour	64	19.7%	7 hours	3	.9%	Mean =	2.1 hours
2 hours	42	12.9%	8 hours	14	4.3%	Median =	1.0 hours
3 hours	25	7.7%	9 hours	4	1.2%	Std.Dev. =	2.9 hours
4 hours	17	5.2%	10 hours	7	2.2%		
5 hours	11	3.4%	over 10 hours	6	1.8%		

Number of days read a newspaper last week

none	1	.3%	4 days	12	3.9%	Total =	306
once	41	13.4%	5 days	18	5.9%	Mean =	5.1 days
2 days	31	10.1%	6 days	6	2.0%	Median =	7.0 days
3 days	22	7.2%	7 days	175	57.2%	Std.Dev. =	2.4 days

Number of magazines read regularly

0	60	18.7%	6	9	2.8%	Total =	321
1	43	13.4%	7	8	2.5%	Mean =	2.9
2	61	19.0%	8	3	.9%	Mean =	2.9
3	63	19.6%	9	3	.9%	Std.Dev. =	2.8
4	36	11.2%	10	6	1.9%		
5	16	5.0%	over 10	8	2.5%		

Number of books read in past 6 months

0	62	19.1%	6	14	4.3%	Total = 325
1	27	8.3%	7	3	.9%	Mean = 4.9
2	44	13.5%	8	8	2.5%	Median = 3.0
3	32	9.8%	9	2	.6%	Std.Dev. = 4.4
4	27	8.3%	10	13	4.0%	
5	14	4.3%	over 10	79	24.3%	

Number of videos watched in past month

0	118	35.6%	6	11	3.3%	Total = 331
1	17	5.1%	7	3	.9%	Mean = 4.5
2	32	9.7%	8	4	1.2%	Median = 2.0
3	37	11.2%	9	2	.6%	Std.Dev. = 6.6
4	21	6.3%	10	19	5.7%	
5	28	8.5%	11+	39	11.8%	

Number of films seen at a theater

0	174	52.6%	6	5	1.5%	Total = 331
1	61	18.4%	7	1	.3%	Mean = 1.3
2	43	13.0%	8	0		Median = 0.0
3	21	6.3%	9	1	.3%	Std.Dev. = 2.8
4	13	3.9%	10	3	.9%	
5	6	1.8%	11+	3	.9%	

TABLE 5
Correlations Between Individual Measures of Mass and Interpersonal Communication, and Social Category Measures

	No. in household	No. children in hsehold	Age	Education	House-hold Income	Gender	Race
No. people talked to							
in household	.24***	.17**	-.08	-.01	.11#	.07	-.08
neighbors	.03	.04	-.01	.00	.01	-.01	-.00
others in neighborhood	.08	.07	-.03	.03	.11#	.02	-.03
others outside neighborhood in public places	-.01	.07 .	03	.16**	.16**	-.09	-.01
elsewhere in city	-.02	-.04	-.10#	.19***	.16**	-.02	-.00
at job	-.02	-.02	-.26***	.17**	.19***	-.08	.02
locally by phone	.03	-.06	-.18***	.16**	.14*	.05	-.01
outside metro area by phone	.01	-.07	-.15*	.12*	.12*	-.12*	-.08
by fax/sent, received	.06	.00	-.18**	.15**	.28**	-.09	-.09
Hours watched TV yesterday	.00	.02	.03	-.21***	-.19***	.01	.09
Hours listened to radio yesterday	.03	.03	-.06	-.05	.06	-.02	-.09
No. days read paper last week	-.18**	-.17**	.36***	.01	.12*	.03	-.04
No. magazines read regularly	-.03	-.05	-.02	.11*	.17**	-.09	-.02
No. books read in past 6 months	-.10	-.08	.07	.16**	.01	-.02	.02
No. videos watched in past month	.23***	.14*	-.30***	-.06	.02	-.02	.04
No. films seen in theater	.05	.06	-.19**	-.01	.08	-.01	.11*

***p < .001; **p < .01; *p < .05; #p < .10

TABLE 6
Strength of Mass Communication Linkages: 1996 Study

Number of hours watch(ed) TV	Yesterday		Usually				
0 hours	45	11.9%	12	3.2%			
up to 1 hour	66	17.5%	71	18.8%			
2 hours	79	21.0%	99	26.3%			
3 hours	63	16.7%	59	15.6%			
4 hours	46	12.2%	61	16.2%		Yesterday		Usually
5 hours	27	7.2%	33	8.8%		Mean = 3.04	3.15
6 hours	19	5.0%	15	4.0%		Median = 2.00	3.00
7 hours	6	1.6%	9	2.4%		Std.Dev. = 2.62	2.24
8 hours	11	2.9%	4	1.1%		Total = 377	377
9 hours	2	.5%	1	.3%			
10 hours	4	1.1%	7	1.9%			
over 10 hours	9	2.4%	6	1.6%			

Number of hours listened to the radio yesterday

0 hours	88	23.3%	6 hours	11	2.9%
up to 1 hour	124	32.9%	7 hours	2	.5%
2 hours	53	14.1%	8 hours	15	4.0%
3 hours	37	9.8%	9 hours	8	2.1%
4 hours	20	5.3%	10 hours	8	2.1%
5 hours	6	1.6%	over 10 hours	5	1.3%

Total = 377
Mean = 2.32 hours
Median = 1.00 hours
Std.Dev. = 2.90 hours

Number of days read a newspaper last week

none	30	8.0%	4 days	20	5.3%
once	36	9.6%	5 days	27	7.2%
2 days	31	8.3%	6 days	10	2.7%
3 days	33	8.8%	7 days	188	50.1%

Total = 375
Mean = 4.77 days
Median = 7.00 days
Std.Dev. = 2.58 days

(continues)

TABLE 6 (cont.)

Number of magazines read regularly

Value	N	%			
0	76	20.2%			
1	34	9.0%			
2	71	18.9%			
3	76	20.2%			
4	44	11.7%			
5	29	7.7%	Total	=	376
6 - 10	39	10.4%	Mean	=	3.10
11 - 20	3	.8%	Median	=	3.00
21+	4	1.1%	Std.Dev.	=	3.16

Number of books read in past 6 months

Value	N	%			
0	80	21.3%			
1	39	10.4%			
2	55	14.7%			
3	44	11.7%			
4	28	7.5%			
5	24	6.4%	Total	=	375
6 - 10	41	10.9%	Mean	=	5.33
11 - 20	31	8.3%	Median	=	3.00
21+	33	8.8%	Std.Dev.	=	6.38

Number of videos watched in past month

Value	N	%			
0	139	37.0%			
1	31	8.2%			
2	40	10.6%			
3	33	8.8%			
4	32	8.5%			
5	28	7.4%	Total	=	376
6-10	53	14.1%	Mean	=	3.36
11-20	10	2.7%	Median	=	2.00
21+	10	2.7%	Std.Dev.	=	4.48

Number of films seen at a theater

Value	N	%			
0	186	49.5%			
1	69	18.4%			
2	60	16.0%			
3	31	8.2%			
4	17	4.5%	Total	=	376
5	7	1.9%	Mean	=	1.19
6-10	4	1.1%	Median	=	1.00
11+	2	.5%	Std.Dev.	=	1.80

TABLE 7
Communication Needs: 1996 Study

Reports of Communication Needs:	Means (0-10 scale)	Standard Deviation	Median	N
Com. in Public Areas Role:	5.99	3.00	6.00	376
(CMU4) "I enjoy striking up conversations with people I don't know when I'm waiting in line, sitting next to someone in a waiting room or while having a cup of coffee somewhere."				
Communication Homopoly:	4.87	3.06	5.00	3.74
(CMU5) "I feel more comfortable talking with people like myself than with people who are different."				
Neighborhood Com.:	5.34	2.64	5.00	3.75
(CMU18) "I wish I had a chance to spend more time talking with other people in my neighborhood."				
Need for Interpersonal Communication:	3.94	3.29	4.00	372
(CMU19) "I hate being alone and sometimes just leave the house to go somewhere so I won't be lonely and can talk with people."				
Need for Solitude:	5.83	2.86	5.00	374
(CMU20) "I value my solitude and welcome the chance to be alone and not have to talk with other people."				
Communication Sender Role across Contexts:	5.37	3.20	5.00	372
(CMU11) "If there was some way I could send a message to everyone in Cleveland using mail by telephone or some computer hookup, I'd do it regularly."				
Mass Com. Sender Role1:	5.68	3.35	6.00	376
(CMU14) "Sometimes I wish I were a columnist for the Plain Dealer and could tell everybody what I thought about what's going on today."				
Mass Com. Sender Role2:	5.24	3.15	5.00	372
(CMU17) "I often feel the need to express myself and wish I had a chance to be a writer or reporter."				

(continues)

265

TABLE 7 (cont.)

Reports of Communication Needs:	Means (0-10 scale)	Standard Deviation	Median	N
Mass Com. Receiver Role: (CMU13) "Even if it cost more, I'd like to have a cable system that had 500 channels so there was always something that fit my personal tastes."	4.76	3.59	5.00	373
Mass Com. Receiver/ Cosmopolitan Role: (CMU7) "I enjoy reading about what's going on in the country and around the world more than news about the local area."	5.39	2.94	5.00	375
Mass Com. Receiver/ Neigh. Locus Role: (CMU8) "I wish there were more news in the media about my neighborhood and less about Cleveland or the metro area in general."	4.57	2.82	5.00	373
Mass Com. Receiver/News vs. Entertainment Role: (CMU9) "I enjoy reading the entertainment, sports, and features in the daily newspaper more than the general news sections."	5.07	3.02	5.00	374

TABLE 8

Communication Routines: 1996 Study

Reports of Communication Needs:	Means (0-10 scale)	Standard Deviation	Median	N
Interpersonal Com. Pattern at Work:	6.74	3.71	8.00	365
(CMU2) "I seem to spend much of my time at work talking with customers, clients or coworkers."				
Family vs. External Locus Pattern:	2.97	3.43	2.00	376
(CMU3) "Many days I don't talk with anyone outside my family."				
Com. Homopoly Pattern:	5.66	3.33	6.00	374
(CMU6) "The people I see most often live in the same part of town I do."				
Interpersonal Com. with Friends Pattern:	7.31	2.45	8.00	374
(CMU15) "I spend a lot of time talking with friends and associates about things I find interesting, like hobbies, personal interests, or current events."				
Clubs/Orgs. as Context for Communication:	7.30	2.32	8.00	376
(CMU16) "I think organizations and clubs are a good way to find people you can talk with about similar interests."				

TABLE 9

Relationships Among Communication Variables: 1996 Study

	Interpersonal Communication Summary and Variability Measures			
	Mean	Variance	Minimum	Maximum
Mass Communication Summary and Variability Measures				
Mean	-.04	-.11*	.04	-.09#
Variance	.06	.03	.09#	.04
Minimum	-.03	-.06	.00	-.06
Maximum	.06	.02	.10#	.03
	Interpersonal Communication Summary and Variability Measures			
	Mean	Variance	Minimum	Maximum
Media Activity Measures				
No. of hours watched TV yesterday	-.15**	-.18***	-.03	-.18***
No. of hours usually watch TV daily	-.06	-.07	-.07	-.07
No. of hours listened to radio yesterday	.00	-.02	.02	-.02
No. of days read paper last week	-.04	-.05	.02	-.04
No. of magazines read regularly	.03	-.02	.17***	-.01
No. of books read in past 6 months	.02	.03	-.04	.04
No. of videos watched last month	.15**	.11*	.10*	.12*

Mass Communication Summary and Variability Measures

	Mean	Variance	Minimum	Maximum
No. of films seen at theater in past month	.11*	.03	.16**	.05
Cable TV	.03	.07	.05	.07
Internet Access	.14**	.11	.16**	.12*

Interpersonal Communication Measures

No. people talked to

	Mean	Variance	Minimum	Maximum
In household	-.07	.01	-.03	-.01
In neighborhood	.03	.14**	-.05	.14**
At work	-.09#	.01	-.02	.00
Elsewhere in city	-.03	-.01	-.01	-.02
People in metro area by telephone	.06	.08	.04	.11*
People outside metro area by telephone	-.03	.04	-.04	.03

Mass Communication Measures

	TV Viewing yesterday	Usually	Listen to Radio	Read Paper	Mag-azines	Books	Video	Films	Cable	Internet Access
Interpersonal Communication Measures										
No. people talked to										
In household	.00	.06	-.10#	-.08	.01	-.05	.04	.05	.03	.02
In neighborhood	-.09#	-.02	.01	-.05	.01	-.00	.20***	.08	-.04	.08
At work	-.14**	-.05	.01	-.04	.03	-.02	.08	.05	.08#	.13*
Elsewhere in City	-.14**	-.07	-.01	.03	-.02	.03	.07	.09#	.03	.08
People in metro area by phone	-.07	-.04	.05	.02	.06	.09#	.06	.09#	.00	.05
People outside area by phone	-.03	-.04	-.02	-.07	.00	-.01	.12*	.04	-.04	.13*

TABLE 10
Correlations Between Social Categories & Communication Measures

	No. in Household	Age	Years in Metro area	Education	Income	Gender
Interpersonal						
Mean	.16**	-.22***	-.17***	.02	.05	-.01
Variance	.15**	-.19***	-.12*	.04	.08	-.01
Minimum	.05	-.12*	-.09#	.07	.16**	-.08
Maximum	.16**	-.20***	-.12*	.04	.08	-.02
Mass Communication						
Mean	.02	.13*	.18***	-.16**	-.08	.00
Variance	.05	.04	.06	-.19***	-.12*	-.01
Minimum	.05	.17***	.17***	-.02	.08	.03
Maximum	.09#	.03	.07	-.18***	-.10#	-.01
No. people talked to						
In household	.28***	-.14**	-.12*	-.06	-.03	.00
In neighborhood	.16**	-.14**	.10#	-.05	-.02	-.00
At work	.12*	-.24***	-.12*	.06	.08	-.02
Elsewhere in city	.06	-.07	-.10#	.06	.05	-.05
People in metro area by telephone	.05	-.10#	-.08	-.01	-.01	.05
People outside metro area by phone	.02	-.07	-.10*	-.01	.08	-.00
Mass Media Use						
No. hours watched TV yesterday	-.10#	.11*	.13*	-.24***	-.20***	-.06

No. hours usually watch TV	-.04	.16**	.21***	-.33***	-.24***	.05
No. hours listened to radio yesterday	-.03	.02	.08	-.09#	.00	.09
No. days read newspaper last week	-.02	.31***	.24***	.11*	.23***	-.01
No. magazines read regularly	.03	.05	.03	.12*	.16***	-.11*
No. books read in past 6 months	.09#	.05	.04	.18***	-.02	.15**
No. videos watched in past month	.09#	-.32***	-.24***	-.01	.06	-.16**
No. films seen at theater in past month	.15**	-.31***	-.23***	.02	.07	-.08
Cable TV	.01	-.05	-.01	.01	.10#	.09
Internet Access	.10#	-.36***	-.32***	.32***	.21***	-.02

Note. For gender, high = female.

271

TABLE 11
Content Categories of and Perceived Functions of Neighborhood Newspapers

Descriptions of Neighborhoods					
Poor, Black central city neigh, low ID low cohesion	Diverse, integrated city neigh., growing Hispanic	Middle class city neigh. borders suburbs	Poor, lower middle class Black suburb	Established wealthier city neigh. apartments	Eastern European ethnic city enclave
Descriptions of Community Papers					
Black entrepreneur profit-making paper	Activist community board, non-profit paper	Paper run for local business group	Black entrep. focus on business	Paper run by support org. of shopping area	White, politically oriented entrep.
Rank Ordering of News Content Categories					
*Calendar of events, etc.	*Calendar of events, etc.	*Development news	*Personal columns	*People features	*Religion#
*Local politics	*Religion	*Social services	*Social services	*Local politics	*Civic groups
*Personal columns	*Civic groups	*Business news	*Schools	*Social services	*Develop. news
*Political columns	*Crime	*Personals	*Political columns	*Business	*Crime
*Business	*Social services	*Personal columns	*City council	*Civic groups	*Local politics
*Schools	*Political columns	*Political columns	*People features	*City council	*Political columns
*People features	*Personal columns	*Local politics	*Local politics	*Crime	*Schools
*Development news	*Schools	*People features	*Business	*Development news	*People features
*Civic	*Development news		*Personals	*Religion	*Business news

272

groups	*Local politics	*Civic groups	*Develop. news	*Personals	*City council
*City council	*Ethnic news	*Calendar	*Crime	*Ethnic news	*Social services
*Social services	*Business news (tie)	*Crime	*Civic groups	*Schools	*Labor
*Crime	*Personals	*Religion	*Block clubs	*Sports	*Sports
*Block clubs	(tie) *City council	*Schools	*Religion		*Personals
*Religion		*Block clubs			*Ethnic news#

"Very Important" Functions Cited by Editors of Papers

Providing news of festivals	Telling res. about orgs.	Providing news of festivals	(Editor was not interviewed)	Providing news of festivals.	(Editor said almost all functions were very important
Linking consumers, adv.	Alerting people to soc. services	Giving res. chance to sell-class.		Linking consumers, adv.	
Alerting people to soc. services	Keeping eye on gov. officials	Alerting people to problems, conflict		Alerting people to soc. service	
Personal items	Discussing pol. issues	Redev.news		Alerting people to problems, conflict	
Keeping eye on gov.	Alerting people to problems, conflict			Editorials	
Covering schools	Redev. news			Redev.news	
Covering churches	Letters to ed.			Local features	
Giving res. chance to sell via classifieds	Articles by residents			Articles by residents	
Entertainment news					
Redev. news					

Note. The average number of column inches for each topic was computed across 10 issues of the neighborhood papers. #Religious news most often is also "ethnic" news in this community. Content which has no church affiliation but is ethnic was coded separately.

273

TABLE 12
Most Important Problems Cited by Neighborhood Residents

Neighborhood	Ordering of area's chief problems	Ordering of area's chief assets	Who's improving things in neighborhood
First-ring, blue-collar, integrating suburb (N = 53)	Schools (25%) Unemployment (21%) Gov. services (17%) Development, business concerns (9%) Politics (6%) Crime (4%)	People, friends family here (34%) Central location (13%) Nothing (11%) Shops, services avlb. in area (6%)	Don't know (28%) No one (13%) City (13%) Organizations, groups (11%) People, residents (9%)
Poor, Black central-city neighborhood low identity, low cohesion (N = 75)	Crime (49%) Development concerns (36%) Youth gangs (20%) Unemployment (15%) Drugs 8%	People, friends, family here (33%) Central location (25%) Nothing (16%) Know area well (13%) Transportation (6%)	Residents (45%) No one (16%) Council rep (12%) Mayor (8%) Orgs. (5%) City (5%) Businesses (4%)
Poor, Black central-city neighborhood, politically active (N = 18)	Crime (44%) Dev. concerns (39%) Politics (17%) Gov. services (6%) Schools (6%)	People, friends, family here (39%) Nothing (28%) Schools (17%)	No one (39%) Council rep (22%) City (11%) Orgs. (11%) Police (11%)

274

Neighborhood			
Middle-class/ blue-collar area, White, city border with suburbs (N = 56)	Crime (64%) Dev. concerns (32%) Gov. services (30%) Schools (14%) Jobs, unemp. (11%) Nothing (9%)	People, friends, family here (45%) Location (43%) Pleasant env. (29%) Services avlb. (14%) Econ. factors (12%) Spirit in area (7%)	Orgs. (73%) People, residents (39%) Council reps (29%)
Diverse, integrated area near city's center, parts redeveloping increasingly Hispanic, with poor whites professionals, Asians, a few White ethnics (N = 392)	Crime (42%) Drugs (30%) Gangs (17%) Youth problems (8%) Development concerns (8%) Trash in area (6%) Schools (4%) Gov. services (4%) Poverty (3%) Alcoholism (3%) No pride (3%) Unemployment (3%)	Central location (39%) People, friends family here (26%) Nothing (14%) Economic factors (7%) Diversity (5%) Clean & safe (4%) Shops, services avlb. in area (3%)	No one (25%) People, residents (24%) City council (12%) Orgs. (11%) Don't know (11%) Businesses (6%) Police (3%) City and mayor (3%) Congresswoman (3%)
White, central city mix of middle/ lower middle-class, blue-collar people, aging area increasingly Hispanic (N = 43)	Crime(37%) Nothing (26%) Development concerns (19%) Government services (14%) Schools (9%)	Central location (67%) People, friends family here (12%) Nothing (9%)	No one (26%) Businesses (21%) Media (16%) Don't know (14%) City council (12%)

(continues)

TABLE 12 (cont.)

Neighborhood	Ordering of area's chief problems	Ordering of area's chief assets	Who's improving things in neighborhood
Diverse, blue-collar central-city neigh. with growing Hispanic influence (N = 97)	Crime (35%) Development concerns (32%) Schools (20%) Youth problems, facilities (11%) Unemployment (7%) Nothing (6%) Government services (5%)	People friendly (30%) Central location (29%) Safe area (12%) Economic factors (11%) Nothing (8%) Shopping available (4%)	Orgs. (26%) People, residents (12%) Don't know (10%) Council rep (9%) Businesses (6%) No one (6%)
Suburban bedroom community, middle class (N = 25)	Government services (32%) No problems (20%) City council (12%) Schools (8%)	Nice, clean area (48%) Quiet area (36%) Location (20%) Nothing (4%)	Mayor (28%) No one (24%) People, residents (16%) Don't know (12%)
White, Eastern Eur. ethnic community, aging blue-collar neighborhood (N = 41)	Crime (80%) Development concerns (56%) Schools (10%) Government services (7%)	Central location (73%) Like area (10%) Economic factors (2%)	Orgs. (61%) People, residents (29%) Businesses (20%)

TABLE 13

Relationship Between Neighborhood Perceptions and Content

| Neighborhood | Chief Problems of Neighborhood Cited | | Residents Surveyed | Content Emphases |
	Editors	Informants		Rank order
First-ring, blue-collar, Integrating, suburb	Racism Acceptance of Blacks	Trouble in schools	Schools (25%) Unemployment (21%) Gov. services (17%) Dev., business concerns (9%) Politics (6%) Crime (4%)	*Calendar of events, etc. *Local politics *Personal columns *Political columns *Business *Schools *People features *Development news *Civic groups *City council *Social services *Crime *Block clubs *Religion
Poor, Black, central-city neighborhood low identity, low cohesion	Economic dev. Improving schools	Drugs Gangs Housing	Crime (49%) Development concerns (36%) Youth gangs (20%) Unemployment (15%) Drugs (8%)	

(continues)

277

TABLE 13 (cont.)

Neighborhood	Chief Problems of Neighborhood Cited			Content Emphases
	Editors	Informants	Residents Surveyed	Rank order
Middle-class/ blue-collar area, White, border's suburb	Crime Drugs Schools -busing	Crime Development of neigh.	Crime (64%) Dev. concerns (32%) Gov. services (30%) Schools (14%) Jobs, unemp. (11%) Nothing(9%)	*Calendar *Religion *Civic groups *Crime *Social services *Political columns *Personal columns *Schools *Development news *Local politics *Ethnic news *Business news(tie) *Personals *City Council
Diverse, integrated area near city's center, parts redeveloping increasingly Hispanic, with poor Whites, professionals, Asians, a few White ethnics	Trouble in schools Crime Poverty	Development of neigh. Perception of area as unsafe	Crime (42%) Drugs (30%) Gangs (17%) Youth problems (8%) Development concerns (8%) Trash in area (6%) Schools (4%) Gov. services (4%) Poverty (3%) Alcoholism (3%) No price (3%) Unemployment (3%)	
Diverse, blue-collar central city neigh. with growing	Economic dev. Unemploy-ment	Schools -busing People not active in	Crime (35%) Development concerns (35%) Schools (20%) Youth problems, facilities (11%)	

Hispanic influence	orgs. to solve problems	Unemployment (7%) Nothing (6%) Gov. services (5%)	*Religion#
			*Civic groups
Suburban bedroom community, middle class	Managing growth of suburb	Nothing specific Need stronger tax base	*Development news
		Gov. services (32%) No problems (20%) City Council (12%) Schools (8%)	*Crime
			*Local politics
			*Political columns
White, Eastern Eur. ethnic community, aging blue-collar neighborhood	Trouble in schools Crime	Crime (80%) Development concerns (56%) Schools (10%) Government services (7%)	*Schools
			*People features
			*Business news
			*City council
			*Social services
			*Labor news
			*Sports
			*Personals
			*Ethnic news
			(largely Hispanic)

Author Index

281

Hughes, J.E., 121(*n*106), *236*
Hughes, M., 165(*n*155), *232*
Hummon, D., 20, *226*
Hunter, A., 7(*t*), 10, 11, 63, *232*
Huntington, S.P., 169(*n*172), *232*
Hur, K.K., 55(*n*62), *233*
Hurlbert, J.S., 120(*n*100), *221*
Ikkink, K., 127, *232*

Inglehart, R., 164, 164(*n*147, *n*149),
    165(*n*158, *n*161-162), *232*

Jackson, R., 24, *228*
Jacob, H., 11, *232*
Jacobs, J., 62(*n*68), 157, *232*
James, A., 127(*n*121), *241*
Jang, H., 121, *232*
Janowitz, M., 6(*t*), 23, 30, 63, 70, 93,
    232, *234*
Jasko, S.A., 127, *240*
Jeffres, L. W., 25, 25(*n*32, *n*34), 31, 32,
    34, 35, 36, 51, 54, 55, 55(*n*62), 56,
    64, 65, 71, 72, 82, 89, 92, 99, 100,
    105, 110, 112, 131(*n*125), 132, 166,
    167(*n*169), 171, 174, *232*, *233*
Jensen, M., 165(*n*154), *233*
Jensen, R.J., 162, *233*
Jimenez, A., 165(*n*155), *234*
Johnsen, E., 69(*n*74), *223*
Johnson, J.D., 121(*n*105), 127, *234*
Johnson, W., 173, *238*
Johnstone, B., 8, *234*
Johnstone, J.W.C., 91(*n*84), *234*
Jones, D.C., 127(*n*122), *234*
Jones, L., 24, *228*
Jones, W.H., 127, *231*
Juster, F., 164(*n*147), *234*

Kadushin, C., 20, *234*
Kang, N., 120, *234*
Kar, S.B., 165(*n*155), *234*
Kasarda, J., 23, 70, *234*
Katz, E., 71, 128, 175(*n*177), *225*, *248*
Kaufer, D.S., 128, *225*
Kaufman, A., 161, *234*

Kaufman, H.F., 158, *234*
Keith, P., 164(*n*153), *234*
Keizer, G., 4, *234*
Keller, S., 4, 6(*t*), 7(*t*), 54, *234*
Kemmis, D., 56, *234*
Killworth, P., 69(*n*74), *223*
Kim, H.J., 127, *234*
Kim, J., 71, 128, *234*, *248*
Kim, K., 128, *234*
Kim, S., 55, 126, *242*
Kim, Y.Y., 8, 55(*n*62), 148, *234*, *235*
Kincaid, D.L., 121, 121(*n*113-115),
    129, *235*
Kincaid, L., 121(*n*105), 129,
    175(*n*177), *242*
Klien, J., 171, *235*
Knoke, D., 119, 199(*n*96, *n*97, *n*99),
    120, 120(*n*100-101), 176(*n*182),
    235
Kochen, M., 69(*n*74), *240*
Korte, C., 161, *235*
Kramer, M.W., 128, *235*
Krannich, R.S., 22, *230*
Krohn, K.R., 130, *229*
Kuklinski, J.H., 119, 119(*n*96, *n*97,
    *n*99), 120, 120(*n*100-101),
    176(*n*182), *235*
Kulik, J.C., 165(*n*154), *228*
Kurian, G.T., 165, *235*

Lacy, S., 35(*n*50), *235*
Lafrance, A.A., 148, *223*
Lai, Y., 164, *243*
Lalli, M., 13(*n*15), *236*
LaRose, R., 55(*n*63), *236*
Larose, S., 121(*n*105), *236*
Larsen, O.N., 54, *227*
Lasswell, H., 91, 143, *236*
Laszlo, E., 118, 143, 143(*n*128), 146,
    146(*n*129-131, *n*133-135),
    147(*n*136), 151, *236*
Latkovich, M., 99, *233*
Laudeman, G., 122, *236*

Subject Index